SCIENTIFIC

PARANORMAL

INVESTIGATION

SCIENTIFIC PARANORMAL INVESTIGATION

HOW TO SOLVE UNEXPLAINED MYSTERIES

BENJAMIN RADFORD

For Randi and Joe, the best of the best.

Publisher Cataloging-in-Publication Data

Radford, Benjamin.
Scientific Paranormal Investigation: how to solve unexplained mysteries /
by Benjamin Radford
p. cm
Includes bibliographical references and index.
ISBN 978-0-936455-11-2
1. Curiosities and wonders. 2. Forensic sciences-- Miscellanea.
3. Parapsychology. I. Title.
BF1031.R33   2010
133-dc21

Printed in the United States of America
Edited by Lisa Jong-Soon Goodlin
Cover by Marty Blake Graphic Design
Book design by Christopher Fix

Rhombus Publishing Company
P.O. Box 806
Corrales NM 87048 USA
www.RhombusBooks.com

Acknowledgements

This book would not have been possible without the support of many people. In addition to those mentioned in the text, I am grateful to many friends and colleagues for inspiration and assistance, including Robert Bartholomew, Tim Binga, Ed and Diane Buckner, Kevin Christopher, Christopher Fix, Kendrick Frazier, Martin Gardner, Jenna Griffith, Ray Hyman, Tom Flynn, Lisa Goodlin, DJ Grothe, Barry Karr, Paul Kurtz, Scott Lilienfeld, Daniel Loxton, Paul Loynes, Joe Nickell, Massimo Polidoro, James Randi, Carl Sagan, Blake Smith, Jim Underdown, Richard Wiseman, and others. The late Barry Beyerstein and Michael Dennett were excellent researchers and good colleagues, and are sorely missed.

Rob Britt, my editor at LiveScience.com, supported my efforts to bring science and skepticism to the public (and stood by me through quasi-threats of lawsuits from disgruntled psychics and *New York Times* reporters). Thanks also to my friends and family through the years who accepted the fact that any trip to another country with me would likely be spent at least partly investigating local ghosts, monsters, and miracles.

Table of Contents

Other Perspectives on Scientific Paranormal Investigation

Part III: Case Studies in Scientific Paranormal Investigation

INTRODUCTION

*"To kill an error is as good a service as, and sometimes even
better than, the establishing of a new truth or fact."*
                                                - Charles Darwin

Scientific Paranormal Investigation is designed to be useful to a variety
of people with different interests. First, for would-be paranormal investigators, those who have read about the world's strange mysteries and
want to try their hand at it, this is a "how to" guide for conducting successful scientific investigations into "unexplained" phenomenon. Interest
in the paranormal has rarely been higher; top-rated TV shows feed the
public's interest in the supernatural. Millions of people watch paranor-
mal-themed television shows on everything from ghosts to psychic detectives, monsters to crop circles, not realizing that they are seeing
entertainment instead of actual investigation. (For a scientific analysis
of the ghost hunting on such shows, see chapter 4, "How *Not* to Investigate the Paranormal: Science and Pseudoscience in Ghost Investigations.") Reading this book won't make you a scientific paranormal
investigator, any more than reading a book on car repair makes you a
mechanic. But it will give you insight into the process and a solid blueprint to work from.

For people with some knowledge of skepticism and an interest in the
paranormal—but who don't necessarily have the time, inclination, or ability to become a paranormal investigator themselves—the collection of il-
lustrative case studies in this book will provide important background

information on the topics. Being knowledgeable about solved cases can be very useful when discussing paranormal topics with skeptics and believers alike.

For the millions who have an interest in the paranormal but who are not necessarily familiar with what skeptics are or what they do, this book provides an understanding of skepticism and how science can be applied to modern mysteries and the paranormal. People are often surprised to learn that paranormal phenomena can be—and indeed has been—subjected to solid scientific analysis. Understanding skepticism will make you a better critical thinker. The principles of skepticism and scientific investigation are identical and apply far beyond exotic topics like ghosts and monsters; they will help you spot logical fallacies and faulty arguments in all areas. The information and case studies here will give the other side of the story all too often missing from mystery-mongering, pro-paranormal books, shows, and magazine articles on the topics.

Many readers with no particular interest in investigation will find first-hand accounts of a wide variety of fascinating topics: psychic cats, blood-thirsty lake monsters, cruel voodoo witches, ghosts, ESP tests, and much more. Anyone with an interest in the bizarre and unexplained will find a treasure trove of mysteries—all examined from a credible, scientific point of view.

This book focuses on the practical aspects of applied skepticism. I have resisted the temptation to delve too deeply into the philosophy and history of skepticism. It's important to understand the nature, scope, and context of skeptical investigation, but others have done a far superior job in discussing these matters than I could. There are wonderful books by the great philosophers of skepticism, from David Hume to Paul Kurtz, and those works appear in the extensive bibliography. I encourage interested readers to seek out the sources and references I provide, as well as the books in the recommended further reading sections. Joe Nickell's books, especially *Missing Pieces: How to Investigate Ghosts, UFOs, Psychics, and Other Mysteries*, are other excellent resources.

I have been involved in hundreds of investigations over the years. Some cases were solved in a few hours by consulting references; others took months of research and preparation. A thorough background in science is helpful, but not necessary to be a knowledgeable skeptic. Many of the keys to understanding skepticism are accessible to the average person. These principles include understanding the basics of chance and randomness; understanding scientific methods; an appreciation of psychology (including how beliefs are formed, and how we fool others and ourselves); and the principles of critical thinking (Occam's razor, logical fallacies, etc.). Many of the so-called soft sciences, such as linguistics and sociology, have made important contributions to skepticism. I can speak knowledgeably about skepticism, science, and many aspects of the paranormal, but I'm not a professional scientist. I do, however, have a solid understanding of how science works, and what makes good and bad science.

Throughout this book I share personal anecdotes. This is inevitable, as my skepticism is an ingrained characteristic, a guide for living. It is not simply a set of principles I pull out of a bag when it comes time to play Sherlock Holmes or Fox Mulder. Investigation is a personal enterprise, and trying to separate out the personal from the professional is not only pointless but counterproductive. (One of the most popular and powerful columns in *Skeptical Inquirer* magazine that Joe Nickell ever wrote was a personal story about intuition, and how it united him with a long-lost daughter.)

In some ways anecdotes are a bane of investigators, for they are not evidence. In this book the anecdotes are offered not as evidence but as examples. Personal, concrete examples illustrating a principle are much more easily learned and remembered than generic guidelines, so I hope the reader will pardon any digressions.

There are thousands of people in the world who call themselves paranormal investigators, ghost hunters, or something similar. Paranormal investigation requires no certificate; anyone can do it with no training, knowledge, or expertise whatsoever. Whether they are effective or not—actually solve any mysteries—is another matter entirely.

There are even some "paranormal investigation" handbooks claiming to instruct readers on how to look into ghosts and the supernatural. The problem is that, with a few exceptions, none of the authors have any background in logic, investigation, or science. They may be writers, but they do little or no actual investigation. Merely collecting ghost stories or Big-foot reports is not investigation. In short, most "experts" on the paranormal have little if any credibility; they are simply folks who have an interest in the topics and decided to write books that mostly ignore the skeptical, rational explanations in favor of mystery-mongering. Readers should re-search the author(s) to evaluate their credibility and history of successful investigation and solved mysteries. If you are going to buy a book or take a course on paranormal investigation, you deserve to have an author or instructor who knows what he or she is talking about.

Many people who are interested in the paranormal believe that one method of investigation is as good as another, that there is no "correct" way to investigate the unexplained. According to authors Marley Gibson, Dave Schrader, and Patrick Burns in their 2009 book *The Other Side: A Teen's Guide to Ghost Hunting and the Paranormal*, "There are a multitude of para-normal investigators with differing philosophies on how to investigate. No one can truly say that his or her methods are better than anyone else's" (p. ix). Christopher Moon, editor-in-chief of *Haunted Times* magazine, agrees, writing in 2010 that "if ghosts/aliens/vampires and the occasional bizarre creature haven't been proven to exist, then how can we say who is going about investigating it the right or wrong way? Simply put, we can't."

Of course we can.

If the goal of investigation is to understand an unexplained phenom-enon, then the methods that produce information solving the mystery are the right ones; the methods that do not help solve the mystery are the wrong ones. It's as simple as that.

The idea that there is no right or wrong way to investigate a phenom-enon (even a supposedly paranormal one) is simply wrong. Paranormal subjects are investigated just like any other subject: through critical think-ing, evidence analysis, logic, and scientific methodologies. Of course, some methods of investigation are better than others. The best way to approach investigation is the same one that professional investigators and detectives use everyday: the scientific method.

Police detectives and crime scene investigators use time-tested, proven techniques and methods to solve crimes. Let's say, for example, police are called to investigate a burglary. There are many different methods that detectives could potentially use to solve the crime. Police could consult a local psychic to identify the criminal, or they might simply wait for the criminal to turn himself in. Another way would be to carefully search for and scientifically examine evidence at the scene for fingerprints or DNA evidence. Any of these methods *could theoretically solve the case*, but only one way—methodical, scientific investigation—has proven useful in solving crimes and mysteries.

What gives me any credibility? It's a fair question, and there are several answers. The first is that I have a background in both science and psychology. The former grounds me in the scientific methods and logic; the latter gives me expertise in the psychological processes that underlie reports of nearly all "unexplained phenomenon." The second is my background as an investigator with the non-profit educational organization The Committee for Skeptical Inquiry, founded by top scientists such as Carl Sagan and Isaac Asimov. I have also served as managing editor for the science magazine *Skeptical Inquirer* since 1998. Third, I engage in actual research and field work, not armchair debunking, with over a decade of personal experience investigating everything from miracles to crop circles to psychics and lake monsters. Unlike well-meaning amateurs, investigating the paranormal is not a hobby or lark for me; it is a career.

Perhaps most importantly, the results speak for themselves. I have solved dozens of mysteries using these methods and techniques, many of them described in this book. The fact that these mysteries have been solved—when most investigations using other "equally valid" techniques remain unsolved—is proof enough that yes, indeed, some investigation methods are far better than others.

I have a long, documented track record of solving mysteries, reported by National Geographic, the Discovery Channel, the History Channel, the Learning Channel, ABC News, *The New York Times*, *Vanity Fair*, *USA Today*, CNN, CBS, CBC, BBC, and other news organizations with three letters. I must be doing something right, because "unexplained" mysteries I investigate keep getting solved. The methods and strategies I use and discuss here have proven themselves time and again. I like to

joke that I'm not afraid of ghosts; they're afraid of me, because they disappear when I investigate.

Being a scientific paranormal investigator is a curious profession. Outside the bubble it's sometimes easy to forget that not everyone spends
their days looking into unexplained phenomenon. It's a fascinating, wonderful, and frustrating job that presents its own unique set of challenges.
I hope you enjoy my take on it.

How I Became a Scientific Paranormal Investigator

The world is a strange and wondrous place. In 1992 a beer shortage led
me on a path that would culminate in me spending much of my life exploring the paranormal. While at the University of New Mexico that year
I won a regional essay contest (my piece examined the reasons for the
1986 Chernobyl and space shuttle Challenger accidents) and as a prize,
I was flown to a college town in Utah to present my paper. While there
my colleagues and I decided to venture out for a few beers. Because we
were unknowingly in a dry county, this turned out to be an arduous and
ill-fated venture. But in the process of going door to door and store to
store, we came across a tiny used bookstore. Amid the shelves of books
on fruit canning and apocalyptic survival guides (Mormon bookstore sta-
ples), I found a few old copies of *Skeptical Inquirer* magazine. One in particular, with a cover article on Nostradamus, caught my eye, and that was
the first time I'd seen anyone criticize the famed prognosticator. The author (James "The Amazing" Randi, as it turned out) offered skeptical,
logical, and reasonable explanations for the prophecies' apparent accuracy. Other paranormal and New Age topics were also discussed, giving
another side to the story. Not all the explanations and arguments convinced me—I wasn't taking the refutations as gospel, but at least I was
hearing a new voice.

I bought the issues and tucked them under my arm as the beer search
went on, and upon returning home I subscribed to the magazine and
joined the non-profit educational organization that published it: The Committee for the Scientific Investigation of Claims of the Paranormal (CSI-
COP, now CSI). Past and current supporters include Johnny Carson, Sir

Arthur C. Clarke, Penn and Teller, and many Nobel prize winners, working scientists, and writers. Five years later I was publishing in the magazine and doing my own investigations, looking into ghosts, pyramid power, psychics, UFOs, mysterious creatures and powers, the Bermuda Triangle, you name it. I became one of only a handful of working, science-based paranormal investigators. But I'm getting ahead of the story.

Like many youngsters, much of my childhood was eaten up by comic books and television. My skepticism was first tweaked by Superman. Though I was never a big Superman fan, I watched Superman films and bought the occasional comic book. Aside from my juvenile, voyeuristic ideas about X-ray vision, I was most interested in Superman's ability to fly. Just how did he do that? How did he actually make himself fly? Did the act of putting his fist forward make him fly? Or did he just think about it and lift off the ground? Did he have some localized mental control over gravity? I wanted to know; I wanted to *understand*. There was no real way to find out, of course. But that didn't stop me from asking the questions, or wondering not only "What if," but also, "If so, then how?"

I then turned my skepticism toward my favorite comic hero, *The Amazing Spider-Man*. After a radioactive spider bit Peter Parker, he gained an ability to stick to walls, a "spider sense" that alerted him to danger, and a few other powers. Once I had questioned the Man of Steel, Spidey was no real challenge. My first question was how he stuck to walls. Okay, I could buy that he could jump onto a wall and stick to it. But how did he *actually* make that happen? Did he stick to everything, or just walls? Why didn't paper, pencils, dollar bills, and everything else stick to his hands, too? He must have been able to turn it on and off somehow, and the convenient switch was apparently in the black box of his mind. Of course I knew that these heroes were just fictional characters, but there seemed to be no answers for my questions.

As a teenager I was fascinated by books about the strange and mysterious world around me. In the summer, I'd walk to the local used bookstore and pull out a handful of crumpled allowance dollars to scoop up paperbacks from the Fifties. Along with Doc Savage, Tom Swift, and Encyclopedia Brown books, I'd pick up a few "true mystery" collections.

I especially remember books by Frank Edwards, with titles like *Stranger Than Science.* Inside those books, I found a banquet of odd and mysterious stories and phenomena spilling from page after yellowed page. These weren't ghost stories or silly pulp fiction novels; these were, as the cover blurb read, "Astounding stories of strange events! All authentic— all absolutely true!" I loved these stories of mystery, supernatural coincidences, prophecies, terrifying creatures, and fascinating oddities. The stories had titles like "The Invisible Fangs," and "The Girl Who Lived Twice," and "A Voice From The Dead?" A blurb on the cover (from the *Colorado Springs Free Press*) called *Stranger than Science* a "fascinating collection of weird, fully-documented stories taken from life that modern science is powerless to explain!"

The assertion that the stories were "fully documented" was perhaps the strangest claim in the book, since none of Frank Edwards's stories cited sources, references, or any documentation whatsoever! (The "science cannot explain" line was quite popular, and also appeared on many other similar books, such as Rupert T. Gould's 1965 book *Oddities: Mysterious, True Events Science Cannot Explain!* I pictured worried scientists—imagined as balding men in horn-rimmed glasses and white lab coats—huddled together, chain-smoking and fretting about the seemingly supernatural mysteries they couldn't explain.)

I continued to gather more and more of these books, and between the library and the bookstore, for a few summers I was a voracious reader. I had books on fortune telling, astrology, and the Bermuda Triangle. I had books on demonic possession, exorcism, palmistry, and dowsing. I had books on mysterious creatures, psychic powers, ghosts, flying saucers, and monsters in dark corners of the world. I assumed that these stories were all (or mostly) true—the authors seemed authoritative. They were learned men and women who had studied mysterious and unusual events, written other similar books, and were apparently well qualified to report the facts of these amazing stories. But I did notice that there seemed to be precious little actual *investigation*; instead, most of the accounts seemed merely copied from other, older sources. There were plenty of theories and bald assertions, but no real scientific investigation, no one doing a reality check on the stories. And there was a disconnect between what I was reading and my experiences. I was just a kid in a small, semi-rural New Mexican village, but I'd never seen ghosts or encountered anyone who could bend spoons with their brains —I didn't even know anybody *who knew anybody* who could. And it wasn't for lack of imagination; as a teen, I spent years at the role-playing game Dungeons and Dragons, and was therefore steeped in the wonders and delights of a rich fantasy world. I spent many hours imagining trolls and orcs, dragons and wizards, elf maidens who looked like Kate Winslet, and battles for treasure and fame. Fantastic creatures, magical spells, potions, and amazing powers were a part of my mind and imagination. But there was always a clear distinction between real and not real. And these mysterious stories, for all their vivid details and astounding claims, somehow didn't seem real to me. I wanted to know what science had to say.

Working as a Scientific Paranormal Investigator

Because the profession of scientific paranormal investigator is such an unusual job, I'm often asked what the job is like. Working at the Committee for Skeptical Inquiry is a little like living *The X-Files*, only without the budget or badges, and with less clever banter. Unexplained mysteries cross my desk daily: bizarre claims and events that have been investigated or need to be looked at or responded to. On occasion I've been described as a "professional skeptic," a label which elicits puzzled and sometimes humorous responses. "You, um, get paid to doubt things? Is that right?" one man asked me. "Because, really, I'm skeptical about a lot of things. Like, my brother-in-law, he says he's going to get a job soon and move out of my basement. But I doubt it. Can I get paid for that?"

I am not paid to doubt things; I am paid to promote science and investigate unusual claims. Our approach is empirical, evidence- and science-based. Science has proven itself incredibly successful in explaining and finding out about the world. If we wish to know why a certain disease strikes one person and not another, we turn to medicine instead of a witch doctor. If we wish to know how to build a bridge that can span a river, we turn to physics instead of psychics. Paranormal or "unexplained" topics are testable by science: either a psychic's prediction comes true or it doesn't; either ghosts exist in the real world or they don't. My job is not to doubt, nor debunk; it is to *investigate*. I have no vested interest in proving or disproving any unexplained phenomena; I get paid the same either way. But the cardinal rule is that an investigator must eliminate all the natural explanations before accepting supernatural ones, and must use sound science.

CHAPTER 1
Science, Skepticism, and the Paranormal

A few years ago, following a talk at a conference, I was challenged by an obviously-less-than-skeptical attendee. "How can proven scientific methods of research be used," he asked, "when by definition, the paranormal is that which defies scientific explanation?"

It's a fair question, but based on a faulty premise. *Paranormal* does not mean something that defies scientific explanation. Using that definition, consciousness (something everyone experiences most of their lives) would be considered paranormal, since science can't fully explain what it is or how it comes about. Or, to use another example, if the paranormal was simply something that science doesn't understand, then germ theory (how germs cause disease) was "paranormal" in the 1700s, simply because scientists didn't understand how it works. Many "paranormal" things can be (and have been) scientifically tested, from Bigfoot hair to psychic powers.

James Randi, in his *Encyclopedia of Claims, Frauds, and Hoaxes of the Occult and Supernatural*, defines *paranormal* as "an adjective referring to events, abilities, and matters not yet defined or explained by science."

Joe Nickell provides a definition of *paranormal* in his book *The Mystery Chronicles: More Real-Life X-Files*, that which is "supposedly beyond the range of science and normal human experience." I use *paranormal* to simply mean something that *appears* to be supernatural or seems to violate natural laws. Its nature might or might not actually be supernatural, but it certainly appears to be, at least superficially.

Many so-called paranormal topics are not "outside the realm of science," instead, if they exist, they will be incorporated into science. Contrary to many critics of skepticism, the reason that many mainstream scientists don't study the paranormal is not because they are too timid to tackle something outside their worldview, but instead because there's little hard evidence upon which to base an experiment or conduct research.

Why Scientific Investigation?

There are many ways humans find out about the world around us. The most common is through personal experience; we see or hear something, learn from it, and move on. For the most part personal experience works well for everyday things like learning not to lock your keys in the car. But personal experience can sometimes mislead us, especially when dealing with things that we don't encounter every day—such as the paranormal.

Personal perception and experience tells us that our planet revolves around us. The sun moves across the sky from east to west, while we don't appear to be moving at all. But personal experience is of course wrong; it is instead the Earth that revolves around the sun. Science reveals that the earth we walk on is also revolving at over 1,000 miles per hour (at the equator), contrary to personal experience. Another example is lightning. For much of human history lightning was a mysterious, perhaps paranormal, phenomenon. Was it thunderbolts from the gods? Until experiments in 1752 (one of which was performed by Benjamin Franklin), the electrical nature of lightning was likely but unproven. Today scientists have a far better understanding of lightning; what was once mysterious and supernatural has now been largely explained. We know it is an electrical atmospheric discharge; yet science, as always, doesn't have all the answers. Lightning yet holds many mysteries, including how it can generate X-rays. Though science doesn't have all the details, it has many of them, and those parts that scientists still don't understand won't be filled by the earlier "mysterious" explanations.

It is one of the great failures of modern education that many people think of science as some irrelevant, arcane pursuit open only to those with a higher education. In fact, science is profoundly democratic, and its methods can be used and appreciated by all. Scientists are distinguishable not by their pocket protectors, nor their twenty-dollar words, nor their stereotypical white lab coats. It is the rigorous methods of investigation and analysis that makes a person a scientist in the true sense of the word. Sure, ideas such as Einstein's theories are mind-bending and can be hard to grasp. But they are only a tiny part of science.

Though there are many pieces of hardware that scientific investigators use to solve mysteries, everything from microscopes to telescopes, forensic kits to chemicals, these tools are useless without the understanding of *why* they are being used—what the principles are behind why one analysis is used instead of another, why one method of inquiry is more fruitful than another.

Science, not mysticism or pseudoscience, created most of the conveniences and essentials we enjoy daily. One area where science is clearly a source of excitement and pride is in space exploration. Images from the Hubble space telescope and the Mars rovers were seen across the globe; people didn't need to be rocket scientists to share in the excitement. In 2004, the world got to see the first ever clear pictures transmitted from another planet. Think for a second about the wonderment and magic of being the first people in human history to get a close-up view of another planet's surface. The truly amazing images from the surface of Mars were achieved not through intuition, or the study of chakras, or astrology, nor any other New Age system of knowledge, but through difficult and expensive science and technology.

Yet science is imperfect, inexact, and done by fallible humans. That's why the Hubble telescope's first images were a billion-dollar blur and had to be refitted with a new lens. Space probes (and, as the world was reminded in 1986 and 2002, space shuttles) crash, get lost, and explode.

On December 3, 1999, the Mars Polar Lander crashed into the surface of Mars. The problem: the developers had made a basic error in units: one group worked in feet while another calculated in meters and failed to account for the conversions. It was an immensely expensive humiliation.

But instead of laughing at science for its fallibility and errors, we should marvel at how well and often it does work, at the amazing advances in knowledge we have gained. Science, even when it fails, succeeds far better than any other human endeavor. The modern New Age movement has been around for decades, and paranormal beliefs (such as divination and astrology) for millennia before that. What public benefits have these brought to the world? Have New Age practices led to better sanitation, better crop yields, vaccines, or advances in knowledge? In some ways I think the New Age is selfish. It is focused on the individual, not the collective. The achievements and advances in science, on the other hand, are for the most part shared by all.

Science is simply a way of examining the world, a very effective method of analysis and investigation. You don't need to be a scientist to do science (or to investigate unexplained mysteries), but you do need to understand the principles involved. As this book progresses and you follow my case studies and investigations, these principles will be illustrated again and again. Drawn largely from the scientific process, psychology, criminal investigation techniques, and logic, these are not boring rules to memorize, but powerful, real-world ideas for critically examining everything from crime scenes to psychic powers to personal decisions. Improbable occurrences do happen; just because something seems bizarre or unusual is reason only to look more closely, not dismiss it out of hand.

Unexplained Versus Unexplainable

It is also important to distinguish between unexplained and unexplainable. Confusing the two is a very common error. There are countless phenomena that at one point were mysterious and unexplained, ranging from how diseases spread to why the sun rises and sets. As the ancient scientist Hippocrates observed, "Men think epilepsy divine, merely because they do not understand it. But if they called everything divine which they do not understand, why, there would be no end to divine things." Eminent biologist Richard Dawkins calls it the "argument from personal incredulity," basically, "If I can't explain it, then no one can."

I have had my share of unusual and seemingly mystical experiences. For instance, I once saw a UFO flying over Albuquerque, New Mexico. Early one morning as I waited at a traffic light facing south, I glanced out my window and saw a huge white disc slowly hovering above the city, between my position and the Sandia Mountains that abut the city. I was amazed, and tried to figure out how large the disk might be. I knew it had to be flying lower than 10,400 feet (the altitude of the mountains), and given its size, I figured that the object had to be several hundred feet long. As I watched carefully, though, I realized that the image was not over the city twenty miles away, but on my window about a foot away from my face. The disc was a reflection of the morning sun off the chrome of the car to my right, which had sidled up next to me as we stopped. When the traffic light turned green, the car moved ahead and its reflection went right along with it. Until I realized that I was seeing an optical illusion, the image looked for all the world like a large, luminescent hovering UFO. For a few exciting moments, I had little doubt about what I was seeing. I've also had apparently prophetic dreams, deja vu, and odd coincidences. Yet each time I was able to find logical, science-based explanations for what I experienced.

The scientific process is not easy; things that are truly useful rarely are. But they are necessary to help investigators separate truth from fiction, error from significance. It's very easy to make a claim about something, while thoroughly investigating a phenomenon can be a difficult job. For example, if a person says she just saw a strange light in the sky, that claim takes literally seconds to make. Investigating that sighting (assuming it's not a hoax or prank) could take weeks or even months while other eyewitnesses are sought, wind conditions are checked, flight plans from any nearby airports are examined, and so on. For this reason, the burden of proof is on the claimant. If someone tells me he discovered a giant ape in his garage, it's up to him to provide proof that what he says is true, not on me to prove there *isn't* a giant ape in his garage. The same applies to all the unusual mysteries in this book. Investigators do not have big budgets and unlimited resources to look into every report of something unusual, and therefore we try to choose the "best evidence" cases, where proving the truth or falsity of a claim will be most significant.

Skepticism and the Search for Truth

One fundamental premise in science and skepticism is that what is true matters. What is true is relevant. Of course, not every question or claim we encounter needs to be examined closely, but if anything is especially deserving of scrutiny, it's our beliefs. Our beliefs dictate to a large extent who we are and how we act. We make important choices in our lives based upon what we believe is true, and not just about paranormal issues but important social and political issues as well. If we believe that power lines near our home cause cancer, we may move our family out of an otherwise safe neighborhood. If we believe that the chemical Alar (at one time sprayed on apples) is endangering our children, we may keep them from eating needed fruits. If we believe that vaccinating our children against diseases may give them autism, we may endanger their lives. If we believe that we are likely to be killed in random violence or terrorism, we may worry needlessly and spend precious funds to avoid minuscule threats. The true state of the world around us is something that I believe we all have a moral obligation to try to understand. Nobody has all the answers; all we can do is to try and weed out the false beliefs to the best of our ability. Every single one of us holds beliefs that are false or only partially true. Perhaps the most important process in human thinking and knowledge is the recognition and awareness that we may be wrong— and the commitment to correct our mistakes.

Physicist Richard Feynman once said that he's smart enough to know that he's dumb. I wouldn't have quite put it that way, but his point is well taken: There is a certain enlightenment in understanding and acknowledging that we are fallible, fool-able creatures, and that not everything is as we perceive it to be. For as often as I hear skeptics and scientists accused of being arrogant, it seems to me that the real arrogance is assuming that natural, human limitations apply to everyone except believers. I'll hear things like, "Okay, so the skeptical investigation showed that this psychic or that dowser was mistaken or fooling himself. But I'm smarter than *that* person...." That may be, but no matter how smart we are, we can all be fooled (often by ourselves).

Skeptics are often accused of being dismissive of believers and their experiences, but I don't think that's true. For example, when I'm speaking to believers in Bigfoot, I point out that we are in complete agreement on at least one thing: the subject is worthy of serious, legitimate study. While many in the public may dismiss Bigfoot claims as being too silly to bother explaining or investigating, I disagree. Whether Bigfoot (or ghosts or auras or psychics) exist or not, many people *believe* that they do, and that in itself is interesting. I would not have spent half of my adult life investigating and writing about the mysteries in this book (and dozens of other topics) if I didn't think they were worth examining with an open mind. Are there people who take an armchair, debunking stance to the paranormal, dismissing claims out of hand? Sure there are. There are skeptics too quick to doubt, just as there are believers too quick to believe. Neither extreme represents these groups as a whole, and neither is healthy.

Open-Mindedness and Skepticism: Possibilities Versus Probabilities

"Simply stated, I 'believe' in nothing and the possibility of everything."

—Loren Coleman (2007)

Often in paranormal issues, the question arises as to whether it is possible that the phenomenon has a supernatural or paranormal explanation. The question, "Is it possible?" which is so revered and often touted, is both a superficial argument and a logical fallacy. The "is it possible" argument, so beloved by many paranormal enthusiasts, is a common rhetorical trick used by criminal defense attorneys to try to create doubt in a jury's mind that their client is guilty: ("Yes, my client's fingerprints were found at the scene. But is it possible that the real criminal drugged him, transported his unconscious body to the crime scene, carefully put his fingerprints on the knife and doorknob, then drove him back to his house and bed, where he woke up the next morning, unaware that he'd been framed?") Such a scenario might be theoretically possible, but that doesn't mean it should be seriously considered as a better explanation than that the defendant is guilty.

The correct, scientific answer is that anything possible. It's possible that (despite a lack of good evidence) ghosts, psychics, lake monsters, and dragons exist. Since no one is omniscient, no one has all the answers and therefore absolute certainty is not a criterion, especially in matters of fact and science. Is it *possible* that smoking doesn't cause lung cancer, but instead some factor no one has yet discovered? Is it possible that O.J. Simpson did not kill his ex-wife and her lover? Is it possible that Princess Diana is actually alive and living in seclusion, that a hired impostor was instead killed in that Paris tunnel? Is it possible that men didn't land on the moon, and the whole event was faked? Is it possible that we are all simply brains in a vat, or characters in someone's dream, and all our experiences seem real but are instead not?

Yes, all these things are possible, and no one can prove conclusively they are not. The question is not what is *possible*, but instead what the evidence shows, and what is reasonable. The "possible" argument is just a superficial red herring. It is, in short, a very weak foundation for either personal philosophy or legal argument.

Several years ago I was confronted by a man who challenged me on this issue, telling me that since I agreed that anything was theoretically possible, and it was such a big world, I should consider paranormal events at least somewhat likely. I replied, "Tell you what: If you're so convinced that theoretically possible things are likely, let's go to the nearest supermarket. I'll buy a gallon of bleach off the shelf, and you drink what's inside. It's *possible* that the jug is actually filled with water or some other harmless substance: Maybe there was a mistake at the factory, or the labels got mixed up, or something else. If you want to focus on the possibility that all the evidence about what's in the container is wrong (the labeling, the smell, etc.), then let's put it to the test and see if you're right." He declined.

Skeptics are sometimes accused of being closed-minded, but I have found that the opposite is true. For example, I often encounter people who are sure that they saw a ghost or a Bigfoot; they are 100% convinced, because, they tell me, "I saw it with my own eyes, and I know what I saw." Which is interesting, because it's clear that *they* are closed-minded, not I. I am open-minded about the possibility that these creatures exist; I don't know (and can't prove) that they do or don't. But the people who "know"— who are absolutely certain—that these things exist are not open minded to the possibility that they *don't* exist. The answer has been decided for them, and no evidence or argument will sway them from their conviction that these things exist.. As long as you are willing to accept evidence either way (especially evidence against what you believe), you are being open-minded and a good investigator.

As Joe Nickell aptly notes in his book *Secrets of the Supernatural,* "Some skeptical investigators refer to themselves as 'debunkers,' which is unfortunate. Although thorough investigation may often result in the debunking of fanciful claims, to call oneself a debunker implies bias, suggesting—rightly or wrongly—that the results are known prior to investigation and will always be negative" (p. 13).

Scholarship, Research, and Precedent

Skepticism, like science or any other body of knowledge, works on precedent. Scientific paranormal investigators need not—indeed should not—approach a case without background information and having researched previous investigations. While the specific circumstances of a mystery may be unique in each case, the type of mystery is not. Any investigation, from aliens to zombies, monsters to mediums to miracles, has many earlier, solved cases as precedents. *Skeptical Inquirer* magazine has examples of solved paranormal mysteries in nearly every issue, and back issues (now available on CD-ROM) are a treasure trove of material from years past. Books by Joe Nickell, Massimo Polidoro, Carl Sagan, Michael Shermer, James Randi, Martin Gardner, and many others listed in the bibliography are an excellent place to start.

Researching and knowing the history of skeptical investigations of paranormal claims is not simply a matter of paying your dues; it is essen-

tial to conducting an informed investigation. If you investigate a poltergeist claim in which there are children in the house (especially teenagers),
reading James Randi's account of his investigation into the 1984 Columbia poltergeist case (and teenager Tina Resch's involvement) will provide
insight. Research might also save you a lot of time and trouble, since
someone else may have already solved the case you're looking into—or at
least proposed a plausible explanation.

This is also tied to the issue of the generally low level of scholarship
in most mainstream and "believer" books on the paranormal and unexplained mysteries. Most such books populating the shelves of libraries
and bookstores omit skeptical and scientific explanations, giving readers
the impression that the mystery has never been critically examined—or
if it has, it has "baffled science." Thus to get a balanced picture you'll
need to research the skeptical literature. There's no point in spending
weeks or months tracking down some obscure "smoking gun" only to
find that it had been revealed a few years earlier in a publication you
missed due to incomplete research.

Of course, no one expects you to obtain and read every skeptical tome.
The breadth of paranormal topics is so vast you'll never be conversant
in everything. But serious investigators should have access to a well-
stocked library of skeptical resources, because often the first step to solving a case (or writing it up as an article) is researching the phenomenon
as a whole, understanding how the new case is similar (or dissimilar) to
previous cases. The Internet is a valuable resource, but information outside of reputable skeptical sources should be used with caution, and their
facts double-checked. The Center for Inquiry library in Buffalo, New
York, holds one of the world's largest collections of skeptical literature
and is available by appointment.

As you gain experience in investigating (and hopefully solving) mysteries, you'll of course have not only other researchers' work to reference,
but your own. For example, in 2008 when I was asked to investigate a
ghostly image caught on surveillance tape in a Kansas gym, I was able to
use a lot of the investigative strategies I learned from my investigation of
the Santa Fe Courthouse Ghost (see Chapter 9) a year earlier. The

"ghosts" were very similar, and turned out to have an identical cause. Future scientific paranormal investigators who are confronted with similar ghost videos can consult my solved cases for strategies and reference.

The Nature of the Unknown

Often in discussions of paranormal topics, the subjects themselves (ghost, Bigfoot, etc.) are treated as if there was a universally agreed-upon definition of what these things are, or what their nature is. But these terms are simply names for specific experiences, not discrete objects or entities. Simply calling something a Bigfoot or ghost does not explain anything, as no one knows that Bigfoot or ghosts exist, much less their nature. The conversation goes something like this:

> "I saw a Bigfoot."
> "How do you know it was a Bigfoot?"
> "It was large and dark and hairy and standing on two legs."
> "Okay, so you saw something large, dark, hairy, and standing on two legs. But no one knows for certain what a Bigfoot is. So how can you positively identify what you saw as a Bigfoot?"

If a truthful eyewitness states, "I saw something in the hallway that I can't identify," that is a valid and accurate statement. If the eyewitness instead states, "I saw a ghost in the hallway," the person is making an unwarranted assumption and a leap of logic—and this is true even if the person actually did see some unknown, paranormal entity.

It's basic logic: You can't claim to positively identify something without knowing the specific nature of that thing. Correctly identifying X necessarily means you must know what X is, what established characteristics distinguish it from Y and Z; there's no way around it. Thus labels like chupacabra, ghost, fairy, Bigfoot, and so on are useful only as descriptive shorthand; for an investigator is it more accurate and useful to think of them as descriptors for an experience.

Once the mystery is approached from this angle, it becomes potentially solvable. A scientific paranormal investigator can no more test, analyze, or examine a Bigfoot or ghost than a botanist can study a wahoozle or a car mechanic can run a test on a frammis. The investigation becomes one not of identifying the Bigfoot or ghost but of trying to understand what the eyewitness experienced, what the person *interpreted* as a Bigfoot or a ghost. This step is one of the most important, and a common reason why investigations fail, or end up with ambiguous results. You must use meaningful labels to understand the phenomenon.

This is not, as some might object, an *a priori* dismissal of the supernatural explanation. If what the eyewitness experienced truly is paranormal, if ghosts or Bigfoot exist, then their nature will be revealed through the scientific process. But before reaching for the paranormal explanation, we must consider known, alternative explanations.

In every single paranormal topic, from UFOs to Bigfoot to ghosts to miracles, there are solved cases and examples of mundane things that were mistaken for the paranormal. Those explanations must be examined and ruled out first. If all the scientific, natural explanations can be justifiably dismissed, we are left with supernatural ones. As Sherlock Holmes states in *The Sign of Four*, "When you have eliminated the impossible, whatever remains, however improbable, must be the truth."

The Importance of Research and Scholarship

I approach paranormal investigation from a background in journalism, which provides two critical elements: skepticism and scholarship. (For more on journalism, see my previous book *Media Mythmakers: How Journalists, Activists, and Advertisers Mislead Us*.) Good journalism and skepticism are inextricably linked. Journalists often cover issues that have two or more sides, and they must carefully weigh what they are told against the facts they have. Journalism demands that reporters not just accept that they are told, but instead question and challenge the information from all sides. This involves checking facts, corroborating reports, and even some investigation. One of the first rules of journalism is, "If your mother tells you she loves you, check it out!"

Whether or not you actually publish the results of your investigation, you will need to have written records of your research. My case files are typically stuffed with written notes, transcripts, photographs, printouts,

CDs with information, and so on—along with plenty of highlighted sections and Post-It notes flagging important information.

The second issue, scholarship, is closely tied to the first. Good investigation (paranormal or otherwise) demands good research. This is where 95 percent of non-skeptical books on the paranormal fail. Even after a decade in the field, I am often astounded by the lack of good scholarship in paranormal studies. If it's a famous mystery (say, the Bermuda Triangle or the 1967 Bigfoot film), there will be a dozen or more authors who have written on the case—and often simply copied information from one place to another.

Providing references and sources is important for an investigator's credibility, as it allows readers and other researchers to check your work, and proves that you didn't just make up facts to suit your theories. A full discussion of what constitutes good research is beyond the scope of this book, though *The Craft of Research*, by Wayne Booth, Gregory Colomb, and Joseph Williams (1995, University of Chicago Press) is an excellent reference. In it the authors write, "Good research should change our thinking. It asks us to accept a new idea, or in the strongest case, to rearrange our system of beliefs in fundamental ways. Such changes we rightly resist without good reasons. So when you ask your readers to change their minds, you owe them your best reasons for doing so." (p.111)

You need to research the topic as though you are a journalist, making sure to get quotes right and facts straight. Good research is partly a defensive exercise in that you should anticipate your readers' questions and objections. You might ask a knowledgeable friend to read over an early draft to see if they have questions. Avoid generalizations, and qualify your conclusions when necessary. If you don't know or can't prove something, be honest about it and explain why the information is incomplete.

As you read through my cases, you will discover a little-known secret in scientific paranormal investigation: Many cases can be solved by simply doing good research. I have solved some mysteries in less than an hour, simply with some critical thinking, source- and fact-checking. To be honest, anyone could have done it, it's just that nobody else did.

Author Larry Kusche, through careful research, debunked many cases of ships that supposedly disappeared in the Bermuda Triangle (some of the ships did sink, but nowhere near the Triangle; others claimed victims who never even existed!). Or see Joe Nickell's case-by-case examination of popular claims of spontaneous human combustion, the appendix to his book *Secrets of the Supernatural*. When important facts are included and the cases are examined under Nickell's close scrutiny, it is the mystery—not the victims—that vanish in a puff of smoke.

If an investigator is looking into a strange flashing light in the sky, it's important to research previous UFO investigations to find out that an escaped party balloon can create exactly that effect (Nickell 2007). If an investigator is researching lake monsters, it's important to research previous cases to find out that eyewitnesses often dramatically overestimate the size of objects they see on water (Radford 2003). And so on.

The oft-contentious battle between skeptics and believers over "who's right" sometimes is reduced to a shouting match. Each side has theories they believe and evidence they think supports those theories. While it's true that skeptics don't have all the answers, it is also true that, in general, skeptics take far more care to get their facts right. Because the standards of argument that skeptics try to uphold are quite rigorous and rooted in scholarly tradition, typically their arguments and conclusions are on solid foundations.

Paranormal Scholarship

It's frustrating to see how often well-established skeptical explanations are simply ignored in the "believer" books and magazines. Often the skeptical viewpoint is intentionally left out to sell more books, but in many cases the authors and publishers simply don't care.

Most general books on "the unexplained" are simply rehashes of old material, borrowed, copied, and reprinted from book to book without any attempt to correct information. Take, for example, *The Encyclopedia of Unsolved Mysteries* (1986 and other editions), a best-seller by Colin and Damon Wilson. The Wilsons are very prolific, due in large part to their habit of hashing and rehashing their own work into many books and articles. There's nothing inherently wrong with writers using their work in various places, but the Wilsons do not bother to correct or update their work. So, for example, if in 1975 they wrote about a baffling UFO case that was revealed five years later to be a hoax, readers who buy a 2000 edition of the book (retitled *The Mammoth Encyclopedia of the Unsolved*) won't know that. The reader will assume that the mystery remains unsolved, whereas it has been solved for 20 years!

Some writers may not have done their research, and are simply unaware of the scientific and skeptical evidence and arguments. Others are aware that the validity and credibility of what they write has been challenged, but they don't care; they want to tell their side, not both sides. Other writers may just be out to make a buck; their purpose is not to actually inform or educate their readers, but to simply tell stories.

The bias toward mystery-mongering is easy to see; simply pick up any popular book on Bigfoot or lake monsters, and in the index, look for the names of noted cryptozoology skeptics (such as David Daegling, Michael Dennett, Matt Crowley, or myself). A few will have them, but most won't. Then look at skeptical books, and you'll see that while the skeptics carefully read, analyze, and respond to the proponents ("Bigfoot believers"), the proponents often ignore the skeptical arguments and evidence. This undermines the writer's credibility, as they are not being honest with their readers. Furthermore, it is a clear sign of faulty scholarship, as it shows that the writer is being selective about scholarship and only using sources that support their theories.

Good science is not about advocacy; while all scientists have their biases and pet theories, their ultimate loyalty should be to the truth. Good scientists acknowledge the limits in their research and conclusions. Skeptical analyses and criticisms presented here and elsewhere are intended to help the search for these phenomena. That's what good science does: it helps separate fact from fiction, truth from error, real evidence from hoaxes. If we can prove that this particular Bigfoot track was a hoax, or that "ghost" sighting was not a ghost, or this argument is faulty, the entire field benefits. Everyone wins, because we know what evidence and arguments are valid and which aren't.

Science, the New Age, and the Search for Truth

Good science is universal. Properly controlled scientific experiments should yield the same results regardless of who is doing the testing. Male or female, British or Turkish, young or old, Muslim or Jew, it doesn't matter. Science's universality is one of its greatest attributes. In this way, science is profoundly democratic and open to just about anyone. While those actually doing science are often highly educated and skilled, the principles of science are everywhere from the library shelves to the local science museum to a simple walk in nature.

Much pseudoscience and the paranormal, by contrast, is individual and idiosyncratic. When asked about the future, different psychics will come up with wildly differing—and often contradictory—information and predictions. Different astrologers will come to different conclusions depending on what methods they use and which school they follow. That fact alone should raise serious questions about the validity of such claims.

Still, New Agers and skeptics might find some common ground regarding personal truth. It is true that people make their own reality to some extent; Joe Nickell notes that "there are no haunted houses, just haunted people." Many people believe in the existence of a literal Satan, and that angels literally watch over them. There are people in the world today who genuinely live in fear of being abducted by aliens or attacked by angry spirits or black magic. Research suggests that many voodoo curses "work" not because they have any real magical power, but because the victim believes the curse will work. They will be fearful, nervous, and stressed. If you live in a world where these forces exist and can harm you, then they just might.

What we believe affects us in ways we might not even realize. Psychological studies have repeatedly borne this out, for example in studies of alcohol placebos. People who imbibe drinks they believe contain alcohol (but do not) act as if they are intoxicated. In one study (Absolut Memory Distortion, *Psychological Science*, 2003, 17, 77-80, by S.L. Assefi and M. Garry) of memory recall, a large group of people were given tonic water, but half of them were told it contained vodka. All were shown a film of a staged crime and were read an inaccurate summary of what happened in the film.

Completely sober subjects who believed they had been drinking liquor showed much higher incidence of false recall of the information than did those who thought they were sober. If you *think* you are drunk or tipsy, you will act drunk or tipsy. This isn't magic or mind control over reality, but mind control over perception. But the same principles apply to the paranormal and New Age to make individual realities become "real."

Science also differs from the New Age and paranormal belief in that it progresses, correcting and building on itself. Technology and medicine are continually advancing and refining. Designs and techniques are improved or abandoned depending on how well they work. By contrast, I don't know of any evidence (or even claim) that suggests that, for example, psychic predictions or dowsing have gotten any more accurate over centuries and millennia of practice. Nor have there been any "advances" in psychic healings or the use of crystals.

Non-scientific Paranormal Investigation

Some may consider the bias toward science and skepticism self-serving. I can already hear the believers' complaint: "Oh, so you're saying that only skeptics do the investigation right, and everyone else is doing it wrong? How arrogant!" The only paranormal investigators doing it right (skeptic or believer) are those using sound science and valid investigative techniques.

Books on ghosts demonstrate a good example of the difference between investigating and writing. The vast majority of books on the topic of ghosts (whether labeled fiction, non-fiction, New Age, or supernatural) are simply collections of ghost stories. They may have subtitles like "Real cases of spirit encounters" or "True stories of victims who haunt" (as in Leslie Rule's books *Ghost in the Mirror* and *When the Ghost Screams*, respectively), but even a casual reading of the books reveals that the authors did little more than take dictation from people who experienced what they believe was a ghost. There's not even a faint whiff of skepticism or investigation of any sort, no attempt to check facts or verify that any of what the authors (and therefore their readers) are told is true. For these authors, if the person they are interviewing seems sincere and believes that he or she had contact with a ghost, well, that's good enough to slap a "real" or "true" label on the cover. There's nothing wrong with ghost stories, but ghost stories are not investigations. It takes little skill or ability to simply collect stories into a book and publish them. As this book shows, actually researching and investigating a ghost story to establish its truth or falsity, on the other hand, takes effort, knowledge, and skill.

From the séances and Spiritualist movement in the 1800s to TV's *Ghost Hunters*, people have been searching for hard evidence of the paranormal for centuries, with a 100% failure rate. People have been trying to prove the existence of ghosts for at least 200 years, and yet we are no closer to finding out what ghosts are. The evidence for ghosts, Bigfoot, or psychic powers is no better today than it was a year ago, a decade ago, or a century ago.

Why is the "final evidence" and conclusive proof so elusive? There are only two possible explanations for this. The first is that these phenomena do not exist, and the evidence for them are the result of hoaxes, honest mistakes, misunderstandings, misidentifications, and psychological mis-perceptions. So far the overwhelming weight of evidence supports this conclusion. This doesn't mean that the search should end—after all, hard evidence may be as close as the next investigation—but the reason for the lack of good evidence must be dealt with.

The second possibility is that these things *are* real and *do* exist—but that the efforts to prove their existence have so far failed because the search is being done in the wrong way, and researchers are not verifying their assumptions and asking the right questions. The methods used to investigate these mysteries over the past decades have, with a few excep-tions, been overwhelmingly non-scientific. Much "research" in the para-normal is notable for its sloppy scholarship, bad logic, and poor scientific methodologies. Many researchers into psychic ability (called psi) readily admit this (see, for example, Hyman 2008). It doesn't seem to occur to the non-scientific paranormal investigators that (assuming the phenom-enon they seek is real) they must do something different.

One common (but apocryphal) definition of insanity is doing the same thing over and over again and expecting different results. For fifty years, the search for Bigfoot has relied on exactly the same methods and

types of evidence: eyewitness sightings, "mysterious" tracks or prints, ambiguous photos and videos. All that effort, and yet not a single verifiable
fact about Bigfoot is known. The search for Bigfoot has so far been a
complete and unqualified failure. For well over a century, the search for
ghosts has relied mostly on sightings and séances. In the last decade or
so ghost hunters have employed new technology (such as EMF detectors
and night vision cameras), yet all the high-tech gear has yet to yield a single piece of hard evidence for ghosts. The same pattern can be found in
nearly every area of paranormal, from ESP to crop circles to astrology:
the evidence gets no better over the years and decades because they are
using the wrong methods.

It's time for the majority of "paranormal experts" and researchers to
change tactics; it's time to use the most reliable methods known to
mankind to help unravel the mysteries. It's time for science.

Not only *should* mysteries be investigated scientifically, but in fact mysteries cannot be solved without scientific methods. My colleagues and I,
using scientific methods, have solved hundreds of mysteries. We have
found answers and solutions to everything from astrology to zombies, ESP
to ghosts. Yet non-scientific (i.e., most) "paranormal investigators" rarely
find conclusive evidence; theirs is an open-ended quest fueled by evidence
that is marginal at best. Look for yourself at the mountains of non-skeptical
books on paranormal topics; see for yourself if their investigations find
any definitive answers or conclusive evidence for the phenomenon.

To be fair, there are times when even TV's *Ghost Hunters* crew finds
explanations for the supposedly ghostly phenomena. When they do, it
is because they are using valid logic and deduction—the tools of science.
When they go beyond science, they invariably are left with unanswered
questions and inconclusive results.

I'm not saying that skeptics don't make mistakes, and I have come across
sloppy skeptics from time to time (and as an editor, I demand accuracy
and fairness in articles that cross my desk). But by and large, I believe that
the reasonable person who compares the average skeptic article or book
to the average "believer" article or book would agree that the skeptics more
often have their facts and arguments right.

Even many believers will be the first to admit this. In a column in the typically less-than-skeptical *Fortean Times* (issue 119, p. 47), contributor Nick Warren commented on the often lax scholarship found in paranormal and believer literature. "One of the most irritating features of fortean studies is the tendency of the same material to be copied from book to book, or periodical to periodical, without any of the authors troubling themselves to check on the citation's origins. Now that so many branches of this endeavour like to accord themselves the status of 'sciences' (UFOlogy, cryptozoology, cereology) this tendency is becoming nothing short of scandalous. Whenever the exercise is actually undertaken, it often happens that the 'mystery' mysteriously disappears....If we wish to be regarded seriously, we must use serious methods of enquiry." (In a remarkable coincidence, Warren cites as examples of bad scholarship the very two books I mentioned earlier as having inspired my interest in the paranormal—Rupert Gould's *Oddities* and Frank Edwards's *Stranger Than Science*.)

As a skeptical writer and investigator, it's disheartening to carefully analyze and study a case, double and triple-check my facts and sources, and be competing with pro-paranormal authors who don't nearly match the effort. In the end, one can hope, their slipshod scholarship will relegate their works to the trash piles, but the reality is that the thirst for mystery-mongering literature will likely keep them in circulation. As they say, the truth never stands in the way of a good story.

The problem is not so much that science or skeptics disregard anomalies or the paranormal, it's that often believers refuse to accept the answers science does find. Skeptics can provide explanations for many "mysterious" things: how a Ouija board works; how dowsing works; why the Bermuda Triangle is a fiction; how the Ghiza pyramids were built; some ghost encounters; spontaneous human combustion; etc. Believers in these phenomena, unfamiliar with skeptical materials, are often unaware of the careful studies and research into the topics, or dismiss the explanations as mistaken or irrelevant. They find fault with skeptics' answers but rarely provide better explanations.

References

Coleman, Loren. 2007. Quoted in *Weird Happens: Investigator Handbook*, by Robert Goerman, from PublishAmerica.

Hyman, Ray. 2008. Anomalous cognition? A second perspective. *Skeptical Inquirer* (32)4, July/August, 41.

Moon, Christopher. 2010. *Haunted Times* magazine Vol. 4, issue 3, Winter 2010, p. 7

Nickell, Joe. 2007. "UFOs over Buffalo" in *Adventures in Paranormal Investigation*. Lexington, Kentucky: The University Press of Kentucky. Pp. 206-210.

Radford, Benjamin. 2003. The measure of a monster: Investigating the Champ photo. *Skeptical Inquirer*. July/August, 27(4).

Further Reading

This list is not exhaustive and is intended to direct readers to a sample of the best skeptical and scientific resources dealing specifically with investigating and understanding unusual claims. Resources dealing with broader issues of skepticism may not be represented here.

How We Know What Isn't So: The Fallibility of Human Reason in Everyday Life, by Thomas Gilovich, 1991.

Mistakes Were Made (But Not By Me): Why We Justify Foolish Beliefs, Bad Decisions, and Hurtful Acts, by Carol Tavris and Elliott Aronson, 2007.

Why People Believe Weird Things, by Michael Shermer, 1997.

Fads and Fallacies in the Name of Science, by Martin Gardner, 1957.

Science: Good, Bad, and Bogus, by Martin Gardner, 1990.

Bad Astronomy: Misconceptions and Misuses Revealed, from Astrology to the Moon Landing "Hoax," by Phil Plait, 2002

Flim Flam! Psychics, ESP, Unicorns, and Other Delusions, by James Randi, 1982.

The Elusive Quarry: A Scientific Appraisal of Psychical Research, by Ray Hyman, 1989.

The Skeptic's Dictionary, by Robert Todd Carroll, 2003.

Encounters With the Paranormal: Science, Knowledge, and Belief, edited by Kendrick Frazier, 1998

Adventures in Paranormal Investigation, by Joe Nickell, 2003.

Real-Life X-Files: Investigating the Paranormal, by Joe Nickell, 2001.

Missing Pieces: How to Investigate Ghosts, UFOs, Psychics, and Other Mysteries, by Joe Nickell and Robert Baker, 1992.

Secrets of the Supernatural: Investigating the World's Occult Mysteries, by Joe Nickell and John F. Fischer.

Miracle Mongers and their Methods, by Harry Houdini, 1993 (reprint).

The Mystery Chronicles: More Real-Life X-Files, by Joe Nickell, 2004.

Looking for a Miracle: Weeping Icons, Relics, Stigmata, Visions, and Healing Cures, by Joe Nickell, 1999.

Psychic Sleuths: ESP and Sensational Cases, by Joe Nickell, 1994.

Lake Monster Mysteries: Investigating the World's Most Elusive Creatures, by Benjamin Radford and Joe Nickell, 2006.

An Encyclopedia of Claims, Frauds, and Hoaxes of the Occult and Supernatural, by James Randi.

The Truth About Uri Geller, by James Randi, 1982.

Guidelines for Testing Psychic Claimants, by Richard Wiseman and Robert Morris, 1995.

Deception and Self-Deception: Investigating Psychics, by Richard Wiseman, 1997.

Secrets of the Psychics: Investigating Paranormal Claims, by Massimo Polidoro, 2003.

Paranormal Claims: A Critical Analysis, edited by Bryan Farha, 2007.

Investigating the Unexplained, by Melvin Harris, 2003.

Pseudoscience and the Paranormal, by Terence Hines, 2003.

The Power of Critical Thinking: Effective Reasoning About Ordinary and Extraordinary Claims, by Lewis Vaughn, 2007.

How to Think About Weird Things, by Theodore Schick and Lewis Vaughn, 2007.

Psi Wars: Getting to Grips with the Paranormal, by James Alcock, 2003.

In Search of the Light: The Adventures of a Parapsychologist, by Susan Blackmore, 1996.

Physics and Psychics: The Search for a World Beyond the Senses, by Victor Stenger, 1990.

Stat-spotting: A Field Guide to Identifying Dubious Data, by Joel Best, 2008.

Innumeracy: Mathematical Illiteracy and its Consequences, by John Allen Paulos, 2001.

Eyewitness Testimony, by Elizabeth Loftus, 1996.

Little Green Men, Meowing Nuns, and Head-Hunting Panics, by Robert E. Bartholomew, 2001.

Critical Reasoning and Logic, by Robert Boyd, 2003.

Clear Thinking: A Practical Introduction, by Hy Ruchlis, 1990.

Understanding Arguments: An Introduction to Informal Logic, by Robert Fogelin, 1987.

CHAPTER 2
Psychology of
the Paranormal

Understanding human psychology is of great benefit in paranormal investigation, in part because often there is little hard evidence to examine and the bulk of the claim is someone's personal experience. "I saw a ghost," one young woman told me during an investigation, or "I think I have psychic powers because my dog can read my mind," as one fourteen-year-old Canadian boy e-mailed me in 2008. Unless there is some sort of supporting evidence or proof, these are simply interpretations of experiences.

There's nothing wrong with personal experiences, but by themselves they are not proof or evidence of anything except that the person experienced something they didn't understand or couldn't immediately explain. Most people who report such experiences are being truthful (i.e., not hoaxing), but being truthful is not the same as being accurate. They may be completely sincere and honest, and simply wrong.

In order for a person to accurately and fully report an experience, they must do four basic things correctly: 1) they must correctly *perceive* the phenomena; 2) they must correctly *interpret* the phenomena; 3) they must correctly *recall* the phenomena; and 4) they must accurately *describe* the phenomena.

Example: A man on a boat in a lake sees something big and dark rise out of the water. When he gets to shore, he tells his wife he saw a lake monster. Maybe he did; maybe he didn't, but some questions must be asked:

1) How accurate is his perception? How good is his vision? What were the lighting conditions: bright daylight, dusk, or nighttime? How far away was it? Ten feet? 100 yards? A quarter mile?

2) How good is his interpretation? Why did he interpret what he saw as specifically a lake monster, instead of a fish, or a wave, or a sunken log? Did it have characteristics that convinced him it could not be something ordinary? Were there any other factors that might influence his interpretation or judgment (for example, alcohol or other drugs, health problems such as diabetes, exhaustion, etc.)? Had he reported seeing the monster before, or been told about the creature? Was he actively searching for the monster, or doing some other activity such as fishing?

3) How good is his recollection? Did the incident happen just minutes or hours earlier? Or was it reported weeks, months, or even years later? Does he have any memory problems? Has he told the same story before? If so, are the accounts different? The more often a person repeats a story, the more likely it is to have been embellished; details creep in or drop out over time.

Perception
Interpretation
Recollection
Reporting

4) How good is his ability to adequately report or describe his experience? How extensive is his vocabulary? Does he speak the same language as the person he's reporting his experience to? Is he too frightened to speak? Are there any other factors that might affect his ability to fully communicate or articulate what he explained?

The same basic questions apply to all eyewitness experiences. Note that an eyewitnesses' account can only be considered completely valid if the person is not affected by factors such as these. If he clearly sees the object, correctly identifies it at the time, but can't correctly recall or describe it later, then the sighting is compromised. If any part of the chain breaks down, if any one of these steps is dubious or missing, then there will be serious errors and mistakes in what is reported.

This of course doesn't mean that all eyewitnesses are unreliable, just that investigators cannot take reports at face value. In our daily lives, any errors that creep into the cognitive process are likely to be minor and insignificant. But in alleged eyewitness accounts of paranormal phenomenon, every detail may be important. The gap between what is experienced and what is reported can create monsters and mystery where none exist.

In my investigations, I have encountered many cases where a sincere person reported a first-hand eyewitness account of something that simply did not happen. For example, in 2008 I investigated the most haunted theater in the Southwest, a place called the KiMo, in Albuquerque, New Mexico (see my article "Ghosts, Doughnuts, and A *Christmas Carol*" in the May/June 2009 *Skeptical Inquirer*). A boy had been killed in an accident at the theater in 1952, and his ghost was said to have supernaturally ruined a performance of A *Christmas Carol* at that theater many years later. Props mysteriously fell over or flew across the stage, actors tripped, forgot their lines, were pushed by unseen hands, lights mysteriously turned on and off by themselves, and so on. While researching the case, I traced the story to the technical director, Dennis Potter, who had worked at the theater for decades. Potter was there that night, and reported what he had seen with his own eyes. Going simply by this first-hand eyewitness report, the case seemed pretty mysterious: hundreds of people in the audience, cast, and crew witnessed some unseen force ruining a play.

The problem is that Potter was the only person who remembered it. I interviewed other people in that production, including actors and the director. They said nothing of the sort happened. Newspaper records show that theater critics don't mention any ruined performance. No one else could be located who could corroborate Potter's first-hand eyewitness account of the very public, ghostly phenomenon. I don't think Potter is crazy or a liar; he simply told the ghost story so many times that he came to confuse fact with fiction. A believer might scoff, saying, "A story like that must have some have some truth to it... nobody would make up details like that." Yet people can and do misremember experiences and events; sometimes they even create them out of thin air and come to believe them.

The main thing to remember about the psychology of the paranormal is the following, which the literature shows is true and uncontested: We are all subject to misunderstandings, misperceptions, and mistakes—and we are all overconfident in the accuracy and validity of those beliefs and perceptions.

The Pattern-Seeking Mind

Understanding the mind's pattern-seeking tendencies is an important element of scientific investigation. Humans try to make sense of the world, and in the process sometimes see patterns and meaning where none exist.

We see this psychological process at work when we find faces and figures in clouds, tree trunks, stains, Rorschach blots, and other ambiguous stimuli. This phenomenon, called pareidolia, is well known in psychology, and it is the cause of many supposedly mysterious and miraculous events.

Examples are all around us; in fact, if you have a New Hampshire state quarter, you have an example of pareidolia in your pocket or purse (take a look). As Carl Sagan noted in his book *The Demon-Haunted World*, "The pattern-recognition machinery in our brains is so efficient in extracting a face from a clutter of other details that we sometimes see faces where there are none."

And it's not just faces, it's also human forms. In one recent example, the idea that there may be life on Mars got a boost from photos taken by the NASA robot Spirit. The images, taken in 2004 and released in January 2008, show a vaguely humanoid figure amid rocks on the Martian landscape. It's not clear from the image what the scale is, and some believed it was alive. The "man on Mars" suggestion started out as a joke on a blog but soon became an international story as conspiracy theorists took hold. A headline in U.K.'s *Daily Telegraph* read, "Bigfoot on Mars? NASA Captures Alien Figure."

We not only see pattern in physical images, but impose them on our experiences as well. My first brush with supposedly significant patterns came as a child at the beach when I was told that every seventh wave was especially big. This intrigued me, and every once in a while I would take a break from making sandcastles (and anatomically generous mermaids) to count the waves. I'd pick an area of beach in front of me, wait for the biggest wave I could find to hit the shore, then start counting. After about ten or fifteen minutes it became clear to me that the number seven, in this case anyway, held no special import or significance. Big waves came and went without apparent pattern or reason.

The phenomenon resurfaced a few weeks after Diana, Princess of Wales, died in 1997, when I remember talking to my mother about Diana's death and the resulting news coverage. Among other things, she wondered aloud who would be the next beloved figure to die. "Deaths come in threes," she informed me. Mother Teresa had also died recently, and that of course left one more prominent person on the deathwatch. The "death in threes" idea seemed strange to me. Tens of thousands of people die every day from disease, accident, suicide, or murder. Out of all those, which are "counted" (and by whom or what?) toward the string of three? Judging by my mother's examples, presumably the deaths only include famous people.

And where do you start counting? My mother assumed that Princess Diana was the first, having been killed August 31, and that Mother Teresa was the second, coming just a week later. But what if Diana instead was the *second* in a set of three (perhaps Jimmy Stewart was first, on July 2), and Mother Teresa completed the set? How would anyone know? I wondered how long my mother would wait for the final installment of the terrible trilogy. If the deaths are ordered in noticeable groups of three, presumably they would come within a certain timeframe, say a few days or weeks. But I realized that if you don't specify or predefine what time frame you're looking for, you won't know if you have it. With any set of events, if you pick and choose which ones you notice, you can make groups of anything (this is a common error that appears in poorly controlled tests of psychic abilities; see Wiseman and Morris's book *Guidelines for Testing Psychic Claimants*). People often see patterns they impose, not necessarily real patterns in the world.

As with the "seventh wave," this and most other similar claims are testable. If a person believes that big waves come in sevens, good things come in fives, deaths come in threes, or whatever, these can be tested to see if they are true. The "deaths come in threes" was a bit of folk wisdom that passed along from person to person, without any critical examination or explanation.

Eyewitnesses and Personal Experience

Studies have shown that personal experience—contrasted with, say, academic experience or second-hand information—strongly influences our perceptions and beliefs. We may hear newscasters discuss the dangers of highways on the nightly news, but the point won't really be driven home until someone we know is injured in an accident. That's just the way the brain has developed: to emphasize emotional, vivid events. Stories are better remembered than statistics; personal experience and emotional events are imprinted much more strongly on our thought processes than those told to us by others. Much of the time this is useful. But because human perception and understanding is subject to many influences and mistakes, it can very easily lead us astray.

Most people recognize on some level that personal experience can't always be trusted. If we are on a jury, we should be more comfortable convicting a defendant on the basis of incriminating fingerprints or DNA evidence than an eyewitness's identification. Carl Sagan wrote in *The Demon-Haunted World*: "American police procedure concentrates on evidence and not anecdotes. As the European witch trials remind us, suspects can be intimidated during interrogation; people confess to crimes they never committed; eyewitnesses can be mistaken....But real, unfabricated evidence—powder burns, fingerprints, DNA samples, footprints, hair under the fingernails of the struggling victim—carry great weight. Criminalists employ something very close to the scientific method, and for the same reasons."

The human brain continually processes thoughts, impressions, sensations, decisions, interpretations, memories, and judgments—perhaps tens of thousands per day. Most of these mental processes are trivial. But some are more significant and noticeable than others, and throughout the day, especially if we are tired, distracted, stressed, or emotional, our brain makes errors. We forget where we parked the car at the supermarket, we misremember people's names, we jump to faulty conclusions. But just as the brain makes mistakes on these trivial issues, those same errors also occur in important issues as well (such as identifying a suspect in a robbery). Personal experience is not always a reliable guide to the world. So we must look to other ways to verify our perceptions; so far science is the best way humanity has devised to do that.

This is common in superstitious thinking; the same principle occurs when, for example, professional tennis players eat exactly the same meals and stay in the same rooms at the same hotels following a big win. They think that their success must have something to do with circumstances beyond their abilities. Poker players will wear the same "lucky" shirt they were wearing when they hit it big, and so on. This is actually a logical fallacy with a Latin name: *post hoc ergo propter hoc* ("after this, therefore because of it"), also known as faulty causation. The human brain seeks causes, and will find them even when they don't exist. We did something, then something bad happened. We did something else, and things were okay, so what we did the first time must have caused the bad things to happen. But that may or may not be true.

When I speak to people who have had special unexplained encounters—say, with psychic powers, or ghosts, or other mysterious phenomena, I'm struck by the confidence with which people aver their beliefs in the face of contradictory evidence. Often they say that they saw it with their own eyes, and know what they experienced. That may be entirely true, but it also raises the question: Can people misunderstand and misperceive the world around them? This is not even a question— it has been firmly, repeatedly, and reliably proven. Innocent people have been jailed for years—even decades—based upon faulty eyewitness testimony. There is no end to the people who sincerely and profoundly believe that they have experienced something unexplainable or mystical. "Until you experience it for yourself," they say, "You'll never know."

People like to believe that they accurately experience, remember, and understand what they see and hear. Yet, as any psychologist or police detective can tell you, our experiences are impressionable and fragile, subject to moods, drugs, expectations, assumptions, and beliefs. We often see what we wish or expect to see; this is not a sign of a foolish or dull mind but a profoundly human one. A man who thinks he cannot be fooled has already fooled himself.

Folie à deux

In most cases, two eyewitnesses are better than one. A second person brings a second perspective to the incident, and might have noticed different details than the first eyewitness. But having a second person corroborate an eyewitness account does not always bring us closer to understanding what happened. This is because sometimes one person's faulty interpretation will be adopted and reinforced by another person.

Sometimes two people—usually people who are related, have longstanding relationships, or have common interests and opinions—will reinforce each other's beliefs. Two, three or more people can share in a collective delusion. Often the subjects report minor, odd experiences, such as strange, untraceable noises, feelings of skin crawling or nausea, etc.

Folie à deux is a form of mass hysteria, and though it is rare, it does occur and should be considered as a possible explanation for an event that could not have occurred as claimed, yet two eyewitnesses swear happened as described. In chapter 5, I describe an instance of folie à deux in a haunted house I investigated. An excellent, fictional example can be seen in the 2006 horror film *Bug*, directed by William Friedkin and starring Ashley

Judd. In the film, a man begins having hallucinations about being attacked by insects and being watched; because he is sincere, a friend of his also begins experiencing his hallucinations. (For more on this, see Arnone, D., A. Patel, and G.M. Tan. 2006. The nosological significance of Folie à deux: a review of the literature, in *Annual of General Psychiatry*, 5:11; Shimizu, M., Y. Kubota, M. Toichi, and H. Baba. 2007. Folie à deux and shared psychiatric disorder, in *Current Psychiatry Reports*, 9:200.)

The Filedrawer Effect

Investigators who research previous cases of paranormal phenomena should be aware of what's called a "filedrawer effect": paranormal phenomena that seem mysterious at first but are soon identified or solved are only rarely reported. With a few exceptions, researchers don't hear about examples where eyewitnesses were confident in their reports, yet proven wrong. This leads to a situation in which the instances where the phenomena were not explained or identified are seen as much more common than the instances in which explanations were found; that is, you are far more likely to read about the one case where a person couldn't explain what he saw, than you are to read about the dozens of other cases where a person didn't know what he saw, but later identified it.

The fact that something initially thought to be unexplainable or mysterious was later found to be an ordinary event does not make the report irrelevant. Quite the opposite, it is very valuable because it adds to our knowledge of real-life examples that were mistaken for paranormal events. Previous explained examples help investigators build the list of possible alternative explanations, which must be ruled out before accepting a paranormal one.

The skeptical literature is full of examples of verified misidentifications: A Bigfoot turns out to be a dark rock; a ghost is revealed to be an unnoticed reflection. But they are only a small fraction of such cases, and notable for the fact that they were proven wrong and exposed. Logically and statistically, it stands to reason that for every case that makes news or gets written up as an article, dozens or perhaps hundreds of similar, everyday examples of misidentifications are not reported. Witnesses may feel silly for admitting they were fooled, or believe their sightings are not worth reporting since nothing unusual was discovered. After all, if I am fooled by a floating log or a large deer mistaken for a lake monster, why would I bother to mention it to cryptozoologists (monster-hunters) and researchers? And even if I did, would they be interested and recognize the value in my report?

This fundamental—but rarely recognized—bias in eyewitness (and investigator) reporting naturally leads to focusing on the unexplained sightings while ignoring or downplaying the explained ones. But to accurately understand eyewitness reports, researchers can't just pick and choose. They must take *all* of them into account—focusing not just on the *unidentified* but also the *misidentified*. Only with this scientific and statistical understanding will a valid picture emerge.

Case Studies in the Psychology of the Paranormal

Here are some case studies from my files illustrating real-world examples of misperceptions, misinterpretations, and other mis-things in the brain.

Faulty Perception: The Case of the Disappearing Dhow

In July 2007, on a visit to East Africa, I visited the Bamburi beach resort, a small hotel north of Mombasa, Kenya. I spent a few days relaxing on a patio overlooking the Indian Ocean, sipping cold beers and taking in the scenery. From my comfortable patio perch I had a magnificent view of palm trees, sunny beach, and the ocean. I watched local hustlers badger strolling tourists into buying their carvings and riding their sullen, saddled camels. I saw chubby American women chasing local African hunks along the beach. In the trees above me I even watched two monkeys with gigantic, neon-blue gonads fight over Doritos and chunks of banana.

But the strangest thing I saw was a disappearing dhow.

The dhows boats are of ancient design, and come in many variations. The smallest ones, common along the east coast of Africa, have a small sail and two stabilizing frames that stick out on either side.

On my first morning at the hotel, I went to the patio where breakfast was served. As I waited for a cup of wretched instant coffee, I surveyed the scenery and skies, planning out my day in paradise. Looking out over the water, I saw a dozen or so identical dhows anchored in the shallow waters a few hundred meters offshore. One in particular caught my eye, because it was closer to shore than the rest, and lay low in the water—intact but apparently sunken (see figure 2.1)

I noticed that it had a small band of white paint on the mast. I wondered why it hadn't been removed (aren't sunken boats a hazard so close to shore?), but my musings were soon ended by a lovely (and very distracting) British girl in a rather skimpy bikini sunning herself on the beach below. I gave the dhow little thought for the rest of the day and soon headed out for a beach jog.

Later that afternoon I returned from a trip into town and headed to my favorite table on the patio. I turned to face the warm ocean breeze and noticed something odd: the sunken dhow was gone. In its place were a dozen or so boats, high in the water and doing just fine (see figure 2.2). I pointed it out to one of my companions, saying that I was surprised someone had salvaged the dhow and hauled it away during the four hours or so since breakfast. The wreck had probably been there for weeks or months, but it was clearly no longer there, apparently removed that day.

The next morning I slept in late, and (being on holiday) I got up a bit before noon. As I waited for my plate of fruit and very mediocre pancakes, I glanced out at the ocean. To my astonishment, the dhow had

Figure 2.1, a "disappearing dhow" in East Africa.

reappeared! I sat up in my chair and squinted against the sun.

"What the hell?" I said, mostly to myself. I got up and walked to the edge of the deck. It was the same boat, confirmed by the small but clear white band on the mast. What was going on? How could the boat disappear, then reappear? Why would someone remove a sunken boat, take it away for the afternoon, then replace it overnight? It was very mysterious, and though this scientific paranormal investigator was off-duty, I set about solving the puzzle.

Figure 2.2, a mysteriously "reappearing dhow," the result of an illusion.

As it was nearly noon, the first step was to immediately order a cold Tusker beer to help sharpen my powers of deduction. Usually I celebrate a solved mystery with a beer, but I wanted to mix things up a bit. I spent about fifteen minutes writing down a few observations in my journal: Despite appearances to the contrary, it was possible—though highly unlikely—that the boat had in fact become invisible. Occam's Razor (see the next section) required that before I explore the idea of mysterious sea vortices or UFO-generated invisibility fields, I look for simpler explanations. The half-naked women wandering the beach nearby did not help my concentration, but none of the explanations made sense. Either the dhow had pulled a Houdini and disappeared while I wasn't watching, or someone was pulling a prank, or moving the boat for arcane reasons, or... or....

Or the boat had *not* disappeared, and was in fact there all along. I looked more closely at the shore and realized I had been fooled by an interesting optical illusion—two, in fact. Both parts of the illusion were caused by the tides. During the morning's low tide, as I had first seen the ocean, the floating boats were farther back in the ocean, leaving the disappearing dhow obviously low in the water and clearly set apart from the others (see figure 2.1 again).

During the afternoon's high tide, however, the dhow no longer appeared sunken because it was buoyed along with the rest of the boats; all of them were at the same water level, and all of them rocked with the waves. The high tide brought the rest of the anchored boats closer to shore, surrounding the sunken dhow with nearly identical boats (see figure 2.2 again). If I hadn't noticed the small white band on the mast, I might not have been able to pick it out from shore.

But why hadn't I noticed that the group of boats were farther away during low tide? The movement of the boats would have been more noticeable if not for the second part of the illusion. I had gauged the boats' locations in the water by their distance from the shoreline, and from there it looked like the boats were at about the same place in the water. But I hadn't realized that the shoreline moved so dramatically with the tides. Neptune was playing tricks on me, deviously moving my reference point so that the boats appeared to be the same relative distance from the shoreline at both high and low tides. I later measured the difference between low and high tide on the beach, and found that there was at least a 160 foot (53 meter) difference.

The disappearing dhow (and the moving shoreline effect) may have been obvious to locals, and it's true that I grew up in the New Mexico desert of the American Southwest, wholly devoid of either oceans or dhows. But I've spent a fair amount of time in and around the world's oceans and beaches, and I'd never noticed anything like it.

Common misperceptions and misunderstandings can make ordinary things seem extraordinary. When people encounter something they can't explain, their first assumption should always be that they might have misunderstood something. Most of the time our perceptions are pretty accurate, but sometimes they are not—and we don't necessarily know when they are wrong unless we are confronted with an obvious paradox, as I was with the disappearing dhow.

Faulty Interpretation: The Case of the Psychic Cat

In college I worked at a restaurant in my small hometown (actually it had a reputation for being haunted—but that's a story for another book). Among my coworkers was a woman name Jeuta, an artistic, effervescent and slightly flaky waitress who lived in the next town over. I visited her one day for tea, and our conversation turned to cats. She had a fluffy one and knew I liked them myself. She said that she believed that cats had special powers, that they could sense things beyond the normal senses. Of course many animal senses are far better than humans'; bloodhounds can track people and cats can see in near-darkness. But she went beyond that to claim that cats —or at least her cat—actually had paranormal abilities. She smiled as I looked intrigued. "Example!" I requested, cocking an eyebrow and crossing my arms.

She stirred honey into her organic herbal tea. "Example: Cats can sense the tops of tables and counters while they're still on the floor." I asked how she knew that, and she explained that when her cat jumps up onto surfaces that are cluttered with items, he rarely if ever knocks anything over. She had delicate art items on many shelves and tables, and of course the cat had the run of the house. (Essentially the cat was allowing her to stay there and feed him for the privilege of his company.)

Jeuta correctly noted that the cat could not see what was on top of surfaces before he jumped, yet he almost invariably managed to alight with what seemed to be paranormal foreknowledge of what he would encounter, thus avoiding accidents. I gave this a few seconds thought, and suggested that perhaps she wasn't giving enough credit to the cat's natural reflexes—which are, after all, legendary. It seemed to me that when the cat jumps, as it arrives at the end of his leap, he has split-seconds to adjust his movement and balance to avoid collisions with whatever is up there. Split seconds isn't much time for you or me, but plenty of time for all but the most slothful of domestic felines.

I didn't discount my friend's explanation—it is indeed possible that cats (or at least her cat) had supernatural powers. But it seemed much more likely that the answer lay in *known* abilities and processes. When it comes to paranormal or supernatural explanations, to borrow a famous line from Pierre LaPlace, I have no need of that hypothesis—science can often explain it quite well. Which explanation is more likely: That her cat has psychic powers, or that it has excellent reflexes? The answer, of course, is that we have proof that the cat has excellent reflexes, and no proof it has psychic powers. This is also a fallacy from personal incredulity (discussed later): Jeuta believed that since she couldn't think of an explanation for the cat's abilities, it had to be paranormal.

Jumping to Conclusions: The *Destination Truth* Yeti Tracks

The Yeti is Nepal's version of the American Bigfoot. Like Bigfoot, it is large, powerful, leaves strange tracks, and has never been proven to exist outside of folklore and myth. Interest in the supposed creature is fueled by occasional sighting reports and odd footprints, but a few years ago an American television crew claimed to have found the Yeti's tracks not far from Mount Everest.

Josh Gates, host of the Sci Fi series *Destination Truth*, claimed that he found three mysterious footprints on November 28, 2007: one full print that measured about thirteen inches long, and two partial prints. Gates said that he could not identify what made them, but that they are "very, very similar" to other strange tracks previously found in the Himalayas and attributed to the Yeti. To Gates and his television crew, this apparently seemed like strong evidence for the elusive creature.

Yet there is a scientific explanation for many Yeti footprints found in the Himalayas. Tracks in snow can be very difficult to interpret correctly because of the unstable nature of the medium in which they are found. Snow physically changes as the temperature varies. As sunlight hits it, this has several effects, often making the tracks of ordinary animals seem both larger and misshapen. As sunlight strikes the impression from different angles, the sides of the tracks melt unevenly. Thus a bear track made at night but found the next afternoon has been exposed to the morning sun and might change into a mysterious track with splayed toes—much like the one Gates and his crew found.

While the track Gates found was apparently not in snow, it was in a medium almost as bad: rocky soil near a river. It can be difficult or impossible to get accurate tracks of even known animals in such hard, uneven terrain. If the soil was soft enough to make a valid impression, as Gates claimed, it is puzzling that he found only one complete track. Unless the creature was dropped from a helicopter, scampered a few feet, and then picked up again, there should be a continuous line of dozens or hundreds of tracks. Or, if the terrain is so poor at capturing tracks that he only found one full print, how accurate can Gates's track be? It's amazing that anyone would claim to have found evidence for the Yeti based on only one ambiguous track found in rocky soil.

Gates and the *Destination Truth* crew interpreted the tracks as those of a Yeti; after all, they were in the area specifically searching for the creature, and as soon as they found something that seemed mysterious, they called the press claiming they'd found evidence. Gates's claims fail Logic 101: Just because Gates doesn't know what made the track doesn't mean that a Yeti did. It's a classic example of jumping to an unwarranted conclusion and an argument from personal incredulity.

Assuming that the track is real, there are several animals that could have made it. Those who live in the foothills of the Himalayas were skeptical about Gates's claim, suggesting that he simply misinterpreted tracks from a mountain bear. Sir Edmund Hillary, who was the first to scale Everest with sherpa Tenzing Norgay, found no evidence of the creature. Famous mountaineer Reinhold Messner also spent months in Nepal and Tibet, climbing mountains and researching Yeti reports following his own sighting. In his book *My Quest for the Yeti*, Messner concludes that large native bears are responsible for Yeti sightings and tracks.

It's not surprising that the track fooled Gates and his crew, since they did little investigation and only spent about a week in the area. Gates is an actor, not a zoologist or animal tracker, and has little or no experience with supposed Yeti footprints. Gates's credibility is not helped by his appearances on the *Ghost Hunters* television show. That series, like *Destination*

Truth, is far more interested in making sensational claims and garnering ratings than actually solving mysteries or scientifically analyzing the evidence.

Finding Significance in Coincidences: The Wikipedia Prophecy

The murder-suicide of Canadian pro wrestler Chris Benoit of his wife and son was bizarre and shocking enough: Benoit strangled his wife and seven-year-old son the night of June 22, 2007, at his home in suburban Atlanta, Georgia. But the story got even stranger when someone noticed that Benoit's entry in the online encyclopedia Wikipedia had been amended to note the death of Benoit's wife. This would not be unusual—except for the fact that the addition was made anonymously at 12:01 A.M., over twelve hours before police found the Benoit family dead. How was that possible? A posting by an anonymous psychic? Was the contributor somehow involved in the deaths? The Internet was abuzz with spooked speculation.

Before going too far with ideas about conspiracy theories or prophecy, there are a few things to note. First of all, contrary to rumor, the Wikipedia entry did not predict Benoit's killing of his wife or his child. It said: "Chris Benoit was replaced by Johnny Nitro for the [wrestling] match at *Vengeance*, as Benoit was not there due to personal issues, stemming from the death of his wife Nancy." There is no mention of Benoit's involvement in his wife's death at all; in fact the entry suggests that the wrestler had the option to participate in the event but chose not to. The "personal issues" explanation for Benoit's absence would seem to be something of an understatement given that he was dead.

Second, death rumors are among the most common types of rumors about celebrities and their families. Many popular performers (including Will Ferrell, Johnny Knoxville, Britney Spears, Paul McCartney, and Brad Pitt) have at one time or another been the subject of erroneously reported deaths. According to the rumor mill, Mikey (from the Life cereal commercials) was killed when he mixed Pop Rocks with soda, and of course Bobby McFerrin (composer of the 1988 hit "Don't Worry, Be Happy") killed himself to end a suicidal depression.

Third, this incident shows how people will often overinterpret mere coincidences as much more meaningful than they are. In Benoit's case, the still-anonymous writer simply made a wild guess (and tasteless joke) based on rumors. The writer admitted, "Last weekend, I had heard about Chris Benoit no-showing [at] *Vengeance* because of a family emergency, and I had heard rumors about why that was. I was reading rumors and speculation about this matter online, and one of them included that his wife may have passed away, and I did the wrong thing by posting it on Wikipedia [in spite of] there being no evidence. I posted my speculation on the situation at the time and I am deeply sorry about this.... it is one of those things that just turned into a huge coincidence." There are probably thousands of other errors and literary pranks on Wikipedia, a few of which may turn out to be strangely prophetic purely by chance.

The Will to Believe: The Case of the Psychic Psychotherapist

While in college, I went to a therapist because I was having trouble focusing on my studies. I could read and study for an hour or so, but then I'd get distracted and go watch television or listen to music instead. I thought he might be able to give me suggestions on relaxing and concentrating. The therapist was pleasant enough, and said he could help me using hypnosis. I paid $40 each for four one-hour sessions. Though I scored well on measures designed to rate hypnotizability (such as describing a miniature dragon flying around the room), nothing happened. Try as I might, I could not be hypnotized. I tried hard to cooperate, but in my heart of hearts I wasn't going to play along and say I was hypnotized when I wasn't. For $40 an hour, I wouldn't pretend to be helped, just as I wouldn't pay a waiter who only pretended to serve me a meal.

Finally, as the third unsuccessful session ended, my hypnotherapist suggested another treatment. It was used, he said, for patients who could not be hypnotized or who had "deeper issues." As I had already invested nearly a month and $150 into trying to improve my study habits, I agreed. The treatment was administered by a friend of his, a pleasant woman who apparently didn't even need to speak to me; all her work was done, I was told, with her mind. Although she didn't officially refer to herself as a psychic, that's what she was doing. I sat in a small, darkened office watching a red lava lamp wiggle and ooze while this woman sat in a chair near the door, her eyes closed. No words were spoken, and in fact she said she could do the work even when I was asleep, so it was okay if I dozed off. Forty silent minutes later, she turned up the lights and said that she had been "through my doors," and found "a locked chest" that she couldn't open. She asked if I knew what was in the chest. It was of course all very symbolic, and I said I didn't really know, though I wondered what my doors looked like, and if the chest contained that miniature dragon I'd envisioned. Poor cramped thing. She said that we could work on that next time and asked if I could pay her in cash.

I did return for one more treatment with her. I did it because both she and the hypnotherapist were very sincere; because I had invested about $200 in my treatment so far; and because, though I had my doubts, in the back of my mind I really hoped they could help me. I'm slightly embarrassed about it now, but it showed me just how powerful the will to believe is. In the end, I didn't really have a problem concentrating, at least no more so than most people. I had created a problem, and the solution lay within myself, not in hypnosis or the paranormal.

PART II: CONDUCTING SCIENTIFIC PARANORMAL INVESTIGATION

There is no one "right" way to investigate claims, except through the use of critical thinking and scientific methods. The techniques I present here have proven themselves useful and effective in solving mysteries. They are drawn from many sources including professional investigations (such as procedures used by police detectives, FBI agents, and investigative journalists), scientific methodologies, formal and informal logic, psychology, personal experience, and other investigators—along with a dose of common sense.

The history of investigation (paranormal and otherwise) shows again and again that this is the most important element of a successful investigation. As a general rule, investigations conducted using these techniques find solutions to the mysteries; investigations that do not usually end up unsolved or with ambiguous evidence.

Each investigator brings his or her own background, expertise, techniques, and talents to investigations. Joe Nickell wrote his own excellent guide to investigation (with Bob Baker): *Missing Pieces: How to Investigate Ghosts, UFOs, Psychics, and Other Mysteries* (1992, Prometheus Books). Joe has been a wonderful mentor, and I learned a lot from him during our many joint investigations and misadventures. Anyone hoping to understand this field should consult his books, as well as those by Massimo Polidoro, James Randi, and others mentioned here.

I can't solve mysteries for you, but I can offer these blueprints and principles; along with the case studies and commentary in the next section, you will be well-prepared to solve the world's greatest mysteries. I've made plenty of mistakes (some of them mentioned in this book), and with each new case I learn new things.

CHAPTER 3
How to Solve Unexplained Mysteries

I n determining the best way to solve a mystery, it is first important to understand the nature of mysteries. Webster's Collegiate dictionary defines *mystery* as "something not understood, or beyond understanding." Yet this definition actually confuses the issue, because the two definitions are not interchangeable; "something not understood" is rather ordinary, while something "beyond understanding" is quite extraordinary. The former implies a temporary ignorance of the true situation due to a lack of information, while the latter states rather dismissively (and omnisciently) that the event is beyond understanding, and in fact has no explanation, no knowable solution.

There is no shortage of things that at one point were not understood, but later clearly understood. For example, for millennia no one knew how diseases were spread until germ theory was developed. Why some people caught the plague and died was a mystery to people in the 1500s, but it is no longer a mystery today. The mystery was solved through scientific investigation—a mystery created by a temporary lack of knowledge, not some supernatural event beyond human understanding.

Some people believe that paranormal phenomena are inherently unknowable. For example, in their guide to ghost hunting, three well-known experts stated, "paranormal evidence is always inconclusive" (Gibson, Burns, and Schrader 2009). I have encountered the same position elsewhere; during a haunted house investigation in California for a TV show, I had a friendly discussion with a member of a ghost hunting group. I asked him why the evidence for ghosts never seemed to get any better, and he replied that ghosts were scientifically unprovable. I pointed out that his team (teasingly dubbed the "Boo Crew" by the show's producers) had brought with them a huge van full of thousands of dollars' worth of cameras, EMF detectors, and ghost hunting gadgets of all description. What was the point of all that, I asked him? If he was certain that ghosts existed—and he was equally certain that their presence could not be scientifically measured—then all the high tech equipment they used was by definition worthless.

I don't understand this fatalistic point of view; it seems like a classic exercise in futility. Part of the problem is that they are not using scientifically valid or useful definitions. They are assuming that a ghost is something they can't explain, instead of a descriptive label for a particular type of experience.

History has shown us that all such mysteries are in theory solvable, and this book is packed with dozens of examples. There is no reason to think that "paranormal mysteries" are any different than other mysteries. If people don't assume that the mysterious disappearances of Amelia Earhart or Natalee Holloway have supernatural explanations, why would they assume that crop circles or ghosts have supernatural solutions?

Mysteries must be approached with the assumption that they are solvable—that given enough information and analysis, they can be understood. This does not necessarily preclude discovering some new entity or phenomenon; if Bigfoot, psychic powers, and ghosts can be proven to exist, they will be incorporated into the known canon of science. They are not, as some might claim, "outside science," instead they would become part of established science. They would join a long list of phenomena that were at one time considered mysterious, but whose nature was finally understood and accepted. Science does not fear or reject "mysterious" and supposedly paranormal events, it embraces them.

Being open-minded to the possibility that you might encounter something unknown to science is fine, but if you go into a case believing that the true solution to the phenomenon is probably unknowable, why bother to investigate? That is a sure-fire scientific inquiry dead-end, akin to "explaining" something by simply saying "it's a miracle" or "it's God's will." True scientific investigation ends once you introduce the supernatural into the equation, because there's no difference between saying, "I don't understand it" and "it's supernatural and therefore unknowable." Saying "I don't have the answer yet" is a perfectly valid, legitimate, and scientific response. But invoking the supernatural by saying "no one can know the answer" is not only arrogant, unscientific, and unprovable, but also discourages investigation.

I don't approach an investigation assuming that I will fail, but instead that if I work hard enough, I can solve the case. If you are convinced that unexplained mysteries and "paranormal phenomenon" are fundamentally unexplainable, then your investigation is already over.

There is also the issue of who, exactly, the event or phenomenon is a mystery to—who is deeming the event inexplicable or unsolvable. What seems odd or inexplicable to one person may be completely understandable to another. Typically, something that is a mystery to a layperson is a solvable problem for an expert. That is why ordinary people hire specialists: to explain or handle things that seem too arcane or mysterious for us layfolk. We hire mechanics to investigate and solve (fix) that strange buzzing sound under the hood. We hire lawyers to investigate ways to get us out of legal trouble (or avoid it in the first place), and solve the problem. We hire doctors to investigate pains and diseases, find the solution to the problem, and treat it. And, more to the point of this book, when confronted with mysteries that are also crimes, we hire people who are trained in investigation and scientific methods (such as police detectives) to research the phenomenon.

Thus many "mysteries" are not really mysteries at all; they are simply phenomena with which the average person has little or no experience. Yet when it comes to the supposedly greatest "unexplained" mysteries in the world—ghosts, crop circles, psychic powers, and so on—people often assume that no expertise or knowledge is needed to investigate or understand the phenomenon. (More on this in Chapter 4.)

Mystery as Missing Context

To an investigator, a mystery is simply an event out of context. A live dolphin laying on a Manhattan sidewalk is a mystery; that same dolphin in a tank at an aquarium is not. Ten thousand gallons of boiling caramel inside a Boeing 747 airplane is a mystery; that same caramel in a candy factory is not. Each mystery or strange event has some surrounding circumstance or context that will render it non-mysterious.

The investigator's job is to find a context in which the mysterious phenomenon makes sense. Think of a completed jigsaw puzzle as a solved mystery. As an investigator you will be given a few pieces of the puzzle (for example in the form of photographs or eyewitness reports). Some pieces of information may be bogus puzzle pieces (such as hoaxes, lies, or incorrect information), and you must verify the truth of each fact before you use it in the puzzle. From a few pieces of the puzzle, you must assemble the rest of the solution.

Often, the mystery is created when the facts are not merely lacking a context, but put into the wrong context. A person claiming that an event is mysterious or paranormal is presenting you with a jigsaw puzzle with a few of the pieces obviously wrong but jammed in there anyway, and saying, "Look! This doesn't fit! This must be a mystery!" They have added their own pieces—fashioned from misinformation, bad logic, or faulty assumptions—to fill in the gaps and constructed the wrong frame around the pieces of evidence. They can't think of any other way to make the pieces fit, and their "solution" is that the event is an unexplainable mystery.

In a real, physical jigsaw puzzle, of course, it's obvious when the solution you propose is wrong, because the pieces don't fit. But this metaphorical puzzle is especially tricky, because it has a flexible frame that makes the bogus pieces appear to fit if you don't look too closely.

In most of the case studies in this book, I began with a few pieces of the puzzle and eventually solved the mystery by finding the correct circumstances around which the strange phenomena made sense. With mysteries, like puzzles, the more you do, the better you get at solving them. You gain experience and expertise; you begin seeing patterns in claims, and learn from your mistakes.

Finding Mysteries

The first question that often comes up is, "Where do you find the mysteries to investigate?" Actually, mysteries are all around you; every town or city has some strange story, from a local haunted house (or "bad place") to a monster sighting to a local psychic. Yet in a way the prevalence of mysteries is a problem; there are far more mysteries than there are investigators (and certainly skeptical ones!). Scientific paranormal investigators must carefully choose which cases to look into, picking those that 1) have specific, investigatable claims; 2) are within your means of investigation; and 3) have sufficient notoriety or information. In fact the best cases are those which are held up (by some writer or "expert") as the "best evidence" for the phenomenon. That way, if you can solve the case, you have undermined the credibility of other, lesser cases in the process.

Typically investigators either choose a mystery that intrigues them (or one that they already have some background in), or they are presented with a case by the news media (for example, a local TV station is doing a report on a weeping statue and requests an investigation).

Types of Mysteries and Investigations

There are four basic types of investigations you'll encounter as a paranormal investigator. These divisions are not hard and fast, and some investigations fall into more than one category, but each of them requires a slightly different focus.

Historical cases are those in which an unexplained event or phenomena happened at some time in the past, usually at a specific place, and is not currently active. This might include the Great Pyramid of Ghiza, the Amityville Horror case, the Nasca lines of Peru, the Bermuda Triangle, the 1947 Roswell Crash site, and so on. My investigation of the Pokémon Panic (Chapter 11) is a historical mystery, as were parts of my chupacabra investigation (Chapter 13). These cases are often solved largely through careful research and analysis. While I always advocate actually going to the place where the mystery occurred, it is not always practical or useful in historical mysteries. For example it's unlikely you will uncover any new information by visiting the Great Pyramid, or taking a cruise through the Bermuda Triangle.

Field investigations are those in which the phenomena are (or may be) still going on, so there is something to actively investigate. Field investigations might include visiting a haunted house with recent reports of some recurring activity, or searching a lake for its monster, or visiting a crop circle (Chapters 5, 7, 8, and 12 are examples of field investigations). These cases are often solved by a combination of field experiments, background research, and careful analysis. More on field investigations later in this chapter.

Forensic research mysteries are similar to historical mysteries, though not necessarily tied to a specific place. Such investigations might include a psychic detective's claim of having solved an old crime, or looking at Nostradamus's prophecies, or re-examining a person's claim of alien abduction. "The psychic and the serial killer case" case (Chapter 6) is an example of a forensic research mystery. Like historical mysteries, these cases are often solved by attention to detailed research and analysis—discovering a "smoking gun" hidden in some obscure newspaper report, or double-checking facts to find that primary sources contradict the "official version." These cases can be especially challenging because the investigator must rely on his or her research skills, and unlike historical mysteries, there may be no actual "place" to visit to further investigate or do original research: it's all in books, files, newspaper reports, original documents, and so on. However, all investigations—every single one, no matter the subject matter—begins with good background research, and sometimes the mystery is solved by doing little more than reading what you found.

Experimental investigations usually focus on a specific person who claims to have some unusual ability or power. Such people include water dowsers, psychics, "energy healers," people who claim to have X-ray vision or the ability to turn invisible, etc. My investigation of remote viewer Lee B (Chapter 10) is an example, and in a later section Massimo Polidoro discusses his experience with similar experiments. These mysteries depend greatly on an investigator's ability to devise and run a valid, well-controlled scientific experiment. Sometimes the testing is easy and pretty straightforward; other times it is complex. It is very, very important that scientific paranormal investigators have a solid understanding of scientific testing protocols before testing any claimants. They should understand control groups, blind and double-blind studies, and statistics; designing and maintaining a strict protocol (for example to rule out hoaxing or random chance) can be difficult, even for experienced, professional scientists. I recommend that aspiring investigators consult independent skeptics groups (such as the Independent Investigation Group of Hollywood, California) to learn more about how to test local claimants. A list of such groups can be found at www.csicop.org and in the back of *Skeptical Inquirer* magazine. Articles and books by Ray Hyman (2003), Richard Wiseman (1995), James Randi, and Susan Blackmore are especially helpful as well.

Of course, many mysteries involve a combination of one or more types of investigation. If you are investigating a ghost photograph, you may be able to solve the mystery by closely examining the photo and getting a description of the circumstances of the photograph (ideally first-hand from the photographer). On the other hand, in some cases you may need to personally visit the spot where the photograph was taken to duplicate the photograph in order to solve the mystery.

Researching the Mystery

Once you have chosen a mystery to investigate, you should research the topic thoroughly, on three levels: A) the general topic; B) the localized version of the topic; and C) the specific sighting, event, or phenomenon.

For example, if you are looking into a Bigfoot sighting on a farm in rural Pennsylvania, you need to not only learn as much as you can about that specific incident (C), but you also should research the history of Bigfoot sightings in Pennsylvania (B), as well as have a general knowledge (A) of Bigfoot sightings, claims, hoaxes, etc.

If you are investigating a local missing persons case where a psychic detective claims to have solved the crime, you should find out all you can about that missing persons case (C), but also do some investigation into the psychic detective herself (B), as well as have a good understanding of the skeptical literature about psychics detectives (A), their history, claims, and methods.

If you're investigating a specific case (and you always will be), why do you need to have background in the general topic? Let's say that during your Bigfoot investigation you meet a Bigfoot hunter named Tom who provides you with information about a sighting he had; if you focus only on that case, you might not discover from further research that he's a known hoaxer—a fact certainly important to know, and one that more general research would reveal.

Sounds like a lot of work, doesn't it? Well, it can be. But don't get discouraged; there are dozens of books out there on any given topic; you don't need to read all of them. Fortunately for you (but sadly for the world), the number of skeptical, well-researched articles and books on these topics is tiny compared to the believer literature. This gets back to the earlier discussion about the importance of research. Instead of approaching research as necessary drudgery, take pride in the fact that you are probably the first person to really do the research and take the first steps to solving the mystery. Sometimes you'll find a "smoking gun" fact or document or photograph that proves that everyone is wrong about the topic. I've spent many sleepless nights while in the throes of an exciting investigation, my mind racing with the implications of the information I've discovered. Solving mysteries that have baffled other people isn't always easy. If the answers were obvious, it wouldn't be a mystery or much of a challenge, and it certainly wouldn't take you to figure it out!

Avoid re-solving mysteries; in skeptical investigation, as in science, there are few definitive answers, and any explanation is always subject to revision upon new information. So if, for example, you are interested in investigating California's Winchester Mystery house, you should read up on all the skeptical research on it. You're welcome to look into solved cases, but unless you are going to improve on a previous investigation, or bring new evidence or a fresh perspective to the topic, there's little point in simply duplicating earlier work.

Applying Scientific Methods to Paranormal Investigation

Earlier I discussed the importance and fruitfulness of using scientific methodology. In many ways solving a mystery is like solving a crime or murder, and police work is based on scientific methods: collecting and examining evidence, constructing alternative theories about how the murder was committed and by whom, using science to test those theories, and so on.

Lewis Vaughn (2008) lists five steps involved in a scientific process: 1) Identify the problem or pose a question; 2) Devise a hypothesis to explain the event or phenomenon; 3) Derive a test implication or prediction; 4) Perform the test; and 5) Accept or reject the hypothesis.

When using these steps to investigate mysteries, identifying a problem will help frame the key questions. Sometimes the question comes down to whether a given phenomenon exists (for example, is there actually a Bermuda Triangle where unknown, deadly forces are at work, or is it merely a fictional construct?). Often the problem is identifying the nature or origin of a phenomenon (for example, there is no question that crop circles exist; the issue is who or what made them).

Devising a hypothesis involves seeking alternative explanations. Usually the first theory (or paranormal explanation) provided to an investigator will be the *last* one examined. Often it is not examined at all, because investigations begin with the most likely explanation, and normal explanations are found before the investigator gets to the paranormal ones.

This methodology is basic to detective work, and applies to any mystery, "paranormal" or otherwise. For example, police know that homicide victims are usually killed by someone the person knows (such as a friend or family member). Stranger slayings are very rare, so detectives naturally begin by looking at the most likely suspects (hypotheses) first. If, in the course of the investigation, it becomes clear that the victim was *not* killed by someone he or she knew, only then do the police begin investigating the less likely suspects (hypotheses). When doctors are presented with a pain or symptom, the most common possible causes are assumed (and ruled out) before testing for rarer disorders. This is a variation of the principle of Occam's Razor (discussed later).

When examining a photograph claimed to be of a ghost, for example, an investigator would devise a series of hypotheses that might include: a hoax; a camera artifact (such as a flash reflection); an optical illusion; a real person mistakenly photographed; and finally a ghost. If the subject is a weeping statute, potential alternative explanations might include a hoax; a natural phenomenon (such as condensation); an optical illusion; and finally that the statue is weeping miraculous tears.

This initial focus on naturalistic, normal explanations has the added benefit of giving the investigator a place to start. Since the nature of paranormal phenomenon is by definition unknown, devising valid hypotheses and tests to examine that phenomenon can be very difficult. A ghost might be any size or form; it may or may not appear in photographs, it may or may not leave "cold spots," emit electromagnetic fields, and so on. With so many variables (and without even an established, evidence-based definition of *ghost*), collecting evidence of ghosts can be like grabbing a fistful of rain.

On the other hand, by starting with alternative, scientific explanations whose characteristics are known, an investigator can accept or reject those hypotheses. This is also where research and experience become very helpful. For example, when presented with a UFO photo, one immediate question is its authenticity: is it a hoax? In order to explore that explanation, it is very helpful to know something about previous hoaxed photographs, specifically hoaxed UFO photos (as well as "UFO" photos that were later revealed to have natural causes). If the investigator is examining reports of a lake monster, one possible explanation might be that eyewitnesses were seeing large fish or other animals; in order to explore that idea, it is important to research what animals live in and around the lake.

Once alternative explanations are selected, they are individually tested. Each explanation or hypothesis will have its own logical implications. In the study of logic this is called a conditional syllogism and takes the form of, "If A, then B," or "If A is true, then B should be true."

If a ghost creates the sound of mysterious footsteps in an empty hallway, *then* an investigator should be able to hear or record them (see Chapter 5). *If* a crop circle is the work of hoaxers, *then* investigators can expect to find certain specific characteristics (see Chapter 7). *If* a ghostly image captured on a surveillance camera is a piece of floating cotton, *then* putting a piece of floating cotton in front of the camera (under the same circumstances) should re-create the ghost (see Chapter 9).

Testing in some cases may mean actual experimental testing. More broadly, testing means carefully comparing the claims against other, independent information (such as checking a psychic's claims against other sources). Sometimes alternative explanations can be rejected quickly, for good reasons. For example, if there are multiple eyewitnesses to some paranormal phenomenon who saw it under different conditions, it is less likely to be an optical illusion.

Once the test is done, the results will guide the investigation. If the hypothesis was successful and fits the facts, then the case is solved; if not, then the next most likely explanation should be tested.

The elements of scientific research design are beyond the scope of this book, but investigators who plan to conduct any sort of experiment should be familiar with the basic concepts of experimental methodology. This includes subject selection, representative sampling, identifying the dependent and independent variables in the experiment, deciding how a dependent variable is to be measured (i.e., personal observation or instrument), and establishing how the results will be analyzed (i.e., what observed effect would confirm or refute the hypothesis?).

Scientific experiments are carefully controlled by the investigator or experimenter: he or she controls some conditions (called independent variables), and measures the variation (dependent variables). To use a basic example, if a scientist wants to see if one potting soil helps plants grow better than another potting soil, she can set up a simple experiment to test this. But she would need to establish careful controls over the experiment to make sure that the results she gets are valid. She would take two identical plants (ideally cuttings from the same parent plant to control for genetics) and expose them to identical sunlight, water, temperature, and so on—essentially controlling a dozen or more variables, so that she can be sure that any difference in growth between the two plants is a result of the dependent variable, the different potting soil. This careful control of the environments is absolutely critical to conducting a valid experiment. If one of the plants was given more sunlight or more water, then that could be the reason it grew better, regardless of which soil it was planted in. Without careful control over the variables and conditions, the experiment is invalid and any results from that experiment are worthless.

While some of these terms and concepts may seem complex and intimidating, anyone can understand the basics with only a few hours' study. There are many resources that give an overview; readers might begin with John Creswell's book *Research Design: Qualitative & Quantitative Approaches* (1994, Sage Publications), as well as Babbie (1990) and Borg, Gall, and Gall (2006).

Examining the "Best Evidence" Photo for Lake Monsters

Here's one example of using the scientific process to solve a mystery. The case involves a photograph taken in 1977 purporting to be of a lake monster known as Champ (said to inhabit Lake Champlain). It is the world's most famous lake monster photo, and widely claimed to be the best evidence for the existence of the creatures.

In brief, the photo was taken by a woman named Sandra Mansi. Joe Nickell and I interviewed her at length in 2002. According to Mansi, she

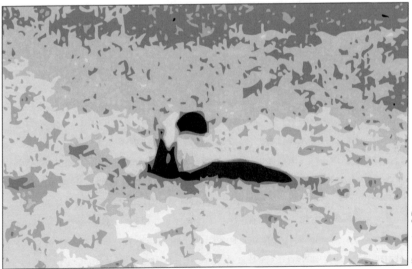

Illustration C.Fix

The Champ lake monster, from Sandra Mansi's 1977 photo.

and her fiancé, Anthony, along with Sandra's two children, were taking a leisurely drive along Lake Champlain. They stopped to relax, and as Sandra watched her children and the lake, she noticed a disturbance in the water about 150 feet away. She thought at first it was a school of fish, then possibly a scuba diver. "Then the head and neck broke the surface of the water. Then I saw the head come up, then the neck, then the back." The photo was baffling and intriguing. (I don't have the space here to fully describe the investigation into this photograph; complete details can be found in Chapter 2 of our book *Lake Monster Mysteries*.)

I began by focusing the investigation not on the general question of Champ's existence, but specifically on Sandra Mansi's eyewitness encounter and her famous photograph. The next step was making a list of possible explanations for her sighting, beginning with what seemed to be the most likely. (Of course, there could be other explanations not on the list.) The list was:

1) hoax
2) hallucination
3) optical illusion
4) wake or wave
5) living, known animal
6) floating tree or log
7) lake monster

It soon became clear that some of the theories were very unlikely, and the pool of alternatives narrowed quickly. The fact that there were multiple eyewitnesses suggested that it was probably not a hoax, nor a hallucination. The fact that it was photographed also helped rule out the hallucination hypothesis. Though photographs can create optical illusions, the object in this photo was clearly an actual object sticking out of the water (even casting a shadow), ruling out an illusion or a wave. The most likely four explanations had been ruled out (though later new evidence might have caused them to be reconsidered), so I moved on to the remaining three hypotheses: an animal, a floating tree, or a lake monster (see table).

Hypothesis / Explanation	Size match?	Known to exist in lake?	Activity?	Appearance?
Living animal	NO	YES	NO	NO
Tree or log	YES	YES	YES	YES
Unknown monster	Unknown	NO	Unlikely	Unknown

Final three explanations for Sandra Mansi's photo of Champ lake monster.

If the object was a known, living animal, then it would have to be something known to exist in the lake (and not, for example, a killer whale). There were a few large animals in the lake (such as sturgeon), though none of them fit the profile of the object Mansi photographed. (If the object was a normal creature, then it would have to be of approximately normal size. Joe and I had performed scientific experiments to see if the size of Mansi's "monster" was as big as reported; we discovered that the "monster" was nowhere near the huge earlier estimates, and instead rose about three feet or less out of the water, and was about seven feet long.) Furthermore, according to Mansi's account, the creature's "head" remained out of the water for five to seven minutes before sinking into the lake. No fish could do that, and there are no known animals that fit the photograph and Mansi's description of the object's behavior. A known, living creature was ruled out.

Only two explanations remained: a floating tree trunk or an unknown lake monster. The more I explored the floating log hypothesis, the more likely it became. A floating log was about the right size; other logs I photographed in and around the lake resembled a serpentine shape; according to Mansi, the "monster" did not react to sounds, suggesting it was non-living; the object's surface, according to Mansi, was "like [tree] bark"; and so on. To demonstrate how an ordinary floating stump could look like the "creature" Mansi sighted, I sculpted a scale model of a tree trunk and created an animated 360-degree view of the object (the video was used in an episode of the TV show MonsterQuest).

I was pretty sure we had finally solved the 25-year-old mystery of Mansi's "Champ monster," but there was one final question: could a floating log act as Mansi had described: surfacing, staying above the water for a few minutes, then slowly sinking away? Through more research (and an interview with a hydrology expert) I learned how submerged, decaying logs can build up gases, rise to the surface, and then sink again, all on their own—exactly as the eyewitness described. The final piece of the puzzle came together, and the mystery was solved.

Analyzing Claim Clusters

Paranormal claims often appear in clusters. While some are one-off, single incident events (such as a UFO sighting), others tend to be presented as a group of incidents that may seem related. This is especially true in reports of ghosts and hauntings. Claimants who experience something they find odd or inexplicable will often unconsciously begin seeking out anything else that seems strange.

Amateur investigators often make the mistake of lumping all the claims together, and assuming that all the reported phenomena are likely to be linked in some way, if not sharing a common cause. While that may indeed be the case, it is essential to treat each claim separately. A person reporting a ghost may believe that the same phenomenon that created a cold spot in the bedroom also made a picture frame fall off the wall in the hallway, but they are very different phenomenon, and likely to have different explanations.

Some minor claims are so peripheral to the main claim (or lacking in supporting evidence) that they need not be fully investigated. For example, let's say that during an interview, a woman mentions that for some reason she thinks that a ghost in her house made her mother sick last Thanksgiving. Assuming it was an isolated incident, that claim may have been made in connection with the haunting, but if it has nothing to do with the current ghostly phenomenon, following up on such a claim would likely be a waste of time. You could interview her mother, but assuming that her mother confirms that she did get ill last Thanksgiving, there would be no way to link it to any ghost; it could have been caused by anything, from food poisoning to a cold. Just because a claimant or eyewitness is convinced that two or more "mysterious" events are linked does not mean they are. Part of being a good investigator is focusing on the important issues that created the mystery and not get sidetracked on irrelevant claims.

Logical Fallacies

There are a number of common logical fallacies that are frequently committed in the defense of erroneous ideas. It is helpful to be aware of them, to learn to recognize them in yourself and others, and to avoid depending on them to defend a point of view. Those listed below are among the most common in discussions of the paranormal.

Ad hominem: attacking the person rather than the argument. (Examples: "UFOlogists are all crazy," or "Skeptics reject my claims because they are closed-minded.")

Ad ignorantum: appeal to ignorance, the idea that whatever is not known to be false must be true, or vice versa. (Example: "ESP is possible because there is so much we don't know about the brain," or "In the woods last night I saw something huge and hairy– it must be Bigfoot!")

Argument from authority: defending a position by citing the authority of the person or people who hold that position. (Example: "Mr. Smith must be correct because he has a PhD" —or is a policeman, or astronaut, etc.)

Equating *unexplained* with *inexplicable*: this is the often overconfident position that because one cannot explain something, there must be no ordinary explanation, and therefore the answer must be paranormal. It assumes that the writer or speaker has all the facts. (Example: "I can't explain that light in the sky, therefore it must be an alien spacecraft," or "I don't know how to explain the Ouija board movements, so it must be spirits.")

Observational selection: selective suppression of evidence, or remembering the hits and forgetting the misses. (Example: "My horoscope said that I'd be lucky, and sure enough, today I found a dollar on the street!" or "Just as I thought of my friend, she phoned me. We have a special connection that way.")

Post hoc, ergo propter hoc: (Literally, "after this therefore because of it"); assuming cause and effect for events related in time. (Example: "After I used my magnetic insoles, my feet felt better. Those magnets really work!")

Special pleading: calling upon unusual, vague, or special arguments to try to explain away failure. (Example: "ESP doesn't work when there are too many skeptics in the room.")

Faulty assumptions: Assuming the existence of unproven forces or entities. (Example: "I'll treat your disease by changing your body's energy fields or vibrations.")

Baloney Detection

In his wonderful book *The Demon-Haunted World*, Carl Sagan (1996) suggests some guidelines for baloney detection, including the following:

1) There should be independent confirmation of the facts of the case, not just from the proponent.

2) Suggest more than one hypothesis to explain a given phenomenon, and try to come up with ways to discriminate between them to see which best fits the facts.

3) Be willing to abandon a hypothesis if it is not useful; don't force-fit a pet explanation to fit the facts.

4) In a chain of argument, each step must come logically from the previous one, and all links in the chain must be valid.

5) Hypotheses and propositions must be falsifiable (able to be proved wrong) and testable. Claims that cannot be proven one way or the other are of limited use.

One basic investigative principle that comes up often is Occam's Razor. This is a philosophical principle attributed to a man named William of Occam, who devised his version way back in the 1300s (for such an important idea, its influence has not spread nearly far enough in the last 700 years). The basic premise is that if you have a phenomenon to be explained and two or more different theories are proposed as solutions, the simplest one (or the one with the fewest assumptions) is much more likely to be the correct answer. For example, if the topic is a ghost that is seen late at night at the foot of a friend's bed as he was drifting off to sleep, is it more likely that he was dreaming (or had a hypnagogic hallucination while falling asleep), or that the ghost of a dead person just happened to appear at exactly a time when he was nearing (or in) a dreamlike state? Either is *possible*, but which is more likely?

James Randi (1995) gives another example, that of a magician's trick of sawing a woman in half and then restoring her. The trick (if done well) certainly gives the impression or experience of a woman being cut in half and put back together unharmed—which would violate various laws of physics. One explanation is that the magician actually did somehow temporarily suspend the laws of the universe just for the trick; another explanation is that the magician has simply used well-known principles of illusion and misdirection to create the illusion. Using Occam's Razor, this is clearly the more likely explanation. Occam's Razor does not mean that the less-likely theories should be rejected without examination, just that the investigator should start with the most likely explanation. A psychic claimant whose powers exactly mimic a magician's tricks may not be using those tricks, but Occam's Razor states that that is the most likely explanation, and must be ruled out.

A related rule of thumb is, "If you hear hoofbeats, think horses not zebras." That is, you should start by assuming the most likely explanation before thinking of less likely ones. Either animal could make the same sound, but unless you are near a zoo (or in Africa), the source of the sound is most likely a horse. For more on logical fallacies see Shermer 1997, Ruchlis 1990, Gardner 1999, and Vaughn 2008.

Guidelines for Skeptical Paranormal Investigation

1) As an investigator, you will be dealing with specific cases and claims. For example, general claims might be that house X is haunted, or person Y is psychic. Specific claims would be that a ghost was seen or photographed on one occasion at house X, or psychic Y can read volunteer's minds. General claims are not testable or falsifiable (you cannot prove or disprove the existence of Bigfoot or psychic powers, but you can prove or disprove specific claimed examples or reports).

2) Establish the claims clearly and thoroughly. It is essential to find out what exactly is being claimed, by whom, and under what circumstances. As psychologist Ray Hyman points out in the dictum named after him ("Hyman's Categorical Imperative"), before trying to explain a claim, make sure that there is something to explain.

Demand specificity and clarity from people about their claims; do not accept fuzzy logic, made-up words, or vague answers to simple questions. Vagueness is a weasel area that can be used to try to explain away failed results. Scientific experiments and tests do not advance on generalizations.

3) Remember that the devil is in the details. Mysteries are easy to create; all you need is to change or omit some important details, or leave false assumptions unchecked. Countless cases of strange or mysterious phenomena have been solved through little more than correctly establishing the particulars and connecting the dots.

4) Be aware of the language and terms used to describe unexplained mysteries; often they are incorrect and misleading. For example, many news reports about psychic detectives have headlines such as, "Psychic Helps in Missing Persons Case," though if you read the story, the missing person has not been found—thus there is no way to know if whatever information the "psychic" gave was helpful. Or take a closer look at the subtitle of Charles Berlitz's 1974 book *The Bermuda Triangle: An Incredible Saga of Unexplained Disappearances*. Note the misuse of the word *disappearances*. The ships and planes that "disappeared" in and around the Bermuda Triangle did not "disappear," nor did they vanish. While a few of the missing vessels have never been located, there's not much mystery as to where they are: they are at the bottom of the Atlantic Ocean. There may (or may not) be some mystery as to why they ended up there, but there's little mystery as to where they went.

5) Remember where the burden of proof lies and be selective about what cases you tackle, so choose those with good evidence. The burden of proof is on the person making the claim, not on the investigator to disprove it.

6) Stay focused on the important issues and questions at hand. When investigating a case, especially a complex one, it is easy to become side-tracked and go in several directions at once. Many paranormal proponents and untrained investigators have a difficult time focusing on one aspect of a case at a time and separating out individual claims to determine if they are true or false. My investigation into the "best case" for psychic detectives (see Chapter 6) is an excellent example; podcast host Alex Tsakiris jumped from claim to claim and tried to lump all the claims together, as if three unproven claims were as valid as one proven one. But that's not how investigation works; each individual claim should be thoroughly evaluated and determined as true or false before moving onto

the next claim. Quality, not quantity, of evidence is what's important. Just as five cups of weak coffee cannot be combined to make one cup of strong coffee, five examples of poor evidence cannot be lumped together to create good evidence. One uncorroborated personal experience is no more useful than a hundred uncorroborated experiences. Another way to put it is "the plural of *anecdote* is not *evidence*."

7) Follow the evidence objectively to its conclusion. Don't begin by assuming that a given investigation will turn out a particular way, and don't go into an investigation trying to prove or disprove it. Seek and consider all evidence, not just that which supports a favored theory or explanation.

8) Do sufficient background research on the topic; have a good grasp of the issues before you begin so you know what to look for and what types of questions to ask. You must ask the right questions to get the right answers.

9) Do good scholarship. Get your facts and quotes right. Double-check original sources; when possible interview original eyewitnesses. Seek primary sources and documents, instead of second- or third-hand information.

10) Get a wide variety of claims about the topic; consult several sources to see the variety of claims. Different sources may contain dramatically different information and provide clues.

11) Look for implications and hidden assumptions underlying claims: If a given claim is true, then what else would (or should) be true? Look for keys and lynchpins in cases; what assumptions are at the crux of the claim? What assumptions, if false, make the mystery disappear? What is the underlying premise for the mystery?

12) Look not only for positive evidence, but negative evidence. Often what did *not* happen is just as important as what *did* happen. One famous fictional example of this type of reasoning can be found in the Sherlock Holmes story "The Silver Blaze." The mystery contains the following exchange between a Scotland Yard detective and Holmes:

Detective: "Is there any other point to which you would
wish to draw my attention?"
Holmes: "To the curious incident of the dog in the night-time."
Detective: "The dog did nothing in the night-time."
Holmes: "That was the curious incident."

The dog in question did not bark at the approach of a specific un-known person, and Holmes "grasped the significance of the silence of the dog: Obviously the midnight visitor was someone whom the dog knew well." That is, the fact that something did not happen (in this ex-ample, a dog did not bark) when we would have expected it to gives us information about what *did* happen.

Examining what is *not* found (and asking why it is not found) can be very useful in helping understand many phenomena. For example, the dead bodies of creatures such as Bigfoot and the Loch Ness monster have never been found. Abducted and missing persons (such as Natalee Hol-loway, Laci Petersen, and eighteen-year hostage victim Jaycee Dugard) were not found by psychic detectives. Crop circles have never been filmed being created—except by humans. And so on. I applied this technique to solving the mystery of the "best case" for psychic detectives, the Amie Hoffman murder (see Chapter 6). In that case, the claim is that police detectives had several important and specific identifying pieces of infor-mation about a serial killer. Part of the mystery was solved (spoiler alert!) when I looked at what *didn't* happen; in that case what didn't happen is that the police didn't find the killer, nor solve the crime, as we would expect them to have done if the psychic's claim was true. In my investi-gation into a famous lake monster photograph, the eyewitness's descrip-tion of what the "monster" did not do was just as important in determining its identity as what it actually did (for more see "Mysteries and Misinformation: How Cryptozoologists Created a Monster," Appen-dix 1 in my book *Lake Monster Mysteries*).

13) Whenever possible, construct timelines for events. If a glass of milk spills before someone touches it, that is a mystery; if it spills after a hand knocks it over, there is no mystery. Establishing the exact chronology of events can make the difference between a baffling mystery and a solved case. For example, my investigation into the Pokémon Panic mystery could not have been solved without establishing a clear order of events, nor could my solving the mystery of the chupacabra's origin in 1995 Puerto Rico.

14) Look for the social context of a claim; reports of mysterious phe-nomena do not occur in a vacuum. For example, the story of the Amityville

Horror hoax was created just as *The Exorcist* was hugely popular in pop culture and the public's consciousness; that fact by itself doesn't "explain" the case, but it does provide a context in which to view the story.

15) Re-creations and reenactments can be very helpful in trying to determine what happened, and how.

16) Keep calm, especially when conducting field investigations. There may be times when an investigator is in an unfamiliar area (such as woods or a reputedly haunted location) searching for something or waiting for something to happen. This guideline seems obvious, but TV shows like *Ghost Hunters* and *Ghost Adventures* are filled with very emotional and suggestible "investigators." Whether they are actually terrified (or just acting terrified for the camera), the fact is that panic and jumping at shadows does not solve mysteries. If something odd or startling happens, a competent researcher must put aside any natural fear and immediately investigate.

17) If you can't find an answer, keep trying. Re-examine all the assumptions, and double-check important facts. Don't be afraid to say, "I don't know." Give it your best guess, based on the evidence, and if you publish an article on it or reach a conclusion, be honest about the limitations of your research.

18) Always treat eyewitnesses and claimants with courtesy and respect. During investigations, you will, by definition, be talking with people who are approaching the topic from a different point of view (or who are already convinced of the validity of only one interpretation of the event they experienced). Remember that good investigation is about finding the facts and revealing the truth; it is not about attacking a person's credibility or motives.

19) Investigators should strive to be open and ethical about their work. Do not accept any pay for your investigation; any payment should be for work done on behalf of a skeptics organization, or more likely for writing an article that is the product of your investigation. Obviously, obey all laws and obtain permission from landowners when using or crossing their property.

Because of the nature of investigation, there may be times when deception is necessary, such as when looking into a psychic who has been accused of stealing from her clients. If an investigator wants to consult the psychic, it is perfectly appropriate to simply act like any other client seeking a reading, and not announce, "I'm an investigator looking into whether you're scamming people!" (Of course, if she's a good psychic, she would know that.) Undercover work is sometimes required. Joe Nickell, for example, has gone undercover many times, at least once at a Spiritualist camp known for shady dealings. I have gone undercover on a dozen or so occasions; one time I posed as a student in a class to expose a professor (teaching on the paranormal, of all things) at a Canadian community college who had faked his teaching credentials.

20) Because scientific paranormal investigation (like anything scientific) is based on precedent, you should be willing to share your methods and results with anyone who asks. If you complete an investigation but choose not to publish or publically present it (say, at a conference or on a Web site), other investigators will be unaware of your work. If you have done a solid investigation and solved a mystery, you deserve credit for it, and your work deserves to be added to the literature. You have a responsibility to others to publish your findings.

As a final note, realize that some questions may remain after proposing a solution, and it is rarely possible to absolutely prove a case to everyone's satisfaction. Mystery mongers, instead of offering better and more plausible explanations, will sometimes try to nitpick at details and suggest that a case remains unsolved if they find some reason to doubt any part of the explanation (even if the other 95% of it is obviously correct). It is not enough for critics to merely say, "I don't think that's right"–they should offer an explanation that better fits the facts. (And if they do, you should accept it.) In real-world cases, information is often incomplete or fragmentary, for many reasons: eyewitnesses can be mistaken, records can be lost, etc. There is often no way to know for absolute certainty what happened. Science does not operate on certainties, but instead on what fits the facts, what is most likely and probable. An investigator is under no obligation to explain phenomena for which insufficient evidence is offered.

Ghost hunters and paranormal investigators who are more interested in being on TV than searching for answers are wasting their time. There are dozens of paranormal groups trying to be the next *Ghost Hunters*, and there are far better routes to fame and fortune. I've appeared on a variety of television shows during my career, usually in connection with investigation I've done. I'm on television because I do investigations; I don't do investigations because I want to be on television.

Nuts and Bolts of Investigation

I have focused on the theory and approach to scientific paranormal investigation, now I'll turn to putting these methods into practice. As I noted, investigations begin with research. I will assume that readers have at least a basic grasp of good research methods—seeking out library books and journal articles, gathering lists of references, and so on. There are plenty of books on how to do good research, and I won't spend much space on it here.

Conducting Field Investigations

In some ways field investigations are the most difficult, demanding, and expensive type of investigation; unless you are lucky enough to have the unexplained phenomenon occur near your home, you may have to travel. Some investigations are very time-sensitive, such as a recently-discovered crop circle or a sudden, unexplained miracle at a suburban home. You must be willing and able to drop what you are doing to go investigate. The sooner you get there the better; weeping statues and crop circles don't always appear at a time most convenient for investigators.

Field investigations in particular require special considerations and preparations, part of an investigative strategy. What do you want to find out, and how are you going to find it out? Research as much as you can about the subject before you go (from news stories and background research, for example), and make a list of questions you want to investigate, people you want to talk to. Contact them ahead of time to introduce yourself and arrange a meeting. Ask who else you should speak to, and ask *those* people who else you should speak to. Sometimes the people with the most important information won't even be on the list, and will only be discovered once you arrive at the location and start asking questions. Joe Nickell's investigation of Toronto's haunted Mackenzie House is an excellent example (chapter 2 in his book *Secrets of the Supernatural*). Go with a plan, but be flexible.

Where, specifically, do you plan to go? If you're investigating a haunted house, the answer is obvious, but if you are investigating a lake monster, you may want to go to the site of a famous photograph or sighting, or to speak to locals, or other people who are already interested or involved in the case. What will do you do once you're there? Will you conduct field experiments, or just gather more information, taking photographs and interviewing people? Establishing your goals early will also help you decide what equipment to bring.

Will you have access to the area? If it's a private residence, or on private property, do you have permission from the owners? If it's a public place, do you know where it is and how to get there? Is there a hotel nearby where you can stay while you investigate? What information do you need, and who has it? Typically an investigator might interview eyewitnesses, librarians, local police, local experts, and so on.

These are the sorts of questions you need to ask. For example, before Joe and I left for British Columbia's Lake Okanagan to search for its reputed monster Ogopogo (Chapter 8), we did extensive research on the beast through books, magazines, TV shows, and our personal files. We combed though a dozen or more references, making notes and highlighting important facts on the case including notable sightings, descriptions, names of eyewitnesses, other leads and sources, etc. I usually devote a single-subject notebook and accordion file just for the case, and keep my notes there. This preparatory research will guide the investigation. We found out that there was a Native Indian legend aspect to Ogopogo, and made a note to speak to an expert about that. We found out that the most famous footage of Ogopogo was shot by a man named Arthur Folden, and we obtained and studied the video. We found out that a place named Rattlesnake Island was supposedly home to Ogopogo, so we made a note to visit that (and send divers down to investigate). And so on, each piece of information suggesting a different angle of research. (To be fair, that particular investigation was conducted with the help of National Geographic Television, and some of the information was provided to us by the show's producer.)

Interviewing Eyewitnesses

Since many paranormal claims come down to personal experience or eye-witnesses, you will often need to personally interview claimants. Do not inject your opinions, or too much skepticism, into the questions or interview; the subject will get defensive. You must be able to be polite but firm, and make it clear from your tone and demeanor that you are trying to help and understand the person, not mock them. Remember that, except in relatively rare instances of hoaxes, the person you're talking to did experience something. The nature of that something may be in question, but until you have more information (probably much more), you won't know whether that experience was a truly unknown phenomenon, a misperception, a prank, or something else.

Always have some record of the interview, using a simple pocket note-book, voice recorder, or both (though be aware that tape recorders make some people nervous and ask first). The last question should be, "Is there anything else you want to tell me, or anything we didn't cover?" Get full names and contact information for all interviewees in case you have follow-up questions. Also be aware that laws about recording telephone conversations vary from state to state. More tips for interviewing eyewitnesses can be found in Robert Goerman's book *Weird Happens* and Vernon Geberth's *Practical Homicide Investigation*.

Throughout your investigation, take careful notes and document everything. If you present your investigation to a group or in an article, all of your assertions and claims should be backed up by facts. You should be able to produce organized, written records of your research in case anything you say or write is challenged. Hold onto your files for later reference, for years if necessary. If someone you interviewed later claims you misquoted him or put words in his mouth, you have the original recordings as proof. (By the way, be careful not to misquote people.)

Investigating Photographic and Video Evidence

Sometimes photographic, videotape, or film evidence is offered instead of, or along with, eyewitness testimony. Ideally, of course, you should interview whoever took the photo or video to get information about the context of the event. If the person is available, get as much information as possible, beyond the simple who, what, where, why, and how. Be very wary of anonymous photos; if the photographer doesn't want to be interviewed or identified, it's likely a fake or hoax.

If practical (and not too much time has passed since the photograph or videotape), you might try to revisit the original location. Depending on what the phenomenon is, you might begin by trying to determine its size or location. See if you can re-create the image, but realize that if you can't, it doesn't necessarily mean that the image is unexplainable, just that the circumstances of the photo (light, people present, environment, etc.) may have changed.

Interviewing Eyewitnesses

Take notes and video- or tape-record the interview for later reference.

Avoid leading questions. Let the witnesses tell you their story; try not to inject your own assumptions and expectations into their accounts.

Get the "Reporter's Basics": who, what, when, where, why, and how. Make sure you fully understand the circumstances of their sightings or experience.

Prepare for the interview by doing research about previous reports.

Remember that most eyewitnesses are sincere, and only rarely will they try to hoax you. Interview subjects should be treated with respect and courtesy.

If there are several witnesses to the same event, interview them separately. They have probably told their story together before, but witnesses can sometimes rely on—and influence—each others' recollections.

Before the interview, do at least some research on the psychology of perception, the ways in which the eyes and mind can fool us. Everyone experiences, recalls, and interprets the world in slightly different ways.

Be sure to ask if the person has had similar experiences previously; sometimes "repeaters" will come to expect to see the monster or ghost, and those expectations can easily bias their interpretations of ordinary objects.

If possible, visit the scene of the sighting with the witnesses; it will help them remember details and give you a better sense of what happened.

Remember that details are very, very important. Every piece of information may be essential, so press for details even if the eyewitness doesn't necessarily think they are important.

In many photographs—especially of purported UFOs and lake monsters—there simply is not enough information contained in the image to
make an accurate, scientifically valid estimate of the object's size. A disc
seen flying in the sky might be miles away and hundreds of yards long, or
a few feet away and only an inch or two long. They might look exactly the
same, especially if there's nothing else in the image by which to judge scale.
If you don't know how far away an unidentified object is from the camera,
it's impossible to know how big it is.

The most important thing to remember when analyzing photographs is
that they are just patches of light and dark on paper; they are two-dimen-
sional images that (allegedly) represent a three-dimensional scene. There are
countless ways that tricks of light and perspective can fool the camera. A
photograph—even a crisp, clear, sharp one—of an alleged Bigfoot, UFO, or
ghost cannot be definitive proof of anything other than that someone photographed something that could be interpreted as mysterious. At best, it is a
guide to corroborating an eyewitness's story (as was the case in the investigation of Sandra Mansi's photo of the Lake Champlain monster).

With the widespread use of photo editing programs like PhotoShop, it's
easy to dismiss strange or unusual photos as fakes or hoaxes. Many of them
indeed are, but don't be too quick to assume that what you're seeing is the
result of digital manipulation or a prank. Very often, strange images can appear unnoticed, created by flash reflections, bystanders, and odd shadows.

Be especially skeptical if the photographer claims that he or she didn't
see the image at the time, and only discovered it later. This is a red flag
that the anomaly is probably a camera artifact—that is, something created
in the process of taking the photograph or videotape, something mechan-
ical inside the camera instead of supernatural outside the camera.

As I mention elsewhere, sometimes what is *not* seen in the image or
video gives a clue as to what was seen. For example, in June 2009 I was
asked to investigate new footage of Champ, the monster said to inhabit
Lake Champlain. The two-minute video was taken with a cell phone camera and showed the silhouette of some object — probably an animal —
moving toward the eastern shore. Many people suggested it was the best
evidence for Champ in decades, though the form resembled the back

and head of a swimming deer, and moved toward the near shore past what appears to be a buoy, which might suggest shallow water.

In this case the video abruptly ends as the animal nears shore, which is suspicious. Surely if the cameraman was intrigued enough by the sight to spend two minutes recording it he didn't suddenly lose interest, stop recording, and head home. According to Loren Coleman (2009), the eyewitness "turned off the camera before he finished seeing it totally disappear, as he was fearful that the automatic saving functions of his phonecam would erase what he already had, since his memory was running low." Yet this "explanation" only deepens the mystery, because that's not how memory on cell phone cameras work; they do not begin recording over previously videotaped material; they simply stop when the memory runs out. Either Coleman is wrong about why the camera stopped filming, or the photographer is wrong about how his cell phone works, but either way the photographer's behavior is suspect. Perhaps he chose to edit out the last seconds of the sequence, when we could all see if it was indeed a deer climbing ashore.

Though this does not prove a hoax, it does raise unanswered questions about the sighting. It's also interesting to note that this footage is unlike other alleged Champ videos and photographs. Many show a round, dark form in the water, but none so closely resemble a large swimming mammal. It also seems odd that an aquatic creature would make such an obvious effort to keep its head above water. If Champ monsters exist, and must regularly surface to breathe (like dolphins or whales) it's amazing that they are not routinely sighted on the populated lake.

In some cases an investigator may be presented with a videotape purporting to contain spontaneously moving objects or phenomena. For example, a TV show might show footage of a psychic dramatically gesturing toward an object, "causing" it to suddenly move.

To use an example from one of my case files, during a haunted house investigation for the TV show *MysteryQuest* in 2009 (titled "The Real Amityville Horror"), I was asked to examine two physical events which had been attributed to ghosts, caught on a security camera. The first was an office chair in a supposedly deserted, after-hours laboratory which can be seen turning halfway around all by itself. The second was a five-foot wall partition which suddenly and dramatically fell over—again, with no obvious cause.

My investigation into these two videotaped ghostly events is too detailed to discuss here, but basically I studied the videotape and carefully measured how far the chair moved, and in what direction. I was able to recreate the exact movement of the chair using a hidden wire, showing that it was likely a hoax. There was probably someone just off camera who worked there and knew how much of the area could be seen by the videocamera. I of course could not prove conclusively that it had been faked—after all, I wasn't there when it happened. All I had to go on was the videotape, and by duplicating it for the TV show's cameras, I proved that it could have been a hoax.

The falling partition was not a hoax, but nor was it a ghost. The short partition wall actually did fall down on its own, and it did look very mysterious. But the real cause was simply material fatigue: the partition was heavy, and had been poorly anchored to loose drywall. Eventually the weight of the partition itself pulled the wall down, and of course it was caught on the security camera. When the staff came in the next day to find the wall down, with no obvious reason for the collapse, they attributed the act to a ghostly presence, and presented the videotape as evidence. (For a similar case investigated by Massimo Polidoro, see "The Mystery of the Moving Tombstone" in the March/April 2010 issue of *Skeptical Inquirer* magazine.)

Many investigators get so wrapped up in trying to understand what they are *seeing* that they neglect to analyze what they are *hearing*. The audio track can provide important clues to what is going on—different voices might reveal who was present, perhaps even how far they were from the camera even if they are not seen. Are there any subtle noises just before or just after something strange happened? What might they indicate?

One excellent resource for scientifically investigating unusual photographs and videos is a small book called *Orbs or Dust? A Practical Guide to False-Positive Evidence*, by Kenneth Biddle. Though the book focuses specifically on ghost photographs, its discussion applies to all supposedly mysterious images.

Investigation Equipment

On television and in films when paranormal investigators or ghost hunters are depicted, they often are seen using all sorts of high-tech gadgetry in the search for the unknown. TV's *Ghost Hunters*, for example, love their high-tech infrared cameras, motion detectors, and so on. There's nothing necessarily wrong with all that, except that the technology can be very expensive (probably beyond the reach of most scientific paranormal investigators), and most people using the equipment don't really understand how the devices work. Perhaps most importantly it is ineffective; the gear doesn't find ghosts. This equipment has never—not once—captured definitive proof of the paranormal. The equipment is not designed for finding ghosts (more on this in Chapter 4).

One of the most important things I learned from Joe Nickell is the importance of being prepared; he has an impressive investigation kit. Mine is loosely modeled after his, plus it has some additional things that I've added over the course of many investigations. Being prepared during an investigation is vitally important. If you're doing a field investigation and you have an idea for an experiment on the fly, there's nothing like the abject self-loathing you feel when you realize that you don't have the equipment you need.

It also helps to have a MacGuyver streak, because you often need to improvise something on the spot. For example, during my investigation into the Santa Fe Courthouse Ghost (Chapter 9), I hadn't realized just how

---

Investigation Toolkit

magnets	rubber gloves	pocket notebook
safety pins	mini-flashlight	lens cleaning wipes
super glue	extra film	audio recorder
fingerprint powder	or memory card	Leatherman tool
Scotch tape	Sharpie marker	tape measure
extra batteries	20 feet of string	10 feet of thin wire
pens and pencils	flour	thread and needles
magnifying glass	lighter or matches	Swiss Army knife
roll of extra quarters	calculator	twist ties
plastic bags	aluminum foil	Velcro strips

high a surveillance camera was mounted. In order to perform an experiment, I needed a 10-foot pole, but I found a cut tree branch nearby, to which I attached a plastic tube with some twist-ties from my kit. It wasn't pretty, but it worked.

There's no definitive list of what you might need on an investigation. Good planning and forethought are important, but there will always be some items (usually small, common things) that you will need or want. Of course you need cameras, video recorders, a tripod, and so on. My investigation kit includes everything from extra batteries (can't have a camera or tape recorder dying at a bad time), to half a roll of extra quarters (I once had to stop an investigation to run to a store and ask for change when my parking meter expired), to common baking flour (a light dusting on a floor might reveal anyone tampering with a weeping statue, for example). I prefer things that are small, strong, and multi-purpose; this list is just a starting point.

As a final note, there is some degree of danger in doing paranormal investigations. The paranormal is a magnet for people with strange beliefs; most of them are harmless, but some are not. I, and other investigators I know, have been threatened. Joe Nickell (1992), himself a veteran of many wild and wooly times, notes, "In making your rounds [as an investigator] you very well may encounter kooks, cranks, creeps, and fanatics who will be quick to hit you, shoot you, knock you down, and so forth if you threaten either their deep-seated beliefs or their fragile self-esteem. Take care. Beware of both fundamentalists and fanatics."

References

Babbie, Earl. 1990. *Survey Research Methods*. Belmont, California: Wadsworth.

Borg, Walter, Joyce Gall, and M.D. Gall. 2006. *Educational Research: An Introduction*. (8th Ed.) New York: Allyn & Bacon.

Coleman, Loren. 2009. Champ filmed? TAPS *Paramagazine*, September/October, p. 21.

Merow, Katharine. 2008. But you deceived me! The necessity of deception in investigation of the paranormal. *Skeptical Inquirer* magazine, July/August 32:4.

Gardner, Martin. 1999. *Gardner's Whys and Wherefores*. Amherst, New York: Prometheus Books.

Geberth, Vernon. 1996. *Practical Homicide Investigation: Tactics, Procedures, and Forensic Techniques* (3rd Ed.). New York, New York: CRC Press.

Gibson, Marley, Patrick Burns, and Dave Schrader. 2009. *The Other Side: A Teen's Guide to Ghost Hunting and the Paranormal.* Boston, Massachusetts: Houghton Mifflin Harcourt.

Goerman, Robert. 2007. *Weird Happens: Investigator Handbook.* Baltimore, Maryland: PublishAmerica.

Hyman, Ray. 2003. How Not To Test Mediums: Critiquing the Afterlife Experiments. *Skeptical Inquirer* January/February.

Nickell, Joe. 1992. *Missing Pieces: How to Investigate Ghosts, UFOs, Psychics, and Other Mysteries.* Amherst, New York: Prometheus Books, p. 151.

Polidoro, Massimo. 2010. The mystery of the moving tombstone. *Skeptical Inquirer,* March/April 34(2), p. 21

Randi, James. 1995. *An Encyclopedia of Claims, Frauds, and Hoaxes of the Occult and Supernatural.* New York, New York: St. Martin's Press.

Huchlis, Hy. 1990. Clear Thinking: A Practical Introduction. New York: Harcourt.

Sagan, Carl. 1996. *The Demon-Haunted World: Science as a Candle in the Dark.* New York, New York: Ballantine Books.

Shermer, Michael. 1997. *Why People Believe Weird Things: Pseudoscience, Superstition and Bogus Notions of Our Time.* New York, New York: MJF Books.

Vaughn, Lewis. 2008. The Power of Critical Thinking: Effective Reasoning About Ordinary and Extraordinary Claims. *New York: Oxford University Press.*

Wiseman, Richard, and Robert Morris. 1995. *Guidelines for Testing Psychic Claimants.* Amherst, New York: Prometheus Books.

Other Perspectives on Scientific Paranormal Investigation

Much of this book draws from my personal experience and case studies investigating the unexplained. But there are many people doing good quality skeptical investigations. In this section, other investigators share their first-hand experiences investigating a wide variety of paranormal topics, and some of the important lessons they have learned. There are many excellent investigators not included here; including all of them would fill up an entire book. Their work can be found in the references and bibliographies, and I encourage readers to seek them out.

The Great Carlos Caper
James "The Amazing" Randi

In 1988, I took an inexperienced layperson—my good friend artist Jose Luis Alvarez—to Australia and created for the TV networks and newspapers a giant hoax through The Great Carlos, a "channeller" who filled the Sydney Opera House with the faithful who were amazed at this wonderful guru-figure who could stop his pulse at will. A week later we announced it had all been a hoax designed to show how easily people can be taken in. Carlos had stopped his pulse and had done other miracles with simple means that got by the most astute investigators.

"Stopped his pulse?" Hold on. Isn't this an impossibility, unless the performer is willing to die? Not at all. Alvarez knew of the conjuror's trick whereby this could be done. It involves concealing a ping-pong ball under in his armpit, on the arm from which the pulse-taker would operate. Simply pressing on the ball—properly located—shuts off the flow of blood to the wrist, and the pulse just stops— not anywhere but in that arm, but the observers were deceived into believing that the heart had stopped! And Alvarez was not about to disabuse them of that notion.

But it was the media, not we, who actually created and nurtured him as a genuine phenomenon. Even before he went to Australia, one TV network paid $16,000—in 1988 dollars, remember! —for a special satellite hook-up so that they could get first coverage on his visit. This was coverage for someone who had offered nothing in the way of evidence, other than a series of faked newspaper accounts in newspapers that never existed, in cities that similarly were created from nothing, and a kid's summer-camp stunt, the pulse-stopping. There was huge excitement upon his arrival there, and the media happily elbowed one another aside for the great privilege of being deceived.

Inside of three weeks, Alvarez had a huge following. Frustrated photographers followed him waist-deep into the water at the seaside to get photos of him chanting, and they used long lenses from rooftops to capture the image of the seemingly reluctant guru. Front-page headlines greeted him several times as he took Sydney on a long, noisy and bumpy media ride. He published a nonsensical book, he was a TV star, and he could have made a fortune—if he'd been a "real" fake.

Alvarez/Carlos was interviewed every day on TV. He made a scene during one interview, and earned front-page news the next day. We manipulated the Australian media at will, giving them just the news they wanted. Scientists consulted by the newspapers refused comment; typically, they backed away from any involvement, refusing to recognize that a succinct opinion concerning what was obviously a farce, could damn it and put us out of business. The Ivory Tower was heavily overbooked during that period.

When we finally exposed the hoax on a full episode of the Australian *Sixty Minutes* television program (which had been the plan from the very inception of the stunt) we became local folk heroes. Restaurants entertained us and refused payment, taxi drivers were honored to serve us gratis, people we encountered hugged us and thanked us for our exposure of a variety of hoax that even today has not vanished. Only the newspapers and the other media who had swallowed our bait were unable to see what we'd done to bring a little sanity to their world, and we were roundly castigated for our efforts. A week later, when a "real" channeller landed in Perth, Australia, the first question she got was, "Did James Randi send you?" and she got right back on the plane.

As an example of manipulation of the media, and as a picture of the reluctance of science to perform the simplest of obligations to bring reason to a silly scenario, the Carlos Caper stands as a sterling archetype.

James Randi, better known as "The Amazing Randi" has been a stage magician, escape artists, and lifelong foe of flim-flammery since the early 1970s. Randi was a founding member of the Committee for the Scientific Investigation of Claims of the Paranormal, and later the James Randi Educational Foundation. He investigated and exposed dozens of fraudulent faith healers and psychics, as well as spoon-bender Uri Geller. Randi has written many books on conjuring, skepticism, and Houdini.

Catching Ghosts
Joe Nickell

Despite the popular antics of inept "ghost hunters," ghosts continue to remain elusive—as if they are only productions of the imagination rather than purportedly still-living entities of a supernatural realm. Nevertheless, actively ghost hunting since 1969, I have actually "caught" a few "ghosts."

True, in most cases I have found plausible explanations for haunting phenomena. At Mackenzie House in Toronto, mysterious footfalls had been heard on the stairs for much of a decade until, during 1972–73, I investigated and discovered the iron stairway in the adjacent building regularly was traversed by a late-night cleanup crew. At various haunted inns, many apparitions have turned out to be due to the percipient experiencing a common "waking dream." And aboard a haunted ship, the mysterious blurring of a dead sailor's picture whenever it was photographed was caused by its nonglare glass softly reflecting the camera's flash.

And then there are hoaxes. At a reputedly haunted restaurant in Georgia, various strange phenomena were reported, including lights that flickered on and off in the barroom. The bartender, whom I interviewed, was initially convinced it was the work of a spirit entity. Parapsychologists who had earlier "investigated" the site using electromagnetic field meters failed to uncover the young worker who admitted that she would sneak up to the doorway, reach for the light switch, then dart away, giggling silently. Similar pranks, minor accidents and glitches, as well as misperceptions coupled with contagion, could easily account for the phenomena reported at the restaurant.

I once caught such a "ghost" in action, namely a hotel desk clerk who was unaware I was looking in his direction as chandelier lights flickered mysteriously. There, as at many other places, ghosts were apparently thought to be good for business.

Such antics are the explanation for almost an entire class of physical hauntings, known as poltergeist cases (after the German term for "noisy spirit"). Typically, small objects are hurled through the air by unseen forces, furniture is overturned, or other disturbances occur—usually by a juvenile trickster determined to plague credulous adults. Such was a case I investigated with Robert A. Baker (1921–2005), a professor of psychology at the University of Kentucky and author of numerous books. Dr. Baker and I were called to an Indiana farmhouse that was experiencing a spate of haunting activity. The main percipient was the young wife and mother. We listened to her story, went through the house, and talked to each family member separately. One little boy, being rather pointedly quizzed by the sage Dr. Baker, suddenly blurted out, "You aren't going to tell on me, are you?" No, the understanding psychologist replied, while insisting that we must nevertheless have an end to the "haunting" activity. We kept in touch with the family for awhile, and apparently the little ghost had heeded Hamlet's imploring, "Rest, rest, perturbed spirit" (Hamlet i.v. 182).

Another supposedly haunted place is The Golden Lamb Inn in Lebanon, Ohio, whose sign proclaims it is "the oldest Inn still operating as a hotel in Ohio." The inn is allegedly haunted by the ghost of Sarah Stubbs, a little girl whose family once managed the hotel. Reportedly pictures hanging on the wall in what was called Sarah's Room were sometimes askew after they were straightened the day previously. I wondered about the phenomenon as I prepared to check into the hotel on February 7, 2002.

As I brought up the subject of haunting, the night clerk revealed a secret: Sometimes, because she found the housekeeping staff so superstitious and credulous, she would slip upstairs at night and "turn the pictures" in Sarah's Room just to "mess with" their minds.

Once again, I had confirmed the value of on-site investigating over armchair debunking. I had caught another ghost, this time at the very beginning of a stay. I have to admit, I slept especially well that night.

Joe Nickell is the world's only full-time professional paranormal investigator, the "Investigative Files" columnist for Skeptical Inquirer *science magazine, and author of over two dozen books. His background includes work as a stage magician (Resident Magician at the Houdini Hall of Fame), private investigator (for a world-famous detective agency), and academic (Ph.D in English, focusing on literary investigation and folklore). This piece is abridged from a column of the same title published in the Skeptical Briefs, June 2008.*

The Testing of Susie Cotrell
Martin Gardner

Back in 1978 a young woman named Susie Cotrell appeared on the Johnny Carson show to demonstrate her psychic powers. She would spread a shuffled deck of cards face down on the table, then have someone draw a card from the mix. Susie would then name the card.

Card magicians who saw the act at once recognized what Susie was doing. She had unwittingly rediscovered a method of card "forcing" that was being routinely performed by Matt Schulien, who owned a German restaurant on Chicago's north side. I was there many times to watch Matt do his table magic, which included what card magicians came to know as the "Matt Schulien force." It goes like this:

A deck is shuffled. Matt would then cut the cards and in doing so obtain a glimpse of the card cut to the bottom. He then mixed the face-down cards on the table, but his thumbs would keep track of the glimpsed card. During the mixing, the card would go back and forth from one thumb to the other while both hands kept mixing. Finally the glimpsed card is left at the spot nearest the person who is asked to choose a card. Nine times out of ten the person will simply take the card nearest her. That, of course, is the card that was glimpsed.

Susie could have learned the Schulien force from a magician, but my guess is that she independently invented it. At any rate, she performed it skilfully. I noticed that on the Carson show, after the deck had been shuffled, Susie bent her knees so that when she cut the deck it was easy to glimpse the bottom card. Susie was declared a powerful psychic by Jule Eisenbud, a psychiatrist who had published a big book about his experiments with Ted Serios, a beer-guzzling Chicago bellhop who, when a Polaroid camera was aimed at his head and snapped, the film would supposedly show photos of memories in his brain, such as snapshots of the Eiffel Tower. James Randi was soon able to demonstrate the same feat on television. The trick made use of a secret tube with a transparency at one end and a lens at the other. Serios would secretly palm the tube and load it into a paper cylinder he called the "gizmo," which he held in front of the camera. Light bounced off his white shirt, went through the tube, and produced the images on the film. Poor Eisenbud, the most gullible of all parapsychologists, never doubted that Serios was a great psychic.

But back to Susie. Her father made the mistake of asking CSICOP (now CSI) to validate Susie's powers. Randi and I served as the investigators, and the testing took place in Buffalo. We first allowed Susie to demonstrate her trick, without shuffling the deck, for a small audience of guest observers. Susie did not know that a camera was secretly recording her hand movements. When we later ran the film backwards you could see the selected card return to the mix while Susie kept it under her thumbs, finally sliding it back either to the deck's top or bottom. If a spectator failed to pick the glimpsed card, Susie had a variety of what magicians call "outs." For example, instead of naming the card she would ask the onlooker to take three more cards, it being almost certain that the three would include the glimpsed "force" card. Susie would then arrange the four cards in a row, and by applying what is called a "magician's force," the glimpsed card would be selected.

After Susie's successful demonstrations, we repeated her performance under strict controls. The deck was now shuffled by Randi or myself. Susie was not allowed to touch the deck until she began the mixing. Now, as expected, Susie was never able to name the selected card. We broke for a brief intermission. When we returned, a deck was lying face-down on the table. Susie didn't realize that I was standing behind her, and I saw her carefully pick up the deck, glace at the bottom card, and replace it. I now regret that I did not let her do the trick without a prior shuffle, then I would dramatically name the selected card myself, but I didn't think of it at the time.

Susie was of course furious with how she had been handled. She got into a loud verbal fight with Randi, demanding that if he thought he knew how she had cheated, then he should demonstrate the trick. Randi refused, on the grounds that he hadn't practiced the trick which she was able to perform so well.

Susie's father was present at the testing. He was absolutely convinced that his daughter's ESP abilities were genuine. In spite of her failures, Susie played the role convincingly of a genuine psychic, deeply offended by how she had been treated by the awful skeptics. She even talked at length about how she was working with retarded children, amazing them with her trick, and telling them that they, too, might possess psychic powers!

Susie, I'm happy to say, has faded away as completely as Ted Serios. Her case shows how easy it is to trap a psychic charlatan if you have on hand an experienced magician like Randi who knows so much about deception, and how to devise traps for exposing fake psychics.

Martin Gardner wrote the "Mathematical Games" column in Scientific American *from 1956 to 1981, and "Notes of a Fringe Watcher" from 1983 to 2002 for the Skeptical Inquirer. He has published over seventy books;* Fads and Fallacies in the Name of Science *(1952, revised 1957) is a classic work of applied skepticism.*

Mr. Polty and the Magic Clock
Susan Blackmore

Way back in 1981 I was asked to help a family terrified by a poltergeist in their home in Bristol, England. My investigation of "Mr. Polty" (as they called him) shows the importance of first believing what people say they have experienced. They may be lying; they may be cheating; but in my experience most are not. Most are genuinely trying to make sense of strange experiences and have—understandably—jumped to the wrong conclusions. It is the investigator's job to take their accounts seriously and then work out what is really going on.

I arrived at the house to be greeted with tales of scary noises in the bathroom, keys rattling in locks when there was no one there, and steps sounding in empty rooms. More intriguing were two events that everyone in the family claimed to have seen: The TV changed channels when no one was near it, and a clock on the mantelpiece that jumped and moved along. I made notes of all they told me and settled down to watch. From then on I stayed a whole day, once a week, for many weeks.

First I asked everyone to keep a diary of Polty events. I could not keep them from making things up, but from their diaries I could check whether one person was always there when weird things happened. They were not.

I then introduced a "Polty box." This was modelled on boxes used at the McDonnell lab in St. Louis, Missouri. It was basically an upside down fish tank containing a pencil and paper (in case Mr. Polty wanted to leave messages), a paper mobile (to be blown by a spirit breath), a spoon (for spoon-bending), and various small objects with their positions marked. I told the family that this was for Mr. Polty to show what he could do. I did not tell them that between the base and the lid I had inserted black velvet and a strip of unexposed film so that I could tell if anyone opened the box.

I don't know what I expected—back in those days I was still hovering between total skepticism, and a touch of hope that I might discover something truly momentous. The box meant I could learn something either way—the spoon might be bent when no one had opened it or I might catch a culprit. Nothing happened.

Meanwhile I solved the TV mystery. At that time few people had remote controls but this TV, unbeknown to its owners, had an ultra-sound detector. Their large dog used to flop in front of the set, and his rattling collar chain made just the right sound to change the channel.

That left the clock, and one day, as I sat there, I saw it jump, just as they had described. Hope again! I began investigating by swapping it for another clock—to determine whether it was the clock or mantle piece that was haunted. This clock did not budge. So I took the original one to a technician at Bristol University who was a clock enthusiast. He was extremely reluctant to examine it; as a Catholic he feared messing with devil's work. (Sigh.)

But I persuaded him that good might prevail and so he provided the key to the whole mystery. The clock, it turned out, was very light but had a heavy, old-fashioned spring that was clogged with years of dirt. As it unwound the coils stuck together and then suddenly released, giving enough energy to make the clock jump along the smooth, tiled mantelpiece.

I took the clock back and explained, very gently, to the family what I had found out. There was disappointment, anger, and relief, but in the end relief prevailed. And Mr. Polty, they told me, quietly slipped away.

Susan Blackmore is a psychologist, writer and ex-parapsychologist, with research and publications on out-of-body experiences, memes, consciousness and anomalous experiences. Her books include The Meme Machine, Consciousness: An Introduction, Conversations on Consciousness *and* Ten Zen Questions.

Avoid Explaining What Needs No Explanation
Ray Hyman

The first principle of skeptical inquiry should be to make sure that an alleged claim happened as described. If the claim is an extraordinary one, and if the evidence for it was not recorded under strict scientific conditions, then the description of the underlying event (or events) is inherently untrustworthy.

In December 1972, Colonel Austin Kibler phoned to ask me to be part of a committee to visit Stanford Research Institute (SRI) in Menlo Park, California. Colonel Kibler was the acting head of the Advanced Research Projects Agency of the Defense Department. This is the agency created by President John F. Kennedy to deal with futuristic aspects of warfare.

Kibler told me that two physicists had been conducting tests on a "psychic" at SRI. If this psychic was real, Kibler told me, then his agency should be involved. To determine if the psychic had genuine powers, Kibler was sending a parapsychologist from the University of Virginia. Kibler wanted me to detect whether the psychic was cheating.

Kibler knew, of course, that I was skeptical of psychic claims. To engage my interest he told me that this psychic, who was an Israeli named Uri Geller, could do anything other psychics could do. In addition, he could bend metal with his mind. He described an incident which he said had occurred at SRI when Geller borrowed a ring. He emphasized that he not be allowed to touch it. He had someone place the ring on a table in the middle of the room. Geller requested that everyone, including himself, stand back from the table. Geller concentrated and, after a brief interval, the ring stood on its side, came apart, and shaped itself into the letter S.

During the day of the visit by the committee representing the Defense Department (the parapsychologist, a representative of the Advanced Research Projects Agency, and me), the investigators showed us records from tests they had conducted with Geller. Geller also demonstrated some of his "mind reading" and metal bending stunts.

However, my major concern was the incident with the ring. I repeatedly tried to get the investigators to tell me exactly what had taken place. For some reason, the investigators kept changing the subject and would talk about Geller's other accomplishments. I persisted. Finally, one of the investigators showed me a brass ring that had been bent from its initial circular shape into a figure 8. When I asked more questions, I learned that Geller had been allowed to take this particular ring home overnight. When he brought the ring to the lab the next morning it was bent.

I kept asking questions. Could Geller bend a ring without touching it? The investigators assured me that he could do it either way. "Did any of you actually see him bend a ring without touching it?" I asked. It took at least another five minutes of persistent questioning before I got them to admit that no one at SRI had ever actually *seen* Geller bend a ring without getting his hands on it. So how come they had claimed that he could bend a ring without touching it? It turns out that Geller had told them so. They simply had taken his word for it.

This is just one example of where a claim was based on faulty evidence. If Kibler had asked me to explain the incident, as he described it, I would have either had to admit a genuine miracle had taken place or invent a highly implausible story. In fact, there was nothing to explain.

Ray Hyman is Professor Emeritus of Psychology at the University of Oregon, a founding member of the Committee for the Scientific Investigation of Claims of the Paranormal, and author of The Elusive Quarry: A Scientific Appraisal of Psychical Research.

Believe nothing until it is officially denied: UFOs and the investigative journalist
David Clarke

One of British journalism's founding fathers, C.P. Scott, said that "comment is free, but facts are sacred." In the study of UFOs comment—often informed by belief, prejudice or just plain ignorance—is plentiful but "facts" are very rare indeed. Even the most basic information surrounding key events in UFO history such as the Roswell incident have become the subject of interminable controversies. It is hardly surprising therefore that experienced journalists have, by and large, avoided becoming embroiled in the minutiae of the UFO controversy.

As a direct result of this neglect, UFO proponents regard journalists with a great deal of suspicion. From my own experience, the most commonly encountered perceptions of journalistic motives include variations on the conspiracy theory that regards the media as pawns in some gigantic worldwide conspiracy to hide "the truth" about extraterrestrial visitors. This paranoid view is ironic because many journalists regard themselves as individuals, whoever their employers may be. Most are genuinely suspicious and inquisitive by nature and thrive upon any hint of a government conspiracy; indeed, a favourite watchword is "never believe anything until it is officially denied." The exposure of a government attempt to conceal alien visits would, for any journalist worthy of the name, constitute the scoop of the century.

On the other hand, most journalists operate within a comfort zone that largely accepts and reproduces the consensus view of the world. They rely upon trusted sources, such as scientists and assorted experts to provide an authoritative last word on controversial topics. Inevitably, UFOs are usually treated in a superficial, light-hearted fashion—not as hard "news" but human interest or entertainment. As a direct result, most coverage of the subject tends to encourage adversarial debates between those who "believe" in aliens and conspiracies to hide the truth and skeptics who pour scorn upon the whole idea. The end result is that prejudices are reinforced and strongly-held opinions are substituted for factual information that might inform future debate.

Since 2005, the introduction of a Freedom of Information Act in the United Kingdom allowed scrutiny of claims that the British Ministry of Defence (MoD) has operated a covert UFO investigation branch. From 2000 onwards I made extensive use of access legislation, backed up with interviews with former military and government sources, in a determined campaign to uncover any facts that might support claims of a "cover-up" made by UFO proponents. Papers unearthed by FOIA requests were largely unclassified and even material declassified from the level of "Secret: UK Eyes Only" contained no evidence of a cover-up by the UK military of visits by aliens. The testimony of all the sources interviewed simply confirmed what the paper trail suggested: there was not a hint of any conspiracy. What my investigation did reveal, however, was a continuing obsession with secrecy (a holdover from the Cold War), a total lack of interest in UFOs *per se* (other than from the narrow perspective of defence and occasional embarrassment at members of its own staff who expressed belief in them).

A direct by-product of my efforts was a policy decision by Defence Minister Des Browne to release the MoD's entire remaining collection of UFO papers to The National Archives in Kew. In total 160 files containing some 10,000 individual sighting reports, policy documents and intelligence briefings are being opened in a rolling disclosure programme. The MoD say they hope that this new policy of openness "may help to counter the maze of rumour and frequently ill-informed speculation that surrounds [our role]."

It remains to be seen if the ministry's optimism is justified, as previous experience has shown that such revelations—such by the crop circle hoaxers—can, perversely, strengthen existing conspiracy beliefs. Ultimately belief lies at the heart of the UFO mystery and the idea of a cover-up is belief-driven. The public want to know the truth about a baffling subject and because the government is involved, it is wrongly assumed they must know the answer. When information is not forthcoming, or when it is released but does not establish the existence of alien visitors, an even deeper cover-up is suspected and so the argument becomes a circular one. The idea of a cover-up of "the truth" about UFOs can never be disproved, only proved; but as Daniel Webster said: "there is nothing so powerful as the truth and often nothing as strange."

Dr. David Clarke teaches investigative journalism and media law at the Department of Journalism and Communication, Sheffield Hallam University, UK. He is the UK National Archives consultant on the release of the MoD files and his book, The UFO Files, *was published in July 2009.*

Using Inconvenient Facts to Assess Claims
Dave Thomas

Generally it's not a good idea to dismiss a claim (or series of claims) because of a single mistake or an "inconvenient fact" that gets in the way. For example, a Holocaust denier might argue that, because the claim that

Nazis actually manufactured soap from human bodies has been proven false, therefore the entire Holocaust was a fiction. Indeed, this approach is one of the classic logical fallacies: "Falsus in uno, falsus in omnibus" ("False in one thing, false in everything").

However, when they are carefully used, "inconvenient facts" can be a useful tool for quickly weeding out spurious claims. When someone is making a slew of claims or assertions, and most of these can't even be checked, I often focus on the few "facts" than *can* be verified. And if these facts turn out to be undeniably wrong—and, if the claimant does not respond, or dismisses any disagreement when approached with the discrepancy —then there is a reasonable basis to dismiss the entire claim.

I spent considerable time examining the claims of a man named Eugene Faulstich (see my piece in the book *Skeptical Odysseys*). Faulstich claimed to have calculated exact astronomical-based dates for thirteen key Biblical events. When he calculated the differences in weeks between all 78 pairs of the 13 dates, and examined the digits in this collection of numbers, he found a whopping 35% were 7's (one would expect 10% for random distributions). Faulstich claimed that he and his colleagues achieved "a new scientific breakthrough in religious studies," and that his group's work showed that "the chronology in the Bible is scientifically provable through the exact science of astrophysics."

The trouble is that most of his events occurred centuries ago, if at all, and were derived from historical eclipses and Biblical citations; they cannot be checked reliably. For example, Faulstich pegged the Crucifixion as occurring on April 6, A.D. 30; his oldest cited date is October 9, 1462 B.C. (that of Moses and the Burning Bush). Most of these dates depend critically on his arcane research methods. Only two of his events are from the 20th century: the hanging of ten Nazi war criminals at Nuremberg in 1946, and Israel's declaration of independence in 1948.

These are "factoids" that can be checked: the war criminals were all hanged on October 16, 1946. However, Faulstich claims this happened two days later—on October 18, 1946—in order to get exactly 100,000 weeks between that day and the crucifixion of Christ.

I corresponded with Faulstich for a long time, and carried out a very detailed analysis of his claims. In particular, I found a set of 13 key dates in *American* history that produced the same anomalous bounty of sevens in the week intervals thus calculated. For example, the interval from the date of the first New Madrid earthquake (Mag 7.5, Dec. 16, 1811) and the United States's severance of ties to Fidel Castro's Cuba (Jan. 3, 1961) is exactly 7777 weeks. Rather than spending decades searching for special dates with magic intervals, I simply submitted a few hundred important events from American history, and let a genetic algorithm come up with the "best" dates—a process that took all of ten minutes.

In retrospect, I could have saved myself a lot of work. Every time I mentioned the Nuremberg "problem" to Faulstich, silence was the result. Encyclopedia citations and news accounts about the hangings did nothing to convince Faulstich that he was wrong about when the executions took place.

If someone won't take into account the "facts" which can be examined, why take their word on the ones that can't? You can't always shoot from the hip—but, when the opportunity presents itself, it's sometimes worth the taking.

Dave Thomas is a physicist and mathematician. Dave is president of the science group New Mexicans for Science and Reason (http://www.nmsr.org), and also is a Fellow of CSI (Committee for Skeptical Inquiry). He has published several articles in Skeptical Inquirer on the Roswell and Aztec UFO Incidents, as well as on the Bible Code. Dave has also published in Scientific American (Dec. 1980 cover article), and has several patents.

The Importance of Improvisation in Investigation
Richard Wiseman

I believe that one of the most important aspects of any investigation involves an ability to improvise. When you examine allegedly unexplained phenomena, you hope that everything will go according to plan: That the medium will try to contact the dead under test conditions, that the psychic will attempt to demonstrate psychokinetic powers whilst being filmed, and that any poltergeist phenomena will happen on cue. Unfortunately, things rarely turn out to be quite so predictable, with mediums often trying to re-negotiate experimental controls just before the start of a test, psychics producing their alleged miracles when the cameras stop rolling, and poltergeists making their presence known when you are least expecting to hear from them. Given that is the case, investigators need to be able to improvise and adapt. The idea is nicely illustrated in an investigation of alleged psychokinetic ability that parapsychologist Professor Erlendur Haraldsson and I carried out a few years ago.

Swami Premananda is a religious leader based in southern India, and claims to be able to materialise small objects in his bare hands. Several witnesses had produced impressive reports of his apparent abilities, and so Erlendur and I contacted Premananda and asked whether he would allow us to test him. Premananda expressed an interest in the idea, and so the two of us travelled to his religious retreat and described what we had in mind. Our proposed test was simple. We would place a transparent plastic bag over Premananda's empty hand, seal it around the wrist, and then film as he tried to materialise an object inside the bag.

Premananda was receptive to the idea, and said that he would meditate for a short while and then attempt the test. He returned a few hours later, sat down, and declared himself ready. I took up my position behind the camera and started to film. Erlendur carefully placed the transparent bag over Premananda's empty hand and sealed the bag around his wrist. Premananda then spent several minutes attempting to materialise an object, but failed. The testing appeared to have finished and it would have been tempting to turn off the camera. However, I had a hunch that Premananda might attempt to produce an object or two under more informal conditions, and so carried on filming.

My hunch paid off. A few minutes later, Premananda suddenly placed his hand on top of Erlendur's hand, and slowly opened it to reveal a small metal statue. Erlendur then took Premananda's hand and placed it into the plastic bag and Premananda apparently materialised some *vibuti* (a fine grey powder used in Hinduism) inside the bag. This turn of events was as fast moving as it was unexpected, and had we not been filming there would have been no way of knowing whether we had just witnessed a magic trick or genuine psychokinetic phenomena. Luckily, a close look at the film resolved the issue. After failing to materialise an object during the formal testing, Premananda quietly placed his hand into his lap. When his hand re-emerged, his fingers were closed and the hand was not shown to be empty before the apparent materialisation of the small statue.

A few moments afterwards, Premananda's hand again moved to his lap and emerged with its back towards the camera, fingers closed. He then had his hand placed into the bag and produced some *vibuti*. All of these movements were consistent with Premananda secretly taking various objects from his lap before "materializing" them. Had we failed to improvise, and simply stuck with the rigid rules of the test, we wouldn't have captured Premananda's alleged psychokinetic ability on camera, and thus it would have been far harder to argue that the phenomena were the result of trickery. So, when it comes to investigating the paranormal, arrive with an open mind, a willingness to go with the flow, and an ability to improvise.

Further reading: Wiseman, R. & Haraldsson, E. (1995). Investigating macro-PK in India: Swami Premananda. *Journal of the Society for Psychical Research*, 60 (839), 193-202.

Professor Richard Wiseman is in the Psychology Department at the University of Hertfordshire. He is author of many books including Guidelines for Testing Psychic Claimants *(with Robert Morris) and* The Luck Factor.

Busting Ghost Busters with the Historical Method
Karen Stollznow

The scientific method is not the sole realm of the physical, natural, or so-called "hard" sciences. The social science of history is a discipline that involves the systematic analysis of the past, and aims to construct an objective, factual account of the past. The historical method can be a part of the scientific method.

The historical method can function as a complementary tool of scientific paranormal investigation, but it can also be a core component. History is fundamental to paranormal research, in that any claim is retrospective. Exploring the history of a claim is a principle phase, before setting up experiments, or treating issues of validity and reliability. We need to know what happened, if indeed anything did happen, before we can test it. Therefore, the scientific method doesn't invariably require the experimental method. Sometimes, history can actually solve the case, or even reveal that there isn't one.

To establish, validate, or refute a claim the researcher needs to acquire and examine observable data, including credible primary and secondary sources, artifacts, documents, scholarly books, records, and reference materials. Obtaining eyewitness accounts is also an important part of the data collection process; but the researcher must differentiate between testimony and proof. Anecdotal evidence is not historical evidence.

History can be a method of falsification. An assertion can be falsified by the documentation of reliable disconfirming evidence. For example, several years ago I investigated Waverley Hills Sanatorium in Louisville, Kentucky. Numerous secondary sources claim that this former tuberculosis hospital is haunted, and that some 65,000 deaths occurred there during the years of operation. Instead, death certificates and a resident physician's autobiography reveal that this figure is a gross exaggeration; approximately 5,500 deaths occurred there, less than 10% of the folkloric legends. As we can see, real history is fascinating enough.

These sources further report the existence of a "body chute" and a room where electro-shock treatment was administered (this in itself is dubious, for a tuberculosis sanatorium). Such claims are disproved by checking the building blueprints that prove these were a transport tunnel and a boiler room, respectively. These sources also report ghostly doctors, nurses, and patients. Like urban legends, the stories change, the names change, and there are no records that verify the existence of these people. However, on a tour of the premises, the site historian presented all of these inaccuracies and apocryphal tales as fact. Eschewing poor quality secondary sources in favor of reliable primary sources provides more plausible alternative theories, and falsifies these claims. Historical research solved these mysteries.

I was invited to investigate an alleged haunted house in the rural Australian city of Armidale, halfway between Sydney and Brisbane. A resident reported a range of paranormal activity, including footsteps and shadows when he's alone in the house; lights flashing on and off; doors and windows opening and closing by themselves; objects disappearing and reappearing in unexpected places; cold spots throughout the house; the pet dog barks at an invisible disturbance; and the sensation of being touched by an unseen hand.

To the resident, these events were frightening and inexplicable, and his immediate premise was that the house was haunted. However, by applying the "simplest explanation" principle of Occam's Razor, these phenomena could be explained heuristically as natural occurrences—weather and activity outside, and structural or electrical problems and household activities inside.

This became an opportunity to observe how a psychic medium would interpret and explain these same incidents. Claiming the ability to communicate with the deceased, a self-styled "ghost buster" was presented with the claims, and invited to visit the house. After touring the premises and conducting a reading, she concluded that the house was indeed haunted. She supplied names, dates, and places as evidence that she had contacted the spirits causing the phenomena. Her information provided testable claims.

This was not her word against mine; it was her word against history. I subsequently consulted with Historian Bruce Ibsen at a local Heritage Center. We found that the historical archives disproved rather than substantiated the ghost buster's claims. Consequently, the subject did not display paranormal abilities. Instead, her reading revealed confirmation bias. With prior knowledge of the reputed haunting events, her results supported the claims, not the history. The ghost busting medium had accepted and expanded upon the resident's initial premise that the house was haunted.

For uncritical, non-scientific paranormal investigators, history seems to equal haunted. In contrast, skepticism is a prerequisite of the historical method. As in the formal sciences, history has a commitment to rigorous research, to discover truth. The application of critical thinking to historical research is imperative; history is distorted by research that is inadequate, uses fallacious sources, and is replete with bias, opinion and hearsay; this creates pseudo-history. History should record fact, not fiction. When we write history, we shouldn't create history.

Dr. Karen Stollznow is a linguist, author, and former editor of the Skeptic *magazine.*

Three Simple Guidelines

James Underdown

There is great variety in the paranormal cases that I and the Independent Investigations Group (IIG) have worked on over the years, but a few simple guidelines can help anyone find answers to most claims, or at least make reasonable guesses. These guidelines all apply to a case we looked into a while ago that concerned a psychic canine named Sparky the Wonder Dog.

1) Do Your Homework. When NBC's *Tonight Show* told Gordie (Sparky's owner) he'd have to prove that his pooch was telepathic to some real skeptics, Gordie sent a videotape of the dog in action to the Center for Inquiry-*West*. The tape showed the dog in a shower stall with Gordie outside the stall holding some large numbers on poster boards. When Gordie asked "How many Sparky?" the dog began barking and stopped when he got to the number in Gordie's hand. The shower glass was wavy and convinced Gordie that Sparky could have only known what the number was through psychic powers.

Readers with a background in skepticism might immediately recognize a similarity to Clever Hans, a horse who lived in early twentieth century Germany who appeared to give math demonstrations to amazed onlookers. It was eventually learned that the horse was picking up on the subtle body language of the humans around him. The humans, by the way, were unaware that they were cueing the horse. Knowing the history of Clever Hans helped us be on the lookout for Gordie signaling Sparky, intentionally or otherwise.

2) Brainstorm the Cheat. In the video, Gordie was dipping the poster board down when Sparky's barks reached the correct number. It looked to us to be a big enough movement for Sparky to see, but the Clever Hans-type trick was so obvious that we got suspicious. Were we were being led off the trail of the real con—a con much cleverer and more complicated? We took some time to brainstorm about what the *real* gimmick might be while we were being lulled to sleep by the Clever Hans bit. Was there a dog whistle in his mouth? Had he memorized the numbers? Did he use a remote electronic shock transmitter... release a scent? We listed as many tricks and devices as we could think of and discussed ways to prevent each them from being employed. When it came time for the test, we were on the lookout for many different sneaky techniques.

3) See for Yourself. Before we had ever seen Sparky in person, we knew a bit about the specific claim, about historical claims like it, had seen tape of him in action, and had thought about what might be happening. It was now time to see for ourselves. I got to see Sparky and Gordie at a cable access TV studio, doing their psychic bit on a small stage. Before they began taping, I asked if I could place a floor plant between them. The plant didn't completely block Sparky's view of Gordie, but it did somewhat impair it. When it came time for Sparky to guess the number, he just barked and barked. Evidently, the plant did block his vision enough to leave him clueless as to what number Gordie was trying to convey.

This firsthand knowledge of the plant's effect helped us put a test together for Sparky at CFI. The test we designed there involved a simple curtain between Gordie and Sparky. When Gordie asked, "How many Sparky?" Sparky just barked and barked. Psychic waves, apparently, do not penetrate plants or curtains

James Underdown is Executive Director of the Center for Inquiry-Los Angeles and is the founder and chair of the Independent Investigations Group. He has appeared throughout the media discussing paranormal, supernatural, and extraordinary claims.

Always Seek Out Original Sources
Daniel Loxton

In my investigations of strange mysteries, one discovery stands out as the most bizarre: that it's possible for me to make discoveries at all.

Very often, I am able to turn to a paranormal topic I know little about, and in a very short time (weeks, occasionally days) make significant contributions to the literature on that topic—either shedding light on a possible solution or solving a mystery. Which is ridiculous. I shouldn't be able to do that from a standing start. When proponents have already spent *decades* discussing claims like Bigfoot, pyramid power, or the Thetis Lake Monster, all avenues of investigation should have been explored.

But, here's the unfortunate truth: paranormal enthusiasts don't do their homework. Rather than digging seriously with an aim to solve these mysteries, paranormal writers pass around unverified trivia like trading cards. They may have exhaustive knowledge of the legendary anecdotes that comprise the canon for their favorite claim, but that information usually comes from third-hand sources—which, in turn, get it from *other* third-hand sources.

When I dig into a paranormal claim, I always start with one simple question: "How did this legend get started?" As with counterfeit art, seeking original sources and probing the provenance of a legend often reveals that the foundation is rotten. Let me give an example:

Take the 1970s fad of "pyramid power." This is the idea that the "sacred geometry" of pyramids focuses an unknown mystical energy. Allegedly, this energy can preserve food or sharpen razor blades stored inside a pyramid (among other, stranger claims). Today there are countless Web sites devoted to this topic, and even a winery that ages its product in a pyramid-shaped building.

All pro-paranormal sources agree that a man named Bovis "discovered" pyramid power while he stood inside the Great Pyramid at Giza — but none seem to ask whether that story is true, or where it came from. They should. The Bovis story is inconsistent from telling to telling. Various versions are set in dates ranging from the 1900s to the 1930s. Bovis is said to have noticed the Great Pyramid contained carcasses from (variously) mice, or bats, or a single cat, or a trash can full of mummified cats.

Where did this vague and unlikely urban legend come from? Published versions all converge on a single secondary source (a dead end). So, I began a wide-ranging hunt for Antoine Bovis's original writings, and turned up a stack of his self-published mystical pamphlets in the hands of an antique dealer in Germany. The punchline? Bovis explicitly denies visiting Egypt. The "standing inside the Great Pyramid" story is a purely fictional embellishment.

Hunting down the original sources is essential. Consider the case of the Thetis Lake Monster. This obscure fish-man is known only from a handful of 1972 newspaper stories. Yet, while the story has percolated for decades in cryptozoological books and Web sites (mutating over time to include unsourced new details) no one ever thought to look for original articles from the region's *other* daily paper. It took me ten minutes in the local library to find a previously unknown early news report describing the terrifying "monster" as *three inches tall.* And paranormal researchers had neglected an even more obvious step. Rather than rely upon third-hand retellings, or even the brief quotes in the original tiny news articles, I tracked down and spoke to the key surviving witness. He flat out told me, "It was just a big lie."

I shouldn't be able to wrap up decades-old mysteries so easily. I wouldn't be able to, if mystery proponents looked more closely at their own key evidence. They could start by adopting one simple trick: *always seek out original sources.*

Daniel Loxton is a writer for Skeptic *magazine, Editor of* Junior Skeptic, *and author of the book* Evolution: How We and All Living Things Came to Be. *He specializes in investigations of classic paranormal claims, especially cryptozoological creatures like Bigfoot and the Loch Ness monster.*

Sleuthing the Psychic Sleuths
Gary P. Posner

A Piper Cherokee plane went missing on a cold January 1984 night in rural upstate Massachusetts. The search was called off after a week, but resumed days later at the urging of Jessica Herbert, whose brother was one of the four passengers. Ms. Herbert had obtained a reading from psychic detective Noreen Renier, and was now armed with the location of the missing craft's resting place. Renier also told her of how her brother, whose leg was broken in the crash, had heroically carried a more severely injured woman to safety and gently sat her against a tree, before himself hobbling down the steep, rocky hillside in search of help.

At least that's the version of events in Ms. Herbert's 1986 deposition testimony, in a libel action brought by Renier against skeptic John Merrell, who had called her a fraud. And Herbert's ex-husband, FBI Special Agent Mark Babyak, testified that he was the one who, on the recommendation of a fellow FBI agent, had suggested consulting Renier. He also recounted how he and still *another* FBI agent/pilot had rented a small plane and, following Renier's psychic directions, began circling an area comporting with her psychic visions. Testifying about the two people who found the wreckage the following day, Babyak said, "It was in basically the area that we had been circling over and that's what, again, drew them to look in that area."

One might think that three FBI agents vouching for a psychic's uncanny abilities ought to be enough to silence the skeptics. But in my chapter about Renier in *Psychic Sleuths* (Prometheus Books, 1994), I spot-lighted this case to illustrate the importance of employing intensely crit-ical scrutiny when evaluating even the most impressively corroborated paranormal claims. And for good reason.

The local press was reporting at the time (and Jessica Herbert knew) that two witnesses saw and heard the plane go down in the distance. So, although the terrain had been slow to reveal its prey, the general whereabouts of the wreckage were no mystery. Dense woods were hampering the search efforts, but contrary to Renier's visions, the locale was not particularly rocky or hilly. And the NTSB's subsequent investigation determined that all four occupants died on impact. No one had carried anyone anywhere, and the woman's body had been decapitated and could not even be recovered until the mangled metal was cut apart.

As for the crash site's discovery, the official search party was one-upped by a father/daughter duo who, on their own initiative, had set out in the general direction the two eyewitnesses had specified. As they progressed and encoun-tered deer tracks in the snow, they decided to follow the tracks, and wound up at the crash site. Neither had seen Babyak's search plane the day before or ever heard of Noreen Renier. And after they read Renier's description of the scene in her 2005 memoir, *A Mind for Murder*, the father told skeptic Merrell, "I don't think she's got *anything* right."

But let's give credit where credit is due. Though Renier may have been somewhat off the mark about the terrain being hilly and rocky, and in fanta-syland about the condition of the victims, she did direct Babyak's search to the proper Massachusetts locale. But did Renier necessarily come up with that location psychically? Is it even fathomable that Jessica Herbert had failed to describe the week-long search to Renier when she called to schedule the reading? And, if she had wanted to, in the day between Herbert's call and her visit, might Renier have even researched the local newspaper coverage of the ongoing saga?

Gary Posner, a retired physician, is vice president of a medical records software company in Tampa, Florida. He is the founder and executive director of Tampa Bay Skeptics, a sci-entific consultant to the Committee for Skeptical Inquiry, and an occasional contributor to CSI's Skeptical Inquirer. His extensive writings about Noreen Renier, and other aspects of the paranormal, can be found at www.gpposner.com.

The Capital Mistake
Massimo Polidoro

As Sherlock Holmes was always eager to point out to his friend Dr. Watson: "It is a capital mistake to theorize before you have all the evidence. Insensibly, one begins to twist the facts to suit theories, instead of theories to suit facts."

In my 20-odd years of investigating mysteries, I have always found this advice one of the most useful. I have often witnessed, among skeptical investigators, long debates regarding the possible solution to a still unsolved mystery. More often than not, this later would turn out to be a mere waste of time, for the solution was usually something different than what was expected.

In the early days of CICAP (the Italian Committee for the Investigation of Claims of the Paranormal), upon receiving letters from people claiming they could do amazing things, we usually started by imagining several possible explanations.

For example, a girl from Venice said she could guess 100% correctly objects hidden in a sealed box. Another one said she could mummify an egg just by placing her hands on it. A man from Florence claimed he was a human magnet, and cutlery would stick to his body. And a Russian lady claimed she could move objects on a table without touching them.

Before having a chance to examine these people, we could not help imagining possible tricks by which these feats could be performed. Trick boxes could be used to "see" through them. Quick hand manipulations could substitute a normal egg for a prepared one. The "human magnet" could use real hidden magnets or even stick glue on his body. And the lady might move objects by secretly breathing on them, or by using invisible threads.

When we finally had a chance to meet the people and see them at work, we immediately realized that they were all sincere people. They were not using trickery; instead they came to us trying to understand what was happening to them. It was also clear that paranormal phenomena had nothing to do with their demonstrations.

Everything was much simpler, provided you could look at the phenomenon objectively. The girl with the boxes was simply deluded: she would use the same three or four objects, ask a friend to hide one inside, and then she would start guessing, saying things like "it has a smooth surface here, and a bit shining there," characteristics that did fit more than one object and, furthermore, she asked for feedback from her friend. All this made her believe she had some sort of X-ray eyes.

The cutlery on the magnet man's body did not fall off because of the natural friction of the skin; however, as soon as we asked the man to bend forward, everything—including the man's delusions—fell on the floor with a loud crash. As for the eggs, we found that the lady did not mummify it in its shell, as we had wrongly assumed, but first broke it in a dish and then let it sit there for a week. Naturally, the egg dehydrated and the fact that she was putting her hands upon it, at intervals, proved to be unnec-essary when several control-eggs were simply let in dishes and turned out exactly identical to the "treated" one.

Finally, the Russian lady was really able to move light objects as she claimed, but the demonstration only worked on Plexiglas tables. The fact is that the movement was caused not by psychokinesis but instead by static electricity.

Not a single one of these explanations was obvious to me upon mere written description, but they all became quite clear once I had a chance to witness a real demonstration and put it to the test. This same principle applies to what you read on a newspaper: never trust a description of an anomalous phenomenon. Even if the journalist is alert and observant, limited space on the page will still prevent the inclusion of details that could actually prove crucial in explaining the mystery.

Massimo Polidoro is an investigator of the paranormal, author, lecturer, and co-founder and head of CICAP, the Italian skeptics group. Web site: www.massimopolidoro.com.

Beware The Lying Camera
Blake Smith

The camera frequently lies; this is an important principle of skepticism. General wisdom is that if a photograph or video image shows something un-usual, then something unusual has been filmed. Yet a little critical thinking might alleviate this "camera-faith" bias. For example, think of all the times that you are willingly fooled by films. In motion pictures, magazine covers, and television a variety of makeup effects, special effects and post-production make beautiful people appear flawless, make men and monsters seem giant or tiny, and make solid objects appear to fly or disappear. And most of us have taken photos where the subject moved, or the light was wrong and the results were blurred or distorted.

A common theme in modern (non-scientific) paranormal investigations seems to be scouring video and photographs to find anomalies. The implication is that unusual and unexplained elements to video and photographs are evidence of the paranormal. Yet if we take into account the error-prone nature of the tools we use to make the photos, then the evidentiary value of their output is diminished.

Another problem is that of pareidolia, the tendency of the human mind to find faces and anthropomorphic shape where none exists. Pareidolia allows us to see the circle, lines, and dots that form a "smiley face" and recognize its implied humanity. But it is also responsible for many sightings of faces in tree bark, toast, clouds, and of course in blurred or damaged photographs where no such image really exists.

When you combine these elements, the value of photographs as evidence of the paranormal or supernatural is very weak before you even consider that many people intentionally fake photographic "evidence." With the rise of the Internet and Photoshop, doctored photos are more rampant than ever, but many perfectly normal lighting effects can create ghostly images, especially if the viewer is looking for (and expecting to see) ghosts.

In 2007, I analyzed some video from a ghost hunting group in Australia. Their video showed what appeared to be a "humanoid" shape moving rapidly across the frame of the video and then disappearing. With the help of an Australian skeptic named Kylie Sturgess I was able to demonstrate that the "object" in the film was actually a light passing across the cemetery's tombstones, and that what seemed to be a humanlike shape was actually just a large tombstone getting very brief illumination. Some of the famous hoaxing techniques (such as intentional double-exposure) are less common with the advent of inexpensive digital cameras, but they introduce their own new pareidolia mechanism: pixelation.

A photograph made with a digital camera can only capture as much detail as the camera's internal computer allows. Most people save their photographs in compressed formats such as JPEG so they take up less disk space. But JPEG is a "lossy" format, meaning that when the picture is compressed, it permanently loses data. Instead of a deep level of detail, zooming in on a section produces only big blocky colors. These picture elements (pixels) can produce their own pareidolia building blocks.

When offered photographic evidence of the paranormal, ask these kinds of questions: Did the person taking the photograph actually see something unusual or did the anomaly only show up after the photo was reviewed? Is the object or effect really in the picture, or is it on top of the picture elements? What is the provenance (history) for the photos or video? Is it possible that image is a hoax? Remember, the camera can add a ghost, angel, or UFO with the same ease that it adds ten pounds.

Blake Smith is a writer, computer tech, and skeptical investigator living in Georgia. He writes on the Web under the name "Doctor Atlantis," though he is neither a doctor, nor from Atlantis.

CHAPTER 4
How *Not* to Investigate the Paranormal
Science and Pseudoscience in Ghost Investigations

ow *not* to investigate the paranormal?

H
I toyed with the idea of just having a two-word chapter here: Watch television. I decided against it, not because it's not true—it very much is—but because millions of people have been badly misinformed by TV shows, books, magazines, and paranormal "experts" about what constitutes valid paranormal investigation, and they deserve more than a glib answer. While this chapter deals specifically with ghost investigations, the principles and pseudoscientific problems described here apply to many other types of investigations, including searches for Bigfoot, lake monsters, psychic powers, and so on.

Ghosts and hauntings are by far the most common type of paranormal investigations due in large part to the hugely popular "reality" cable TV show *Ghost Hunters* and its spin-offs and imitators (*Paranormal State*, *Ghost Adventures*, etc.). Such shows depict teams of ordinary folks (with no particular investigative or scientific backgrounds) as successful ghost investigators, and suggest that just about anyone can do it. Another reason for the popularity of ghost investigations is that, compared to other supposedly "unexplained" phenomenon, ghost reports are very common. Not everyone lives next to a lake reputed to hold a monster, or a wheat field where crop circles mysteriously appeared. But nearly every town or city has at least one (and often several) reputedly haunted places. Any old building, school, abandoned mine, decrepit house, or cemetery will do. Because the evidence for ghosts is so general and ambiguous (ranging from "spooky feelings" to ghostly photos and "spirit voices" or EVPs), any location may generate "evidence" if enough people look hard enough (and the standard of evidence is low enough).

Ghost investigations can be a deceptively tricky endeavor. Very ordinary events can be—and have been—mistaken for extraordinary ones, and the main challenge for any ghost investigator is separating out the truth from the jumble of myths, mistakes, and misunderstandings. Often it is very easy to accidentally create or misinterpret evidence: Is that flash of a light on a wall from flashlight reflection—or a ghost? Are the faint sounds recorded in an empty house spirit voices—or a neighbor's radio? It's not always clear, and investigators must be careful to weed out the red herrings and false clues and focus on the real ones. (When I refer to "ghost hunters," I'm referring to ghost investigators in general, not specifically to the *Ghost Hunters* TV show team unless otherwise noted.)

T.A.P.S. and other *Ghost Hunters*

The most famous ghost hunters in the world, Jason Hawes and Grant Wilson (co-founders of the Atlantic Paranormal Society—T.A.P.S.—and stars of the TV show *Ghost Hunters*), agree that science is the best way to approach investigations. They have always claimed to use good scientific methods and investigative procedures, for example writing, "T.A.P.S. uses scientific methods to determine whether or not someone's home might be haunted," and "We approach ghost hunting from a scientific point of view" (Hawes and Wilson 2007, 270).

Yet in their 2007 book *Ghost Hunting*, Jason Hawes spends a grand total of *four paragraphs* (out of 273 pages) on a chapter titled "The Scientific Approach." Hawes says little about science or the scientific methods—in fact it's the shortest chapter in the book. As for his understanding of science, Hawes writes that "Scientific knowledge comes from systematic and objective observations, which help us make deductions we can trust. It also means we have to test those deductions through controlled experiments that can be repeated by others under those same conditions.... We're determined to come as close to scientific accuracy as we possibly can. That's the only way we're going to produce reliable evidence and advance the study of the paranormal" (Hawes and Wilson 2007, 13-14).

Jason Hawes is correct, as far as he goes. He is right that only scientific investigation will shed light on ghostly phenomenon. But he is wrong in his belief that he and his T.A.P.S. crew are doing good scientific investigation. After watching episodes of *Ghost Hunters* and other similar programs it quickly becomes clear to anyone with a background in science that the methods used are both illogical and unscientific.

Ironically, Hawes and Wilson formed T.A.P.S. because they were dissatisfied with the lack of good investigation methods they saw among ghost hunters. According to Jason Hawes, "Finally I said, 'Screw the rest of what's out there,' referring to other ghost hunters and their methods. 'Let's do it our own way'" (Hawes and Wilson 2007, 5).

Unfortunately when the T.A.P.S. team developed their "own way" of ghost investigation, they started from scratch and did not consult professionals from relevant fields. Had their procedures been developed by scientists or investigators, their research methods would have been much more scientific. Some of the T.A.P.S. crews' methods were slightly better than other groups (for example they were among the first to dismiss "orbs" as ghosts), but they were not much more scientific.

A typical ghost hunt follows a pattern. First, the group hears about the claim, and goes to the location to interview one or more people who reported some unusual event. Next, armed with reports and speculation about what might be going on, the team spends hours bringing out and setting up high-tech gear (cameras, audio recorders, EMF detectors, infrared cameras, etc.) around the reputedly haunted location. Then the group does a stakeout that lasts anywhere from a few hours to overnight. During this time they walk around taking photos, temperature readings, recording audio and video footage, and so on. The lights are turned off, and sometimes psychic mediums, dowsing rods, pendulums, and the like are used to try and communicate with a spirit. Other times a test (or "control") object (such as a teddy bear, ball bearings, a toy, a candle, etc.)

will be placed in a conspicuous place, and the ghost asked to affect or move the object.

Usually as the investigators, either individually or as a team, walk around the darkened place they may hear noises or bump into things. Often any "strange" sounds or smells or lights or other experiences will be considered potential ghost activity. Sometimes the ghost hunters will find an explanation for this (and the original claimed) phenomenon, other times they won't. Nothing terribly dramatic will happen, and at the end of the specified time, the investigators have some phenomenon (recorded sounds, video, etc.) to be analyzed at a later time; the stakeout ends and everyone gets some sleep.

Later the investigators go over every bit of audio and video they recorded, combing through for anything that anyone thinks might be strange or unusual. Depending on how much recording they did, they may have dozens or hundreds of hours, and usually they are able to find a few faint "unexplained" noises (that might be EVPs, or ghost voices) or lights or odd electromagnetic field readings. If the team uses psychics, they will give their impressions. Usually at this point the team has found at least a few pieces of evidence that they can associate with a human presence. For example, a psychic may say she sensed an older male presence in one room or area; or a faint sound recorded at some location might be thought to resemble a child's voice; or one of the investigators might suggest that a shadow on a wall looks like a tall, thin woman.

Often the investigators research (or further research) the history of the house, poring over early records and newspaper archives, perhaps interviewing previous owners, looking for anything having to do with the house, its previous occupants, or even the nearby land and houses. Once they have a rough history of the place, they will look for matches: Is there anything in the location's history that can support or confirm the "evidence" they gathered during their investigation?

Often the answer is yes: If it turns out that an elderly woman lived in the house at any point since it was built (and especially if she died there— or even *might* have died there), that "confirms" the psychic's impressions. If a young girl lived there at some point (especially many years ago, and therefore might have since died), then the sound that could be a girl's voice is probably her. And so on. In this way, the investigators believe they are being successful when they find a correlation. They congratulate themselves on a good ghost investigation, explain their findings to the location's owner, and then either call the local news media or write up a report for their Web site listing the phenomena they couldn't explain.

While this is standard operating procedure for many ghost hunting groups and paranormal investigators, there's a whole catalog of errors, logical fallacies, and investigation mistakes in this scenario, from start to finish. Most of these mistakes fall into two categories: They either create false evidence (red herrings, or what in science are known as false-positives, or Type II errors); or the practice is illogical and violates basic scientific methods.

It's important to note that ghost hunters and paranormal investigators often call themselves skeptics, claiming (and sincerely believing) that they are employing science and scientific methods. Whether they claim to be scientific is irrelevant. As the common saying from Matthew (7:16) goes, "Ye shall know them by their fruits." If you want to know whether an investigator or group is scientific or not, examine their methods and results. Do they use the pseudoscientific methods described here? What is their track record of solved cases? Do their investigations end up with inconclusive and ambiguous results, or solved mysteries?

They are not scientists, and studies have repeatedly found that the general public has a very poor understanding of science. Indeed, there's no reason to expect the average person to understand the basic principles of science, any more than the average person would be expected to understand the basics of economic theory, dentistry, or accounting. Most ghost investigators are intelligent, sincere people who have simply never been exposed to the real scientific side of ghost hunting, and instead take their cues and methods from "experts" and what they see on TV shows.

This is not to suggest that ghost investigators must be scientists. A few of them are—Richard Wiseman, Susan Blackmore, and Dr. Steven Novella, a clinical neurologist at Yale University—are a few examples. But most first-rate paranormal investigators are not scientists; I am not a working scientist, and neither are James Randi, Joe Nickell, Massimo Polidoro, and others. What we share is a solid understanding of the fundamentals of science and its methods.

Typical Mistakes in Science and Logic

1. Thinking that all methods of ghost hunting or investigation are equally useful or valid.

I touched on this earlier, but it bears repeating and is especially relevant to ghost hunting: Many people believe that one method of investigation is as good as another, that there is no "correct" way to investigate the unexplained.

Why it's a mistake: If the goal of investigation is to understand an unexplained phenomenon, then the methods that produce information solving the mystery are the right ones; the methods that do not help solve the mystery are the wrong ones. It's as simple as that. Paranormal subjects are investigated just like any other subject: through critical thinking, evidence analysis, logic, and scientific methodologies. The best way to approach investigation is the same one that professional investigators and detectives use every day: the scientific method. Assuming that all methods of ghost investigation are equally good is not only incorrect, but causes many ghost hunters to waste untold time, effort, and money following worthless techniques that don't get results.

2. Considering subjective feelings and emotions as evidence of ghostly encounters.

Members of ghost hunting groups (and TV shows like *Ghost Hunters*) often report descriptions of personal feelings and experiences like, "I felt a heavy, sad presence and wanted to cry," or "I felt like something didn't want me there," and so on. They also describe in detail how, for example, they got goose bumps upon entering a room, or grew panicked at some unseen presence, assuming they were reacting to an unseen ghost. For example, one member of the *Ghost Adventures* TV show, Zak Bagans, said that during investigations he sometimes feels "overtaken" or "overcome by a spirit," and other times he has begun crying (Avakian 2010).

Why it's a mistake: Subjective experiences are essentially stories and anecdotes. There's nothing wrong with personal experiences, but by themselves they are not proof or evidence of anything. Most people who report such experiences are sincere in their belief that a ghost caused their panic, but that belief does not necessarily make it true. The problem, of course, is that there is not necessarily any connection between any real danger or a ghostly presence and how a person feels. Many people suffer from irrational phobias and panic attacks, terrified of any number of things such as insects, airplane travel, and crossing bridges. Their fears and panic are very real—they truly are sweating and terrified. But it's all psychological; it has nothing to do with the outside world. In the same way, the power of suggestion can be very strong, and a suggestible ghost hunter can easily convince herself—and others—that something weird is going on.

3. Failing to consider alternative explanations for anomalous or "unexplained" phenomena.

Ghost hunters often over-interpret evidence and fail to adequately consider alternative explanations—including assuming that "orbs" are ghosts, EVPs are ghost voices, and so on.

Why it's a mistake: The designation of "unexplained" or paranormal must only be accepted when all other normal, natural explanations have been ruled out through careful analysis. The explanation for orbs as flash reflections of dust, insects, mist, et cetera, has been widely discussed for years (Radford 2007, Biddle 2007). Many ghost hunters who accept the scientific, skeptical explanation for orbs continue to record EVPs as ghost voices, despite the fact that the scientific evidence for the validity of EVPs is as poor as it is for orbs. (In fact, their origins are identical: The scientific explanation for EVPs, a psychological process called apophenia, has been thoroughly discussed in the scientific and skeptical literature.) Not a single orb has ever been proven to be a ghost, and not a single EVP has been proven to be of a dead person. This method of inquiry has proven to be completely fruitless.

Another common error is overinterpreting supposedly anomalous phenomenon. Ghost reports are filled with phrases like "one investigator heard a young girl singing softly" or "the shadow of an old man appeared in a hallway." How, exactly, does the ghost hunter know for a fact it was a young girl's voice or an old man's silhouette? I know adult women who could convincingly mimic the soft singing of a young girl, and cast a shadow that might look exactly like an old man's. It is of course *possible* that the sound and shadow is of a young girl and old man, respectively, but an investigator must be careful not to go beyond the established facts and assume that their interpretation is the correct one. Once you have made a specific, declarative statement like "a young girl singing softly," you have locked onto that interpretation, and not kept an open mind about other interpretations.

Unless a person verifies the source of a sound, it is logically impossible to identify with any certainty what created that sound. An adult, an animal, a breeze whistling through an unseen passage, or something else, might sound like a child's voice. Many ghost hunters mistakenly assume that whatever they are told is valid and accurate (for example, John Kachuba, in his book *Ghosthunters*, writes "I took my interviewees at their words, and so should my readers"). Because eyewitness reports have been proven to be often unreliable, scientific paranormal investigators cannot simply take eyewitnesses "at their word" no matter how sincere they are. Even if the *description* of their experience is accurate, the *interpretation* might not be.

This also brings up another basic problem that plagues ghost hunters: how do they know that whatever is causing the mysterious phenomenon is necessarily the disembodied spirit of a dead person? Why couldn't it be an invisible gremlin, or a miraculous act of God, or anything else? A ghost is only one of many possible interpretations, and "explaining" a phenomenon by saying "a ghost caused it" is really no explanation at all.

4. Using unproven tools and equipment.

There are two basic types of equipment and tools that ghost hunters use: metaphysical ones (psychics, dowsing rods, pendulums, séances, etc.) and scientific ones (electromagnetic field detectors, thermometers, FLIR cameras, etc). These devices are commonly used, and sold, as ghost hunting equipment.

Why it's a mistake: In their work, scientists and investigators only use equipment that has been proven to work and is designed for the purpose for which it is used. Police detectives don't use dowsing rods to identify suspects, and doctors don't use EMF detectors to test for genetic diseases. It's not that EMF detectors aren't useful—they very much are, in certain fields—but they have nothing to do with what the doctor is investigating. The same holds true for these unproven tools.

Metaphysical Tools

Psychic abilities have never been proven to exist. Some people—especially those who claim to be psychic or "intuitive" —may disagree, but the fact remains that such powers have never been scientifically validated. This is not the place for a lengthy discussion on the reality of psychic powers; the scientific evidence can be found elsewhere.

But, for the sake of argument, let us suppose that psychic power exists, and that some psychics have some unknown, unprovable ability to provide unique information about a haunted location or spirit. This would still be of little or no value to a scientific paranormal investigator. To see why, let's examine some claims.

In the book *The Other Side: A Teen's Guide to Ghost Hunting and the Paranormal*, authors Marley Gibson, Patrick Burns, and Dave Schrader write, "Certain studies suggest that even the best psychics are accurate only 30 percent of the time... Remember again that a lot of psychics will be wrong more often than they are exact" (p. 49, 51). I don't know where the authors—who, by the way, all believe in psychic ability—got the 30% figure (instead of random chance), but let's assume they are correct. If the accuracy of psychic power is 30%, this is a terrible success rate.

No scientific test is accurate 100% of the time, but any investigative tool or technique that was accurate 30% of the time would never be used by a responsible scientist or investigator. And remember: that rate is for the *best* psychics. If the ghost-hunting psychic isn't one of the best, the accuracy rate would presumably be lower—twenty percent? Ten percent? Zero percent? Who knows?

Imagine if, during the course of an investigation, a ghost hunter used a psychic who gave 30 different pieces of information about the haunting or spirit. Assuming your psychic is one of the best, she will be wrong about 21 pieces of information, and correct about 9 of them. Making matters worse, there's no way to know which 9 clues she is correct about. To find out, each piece of information would have to be investigated, and three out of four will be wrong. It's an incredible waste of time and resources—*and that's assuming psychic powers exist.* No scientific investigator in his right mind would use a psychic.

Steve Gonsalves, of the T.A.P.S. group and the *Ghost Hunters* TV show, wrote in the February 2007 issue of the *TAPS Paramagazine* that "the legitimacy and findings of remote viewing [psychics] are obviously questionable, but... if you believe in mind power and ESP, then I say, 'Why not?' It certainly won't hurt..." To an investigator who wastes hours trying to verify wild leads provided by psychics who can't validate their powers scientifically, it certainly *can* hurt.

The exact same problem occurs with the use of dowsing rods, pendulums, tarot cards (Belanger 2005), and other metaphysical and New Age items: they may be fun to play with, but they have never been scientifically proven to work. There's no evidence that dowsing rods can detect water, much less ghosts. Any "evidence" that these tools and devices provide are far more likely to be red herrings than valid pieces of evidence.

Scientific Tools

Many ghost hunters consider themselves scientific if they use high-tech scientific equipment such as Geiger counters, Electromagnetic Field (EMF) detectors, ion detectors, infrared cameras, sensitive microphones, and so on. Yet the equipment is only as scientific as the person using it; you may own the world's most sophisticated thermometer, but if you are using it as a barometer, your measurements are worthless. Using a calculator doesn't make you a mathematician, and using a scientific instrument doesn't make you a scientist.

The use of these devices rest upon nothing more than assumptions and pure speculation (Radford 2006a, 2006b). For any of these pieces of equipment to be useful there must be some proven connection to ghosts. For example, if ghosts were known to emit electromagnetic fields, then a device that measures such fields would be useful. If ghosts were known to cause temperature drops, then a sensitive thermometer would be useful. If ghosts were known to emit ions, then a device that measures such ions would be useful. And so on.

The problem is that there is no body of research that shows that any of the energies these devices are measuring have anything to do with ghosts. Many things are known to emit electromagnetic fields and cause temperature drops; ghosts are not among them. There has not been a single study that shows that these things can detect a ghostly presence. Until someone can reliably demonstrate that ghosts have certain measurable characteristics, devices that purport to measure those unknown characteristics are irrelevant.

Every single reading, whether a fluctuation in a field or a drop in temperature or anything else, can always be attributed to something other than a ghost: even if an investigator gets an "anomalous" reading, there's simply no way to prove it was caused by a ghost. The evidence gathered by these devices will be inconclusive at best. What's the point in using a tool that—even if it works as you think it does—can't prove anything one way or the other?

There's no logical reason to think that an EMF detector would be any more useful in detecting ghosts than a broken inkjet printer or a fuel gauge from a 1983 Buick. I don't use EMF detectors to find ghosts for the same reason I don't use a toaster to clean my laundry.

Some investigators claim that they don't use the equipment to detect ghosts; instead they use it to rule out natural explanations for a ghostly phenomenon. The problem is that the naturalistic "explanations" they claim to be ruling out often have nothing to do with the original ghost claims. For example, let's say that a person believes his house is haunted because he hears faint voices at night, an odd glowing form appeared in a photograph of the house, and small items have inexplicably fallen off a kitchen shelf. Ion counters, FLIR cameras, and EMF detectors are of no benefit in addressing these claims. They cannot reveal the true identity of a glow in a photograph, nor will they explain the origin of the voice-like sounds, nor what caused an item to mysteriously fall off a shelf. The ghost investigators are not "ruling out" any natural explanations with this equipment, because the gear has nothing to do with the claims. Establishing the location of an electromagnetic field or a cold area is of no value; it doesn't "explain" anything.

Many ghost hunters, including the T.A.P.S. team, use EMF detectors to search for electromagnetic fields because they believe that intense magnetic fields can create hallucinations, which in turn might create the illusion of ghosts. It's an interesting theory; unfortunately it's just a theory, not a proven effect. It is true that hallucinations (such as out-of-body experiences) can be triggered by stimulating specific areas of the brain with fixed wavelength patterns of high-level electromagnetic fields. But this only happens with very specific, controlled frequencies of waves carefully directed at specific parts of the brain in a clinical experiment. There is simply no evidence that electromagnetic fields generated by common household appliances can generate EMFs of the frequency and power that can induce hallucinations (Novella 2010).

Cameras and other recording gear can be useful in an investigation, but it all depends on the purpose, on what the investigator is using it for. A camera set to record the entrance to a door might be very useful in making sure that no one enters unnoticed to pull a hoax or prank. If there is a specific claimed phenomenon that is said to occur, the camera may be a useful tool to record the event if it happens. But simply setting a camera up to record for hours on end with no particular purpose is an easy way to collect bogus evidence.

5. Using improper and unscientific investigation methods.

In addition to misusing scientific equipment, ghost hunters often misuse (or ignore) good scientific research methods.

Why it's a mistake: Examining all the errors in ghost investigations would take an entire book; instead I will highlight the three most common mistakes I have encountered, drawing from personal experience and TV shows like *Ghost Hunters* and *Paranormal State*.

Investigating with the lights off

Nearly every ghost-themed TV show has several scenes in which the investigators walk around a darkened place, usually at night, looking for ghosts. Purposely conducting an investigation in the dark is the equivalent of tying an anvil to a marathon runner's foot. Think about it for a second: if you are trying to identify an unknown object, is it better to look for it under bright lights, or in a darkened room? There are no other objects or entities on earth that anyone would think are better observed in darkness instead of light; why would ghosts be any different? Humans are visual creatures, and our eyes need light to see—the more light the better. Darkness, by definition, severely limits the amount of information available. Searching at night in the dark puts investigators at an immediate and obvious disadvantage in trying to identify and understand what's going on around them.

While some report seeing ghosts as glowing figures, many people report them as shadows or dark entities. Searching a dark room for a shadowy figure is an exercise in futility. Unless a ghost or entity has been specifically and repeatedly reported or photographed emitting light, there's no valid, logical reason that ghost investigators would work literally (and figuratively) in the dark. If the purpose of the investigation is to get spooky footage, turn the lights off. If the purpose is to scientifically search for evidence of ghosts, leave the lights on.

Sampling errors

Elsewhere I explain why a ghost stakeout or overnight investigation is a bad idea, but there's another, less obvious basic scientific mistake. Usually ghost hunters will begin their stakeout by taking readings from their high-tech equipment. While a thorough investigation into *specific claims* or phenomena (such as why a door opens on its own, or the source of a strange noise) can be conducted in a matter of hours, a complete investigation into a haunted location can't be done in a few hours, or even during an overnight stay. The reason is very simple: a few hours or overnight is not enough time to gather enough information to establish a valid set of baseline (or control) measurements for what "normal" (i.e. presumably ghost-free) conditions are at the location.

To know what is extraordinary for the area, an investigator must first determine what is ordinary. Many ghost hunters understand this general principle, but greatly underestimate the importance of valid sampling. In environmental science, measurement sampling, for example checking for water or air contaminants, is a very complex process: choosing how to sample, where to sample, what to sample, how often, with what tools, etc. is critical to getting useful measurements. This is why for valid experiments, scientists must take dozens—sometimes hundreds—of independent measurements, and analyze the results to derive a statistical average (along with a range of normal variation), which can be used as a basis for research. The timeframes and number of samples that ghost hunters use are far too short to yield any scientifically meaningful baseline numbers.

There's also the logical problem of comparing readings (EMFs, temperatures, etc.) taken at different times. As any scientist or statistician can tell you, two data points are meaningless. All you can tell from two sets of readings is that either the number has changed or it hasn't. How can the investigator know that the baseline readings they got "before" the investigation started were not detecting ghosts? Think of it this way: Just because Measurement A was taken a few hours before Measurement B does not mean that Measurement A is the "normal" one (the control) and Measurement B represents an anomaly. Maybe Measurement A was the anomaly; or maybe Measurement B was the anomaly; or maybe both Measurements A and B were within the ordinary range of variation and if the investigators took Measurement C they would find *that* to be the anomaly. There's no way to tell which of these interpretations is correct without many more samples (data points).

A scientific ghost investigator would have to make at least a dozen separate visits to the location (at different times of the day and under different conditions) to carefully measure and record whatever variables (temperature, humidity, light, vibrations, sounds, electromagnetic fields, etc.) they will be measuring during their stakeout. The more times an investigator samples the location, the more complete and more accurate the information will be.

Of course, following scientifically valid sampling methods is not especially fun. Taking measurements and creating a data set in preparation for an investigation is neither interesting nor spooky; it is boring, tedious, mathematical drudgery. Why bother spending weeks with numbers and textbooks when you can be walking around an abandoned hospital with flashlights, spooking your friends and jumping at shadows?

Ineffectively using recording devices

As we have seen, devices such as EMF detectors and ion counters have no use in ghost investigations. Ordinary cameras and audio recorders, however, can be helpful if used correctly. Unfortunately, many ghost hunters (including the Ghost Hunters) don't know how to use the equipment effectively.

For example, in Episode 401 (airdate March 5, 2008), the TAPS crew investigated Philadelphia's Fort Mifflin. While there, lead investigator Grant Wilson acted startled on camera while looking through a crawlspace (in near-darkness, of course). He claimed he saw a human face staring back at him only a few feet away, but predictably the television crew trailing him didn't capture it on video. This type of incident has happened dozens of times over the six seasons of the Ghost Hunters television show: One or another ghost hunter claims to have seen or heard something just off-camera, and therefore without any proof. Was it real, a hoax, an illusion, or hallucination? Without some recorded evidence, it's just another personal story. The solution is obvious: head-mounted wireless digital cameras. They were finally used occasionally in a few later episodes (though not consistently by all the crew), and it's odd that it took five years for the high-tech T.A.P.S. crew to realize they were a good idea.

Another example is the use of voice recorders. Most ghost hunters, including the T.A.P.S. team, use handheld voice recorders in an attempt to capture a ghost voice or EVP. Often the ghost hunter holds it while standing in the middle of a room and addressing the supposed spirit, or while walking around. Sometimes a voice-like sound or noise will be heard at the time; if so, the ghost hunter(s) will ask more questions, and if not the sound or EVP will be saved for later analysis.

Unfortunately, this protocol is not effective. To identify the nature of the sound (human, ghost, cat, furnace, etc.), an investigator must first determine its source, and that in turn involves locating the sound's origin, which can be very difficult for a ghost hunter to do, especially in a darkened room. If the sound came from an open window, that would suggest one explanation, while if the sound's origin could be located to the middle of an empty room, that might be more mysterious. Locating the source of a sound is nearly impossible using only one recording device.

The way to scientifically determine the source location of a sound is with more than one microphone—at least three, and the more the better. By placing sensitive microphones throughout the location (and certainly in the four corners of a room and outside), the signal strength of the sound can be measured at each microphone.

Sound is created by longitudinal compression waves in the air, moving away from the source of the sound. Soundwaves also have several measurable characteristics, including frequency, amplitude, speed, and wavelength. Along with a basic knowledge of acoustics and math, these characteristics allow the investigator to triangulate within a few feet where the sound came from. Ideally triangulation should be done in real time so that the ghost hunters can immediately investigate.

6. Focusing on the history of a haunted location instead of the specific phenomenon reported at it.

Ghost hunters often spend considerable time and effort researching the history of a house or building, scouring local records and newspapers to determine when the place was built, by whom, who may have lived or died there, stories, legends, lists of past owners, tragedies, and so on. This is a staple of many ghost investigations, in which the first hour or so is spent listening to (real or fictional) stories about the history of the place.

Why it's a mistake: While the history of the location is interesting, it almost always has little or nothing to do with the current haunting claims or phenomena. If a ghostly figure is reported in a stairwell, a spooky face is photographed in a bedroom, or mysterious noise is reported coming from the attic, knowing who built the place in 1928 (or the name of the little girl who died there ten years ago, or whether two or 200 people died there) is irrelevant. It has nothing to do with the face or noises, which must be investigated completely independently. Sometimes ghost hunters will hear or record what they believe is the sound of a voice and assume it must be a ghost, then get so wrapped up in researching the house's history trying to "identify" the ghost that they neglect to fully investigate the source of the sound.

Time spent researching the location's history is usually wasted unless there's some reason to think that a building's structure may be related to some specific unexplained phenomenon. For example, knowing when a house was built might give you an idea of its construction materials and architecture. This knowledge could help identify odd sounds resulting from a bygone era's plumbing and heating systems.

7. Doing a stakeout or "lockdown."

A stakeout is typically an overnight "investigation" into a haunted location, usually with a half dozen or more people wandering around the premises, setting up cameras and other gear, etc. Nearly every ghost-themed "reality" television show features this (especially Ghost Hunters and Ghost Adventures), and it is standard procedure for most ghost-hunting groups. It's also a sure sign of pseudoscience and amateur investigation.

Why it's a mistake: As an investigative procedure in ghost hunting, the stakeout (or "lockdown," as it's sometimes melodramatically called) has a 100% track record of failure; out of the hundreds of stakeouts conducted by ghost hunters, not a single one has yielded any significant evidence for ghosts. (As I noted, they might have better success if they left the lights on.)

A stakeout is essentially a scientific experiment without the science. Scientific experiments are carefully controlled by the investigator or experimenter: he or she controls some conditions, and measures variation in the result (see the discussion on experiments in Chapter 3). Without careful control over the variables and conditions, the experiment is invalid and any results from that experiment are worthless.

This is directly relevant to ghost investigations, because in a stakeout the experimenter by definition cannot control all, or even the most, of the variables and conditions in the experiment he's conducting. Making the problem worse, ghost hunters often have little or no training in proper investigation procedures and usually create as much evidence as they uncover. I have witnessed many cases where ghost hunters waste time investigating "evidence" that they themselves created because of sloppy technique and carelessness. It's very much like a dog chasing its own tail, and it would be funny if it wasn't such a serious problem.

It's important to remember that nearly anything anyone thinks is odd for any reason can be offered as evidence of a ghost. There is an impossibly broad spectrum of phenomena that have been claimed as signs of ghosts, including lights, shadows, noises, silence, heat, cold, moving objects, smells, uneasiness, and so on. If the presence of a ghost could be narrowed down to a specific phenomenon—for example, if everyone agreed (or it had been proven) that ghosts give off red light, or a certain high-pitched sound—then the problem of not having a controlled location would be greatly reduced. An investigator wouldn't need to rule out every possible source of sound, smell, light, etc. but instead rule out merely any sources of red light or a high-pitched sound. But because just about any phenomenon can be attributed to ghosts, there is no way to rule out or control for the conditions. A ghost stakeout or lockdown is unscientific, and a waste of time.

There is one limited exception when a stakeout is warranted: if there is some claim or *specific reason* to believe that the ghostly phenomena will appear at a certain time, or under certain conditions. This can help establish or refute a cause-and-effect link. For example, if a mysterious sound or light is claimed to happen at a specific time (say, around midnight), or under certain conditions (such as a full moon or the anniversary of a death), then it is reasonable to be present and ready to investigate should the phenomenon present itself. However, simply sitting around waiting for some unspecified event to happen is non-scientific and almost guaranteed to create false positive evidence.

8. Doing a post-mortem evaluation of evidence gathered during a stakeout or lockdown.

Ghost hunters often do an overnight investigation, recording dozens or hundreds of hours of audio and videotape to be painstakingly reviewed at a later time in a search for any anomalies that were not noticed at the time of recording. This pseudoscientific procedure is standard practice for the T.A.P.S./*Ghost Hunters* crew.

Why it's a mistake: As noted above, the stakeout is inherently un-scientific, and therefore any evidence gathered during that investigation will be of little value. If the procedure for collecting data is flawed, then any results from that procedure will be flawed: garbage in, garbage out. Beyond that, it's a mistake for other reasons. Except in rare cases, review-ing evidence after an investigation concludes is of very limited value. Even if something strange or unusual is recorded, the chance to meaningfully investigate the phenomenon (say, a noise, light, or moving object) has passed. Good investigators must fully investigate any unexplained phe-nomenon *at the time it is occurring*; noticing something strange on an audio or videotape days or weeks later is pointless.

In statistical analysis, this process—which is discouraged because it often creates Type II errors, or evidence where none exist—is called *retrospective substratification*, also known as data mining. It happens when an experimenter collects a lot of data, but doesn't find the effect they expected, or were looking for. Let's say, for example, a ghost hunter sets a camera to record a so-called "trigger item," an object that the spirit is asked to move or manipulate (such as a teddy bear). The item is videotaped from dusk until dawn, and later during the "evi-dence review" the ghost hunter watches hours and hours of footage of a completely stationary teddy bear doing absolutely nothing. The test's hypothesis that the ghost would make the teddy bear move (maybe float in the air, spin around, or puke green slime) has been falsified: it did not happen. But if at any point during the many hours there seems to be a faint light or sound or movement, the experimenter may decide that it might be the ghost. (Or, of course, it might have been a flying insect, an unnoticed headlight or flashlight, a video glitch, or any number of other things.) The point is that the ghost hunter did not accept that the original intended effect was not found, and kept looking and lowering the bar of evidence until some apparently minor, likely mundane, event was considered evidence. Everyone would agree that a teddy bear suddenly floating in the air might be considered strong evidence of the paranormal, but no scientific investigator would agree that a faint sound is good evidence.

There is some value in reviewing videotapes for a specific purpose (for example to determine who was in a location or to help rule out hoaxes and mistakes). At one investigation I did for the TV show *MysteryQuest*, one of the ghost hunters used a FLIR camera to detect a foot-long vertical warm spot on a pillar. No one in the room could explain what caused it; one ghost hunter suggested it was a sign that a ghost had been watching them. In fact I had seen one of the ghost hunters leaning against the pillar a few minutes earlier, and the warm spot matched exactly the height and shape of the man's upper arm. All the ghost hunters swore that none of them had leaned against the pole, and when I suggested they review the tape, they saw I was correct. If they had not been recording that area (or if I hadn't seen the investigator create the warm spot), it likely would have remained mysterious.

9. Lack of any systematic scientific testing of hypotheses.

Despite a lack of hard evidence about the nature of ghosts, there are many popular claims and theories about them; almost none have been tested.

Why it's a mistake: Many theories about ghosts make testable claims and predictions, yet few good scientific tests have been conducted. For example, if an investigator believes that ghosts inhabit a building, and also that ghosts give off electromagnetic fields, then logically a "haunted" building should have higher levels of electromagnetic fields than a comparable control building that the investigator believes is not haunted. If an investigator believes that a device such as "Frank's Box" (a so-called "telephone to the dead") can actually communicate with the dead, there are ways to test that theory. And so on.

To address one common claim, batteries are said to become mysteriously drained by ghosts in haunted locations (Kachuba 2007). Some think it's because ghosts are primarily energy, and feed off the batteries to manifest themselves. There's plenty of speculation—but little experimentation. Yet this is an easily testable, verifiable claim: Either batteries in a supposedly haunted location lose their charge more quickly than identical batteries in a control location, or they do not. I personally conducted just such a test at "The Haunted" Wolfe Manor (aka Andleberry Estates) in Clovis, California, in 2009. I purchased four sets of identical batteries (two each of "C" and "D" cells), and placed half of them in Wolfe Manor, and the other half off-site. Twenty-four hours later I used a battery meter to check the cells' charges; my experiment showed no electricity drainage at all in the "haunted" location batteries or anywhere else. This was a simple, basic scientific experiment that just about anyone could do, yet as far as I know this was the first time that any ghost hunter had tested this claim.

Why is there so little actual scientific experimentation of ghost claims? I think there are several reasons. First, conducting scientifically valid experiments is not easy; it requires knowledge of basic experimental design (such as controls, control groups, single- and double-blind testing protocols, etc.). These ideas are not difficult to grasp, but they do require a greater understanding of science and its methods than the average person possesses. Most people have never done a scientific experiment in their lives, outside of a few in high school biology class.

Second, controlled experiments are not nearly as much fun as wandering around a haunted house at night with friends looking for ghosts. It's largely boring work that involves careful and repeated measurements; it is not "fun," but it is the best way to try to validate the existence of ghosts.

Not doing the necessary research is also a big mistake because it is exactly this type of experimentation that could prove that ghosts exist. All other types of evidence—all the anecdotes, stories, legends, orb photos, EVPs, and so on—have been (and likely will remain) inconclusive and ambiguous at best. But if a ghost investigator conducted a series of well-designed experiments proving that there was some measurable difference between a haunted location and a non-haunted one, that would be valid, scientific evidence to build on and that discovery might change the world.

Some claims are impossible to test, and are therefore unscientific. One of the hallmarks of good scientific methodology is that a claim, proposition, or hypothesis must be falsifiable; that is, there must be some way to determine whether an event occurred or it didn't, a phenomenon exists or it doesn't. If I claim that an invisible, undetectable polar bear is living in my garage, that may be true but is not a testable, falsifiable claim, because if an investigator searches for evidence and finds none at all, I can just say, "Of course you couldn't find evidence for it, the polar bear is undetectable."

Pseudoscientific ghost hunters are essentially operating on the premise that what they are looking for can choose whether or not to exist (or at least be detected). This renders their investigation unfalsifiable and inherently unscientific, because even if there's not a shred or hint of evidence, the ghost hunter can claim that there are many ghosts present, but they choose not to make themselves known. Ghosts are the only things in the universe that are claimed to be able to exist at will; nothing else that has ever been studied is claimed to have this ability. It's the equivalent of explaining something by saying, "God did it," and it's a logical fallacy called special pleading. It can't be proven or disproven, and reduces ghosts to a mere brain teaser.

In the world of ghost hunting, the fact that the ghost hunters *cannot* explain phenomenon is taken as a sign of their expertise. That is, they will confidently proclaim a location haunted if they could not find an explanation for some (apparently) strange phenomenon or other; they couldn't figure it out, couldn't solve the mystery. Unscientific ghost hunters set up a no-lose situation for themselves: If they are able to debunk or find ordinary explanations for ghostly phenomenon, then that shows what good investigators they are because they cleverly figured it out. On the other hand, if they *can't* figure out an explanation for some phenomenon, then that *also* demonstrates what good investigators they are, because they claim it is evidence of ghosts! And if they don't find any evidence of ghosts, that of course does not prove that ghosts don't exist, it can just be interpreted to mean that there were no ghosts active there at the time the ghost hunters were there; or the ghosts simply chose not to show a sign of their presence. The door is left wide open for later investigations. Follow-up investigations are likely to find some "anomaly," especially given the lax standards of evidence, since all that is needed to create evidence for ghosts is for one person to say, "I don't really understand this," thus virtually guaranteeing that many "haunted locations" will be deemed to have some "unexplained" activity, whether ghosts reside there or not.

Imagine if other investigative professions operated the same way, claiming success when they were *unable* to solve a problem: Police detectives unable to solve crimes would be promoted; doctors unable to correctly diagnose diseases would be congratulated and receive awards; mechanics who couldn't explain and fix automotive problems would be successful. Usually, inability to accomplish a goal (such as explaining a mystery) is seen as an obvious failure; for ghost hunters, it's a sign of success.

References

Avakian, Laura. 2010. Surviving lockdown: Behind the scenes with the Ghost Adventure crew. *Haunted Times* 4(3), p. 19.

Belanger, Jeff. 2005. *Communicating With the Dead.* Franklin Lakes, New Jersey: New Page Books, 37.

Biddle, Kenny. 2007. *Orbs or Dust? A Practical Guide to False-Positive Evidence.* Paranormal Investigators & Research Association.

Geberth, Vernon. 1996. *Practical Homicide Investigation: Tactics, Procedures, and Forensic*

Techniques, 3rd edition. New York, New York: CRC Press.

Gibson, Marley, Patrick Burns, and Dave Schrader. 2009. *The Other Side: A Teen's Guide to Ghost Hunting and the Paranormal.* Boston, Massachusetts: Houghton Mifflin Harcourt.

Gonsalves, Steve. 2007. Unplugged column, *TAPS Paramagazine*, February 2(6), p. 36.

Gonsalves, Steve. 2009. Unplugged column, *TAPS Paramagazine*, September/October 3(11), p. 28.

Hawes, Jason, and Grant Wilson. 2007. *Ghost Hunting: True Stories of Unexplained Phenomena from the Atlantic Paranormal Society.* New York, New York: Pocket Books.

Kachuba John. 2007. *Ghosthunters: On the Trail of Mediums, Dowsers, Spirit Seekers, and Other Investigators of America's Paranormal World.* Franklin Lakes, New Jersey: New Page Books, p. 23.

Mancuso, Christopher, and Brian Cano. 2010. The urban explorer's backpack. *Haunted Times* 4(3), p. 52.

Merrell, Don. 2008. Ghosts and Ion Counters. *Skeptical Inquirer*, November/December 32(6), p. 60.

Moon, Christopher. 2010. Editor's note, *Haunted Times* 4(3), p. 7.

Novella, Steven. 2010. Getting into the Spirit of Things. MonsterTalk podcast, March 2.

Radford, Benjamin. 2006a. Go, Go, Ghost Gadgets. *Skeptical Inquirer*, 30(5), September/October.

Radford, Benjamin. 2006b. The Shady Side of Ghost Hunting. Web published at LiveScience.com, October 27.

Radford, Benjamin. 2006c. Ghost Photos: A Close Look at the Paranormal. Web published at LiveScience.com, October 30.

Radford, Benjamin. 2007. The (Non)Mysterious Orbs. *Skeptical Inquirer*, 31(5), September/October.

PART III: Case Studies in
Paranormal Investigation

In-depth case studies are one of the best ways of learning, as the reader can follow along with the writer and learn from the choices made—both good and bad. I have investigated hundreds of mysterious and paranormal cases in the past twelve years. Many of my investigations have appeared in the book *Lake Monster Mysteries*, several of Joe Nickell's books, in *Skeptical Inquirer* and *Fortean Times* magazines, *Skeptical Briefs* newsletter, and other publications around the world. Invariably, some cases are more successful and definitive than others, and in selecting which cases to highlight, I chose those that I have personally investigated (and therefore can explain the investigation techniques behind) and that illustrate important principles of scientific paranormal investigation.

A few of the cases included here have been previously published, though I have expanded the pieces considerably and rewritten some to make the investigative strategy clearer. Each case study is followed by commentary highlighting issues in the investigation process. While most of the cases I mention focus on field investigations, some mysteries were solved simply through research and detective work.

Throughout the case studies of investigations, I highlight skeptical principles as they apply to each case. We see, for example, the importance of meticulous research and fact-checking in my examination of the White Witch of Rose Hall and sea monsters; how easy it is to fool ourselves—and be fooled by—others in the investigation into psychic powers; and why eyewitnesses are often unreliable. The same principles apply in different ways to different cases.

CHAPTER 5
The Demonic Ghost House

Buffalo, New York

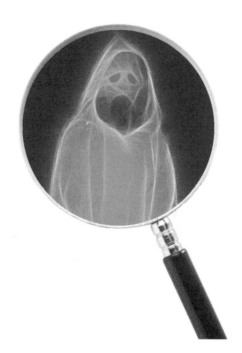

The ancient belief in ghosts and hauntings remains among the most common of paranormal ideas. A 2005 Gallup poll found that 37 percent of Americans believe in haunted houses, and 21 percent believe in communication with the dead. Part of the reason for the enduring interest is pop culture, as seen in films like *The Sixth Sense*, *Ghostbusters*, and *The Amityville Horror*. But our human fear of mortality also plays a significant role; because death is so final, many of us want to believe in an afterlife, and that some day we will be reunited with our deceased loved ones. Ghosts and spirits are actually only a small part of a wider spectrum of similar beliefs, including near-death experiences (NDEs); reincarnation, channeling, spiritual possession, and Spiritualism. Though ghosts are often regarded by the public as scary or harmful entities, those who search for and investigate ghosts often suggest that the spirits are simply trying to communicate messages, connect with loved ones, or find their way to another world—not frighten or harm us.

There are many ideas and theories about ghosts: what they are, what they do, why some people see them and others don't, and so on. For the

Figure 5.1, a home near Buffalo where paranormal events were reported.

scientific investigator, however, theories must be drawn from facts. Without valid evidence to support them, various theories about ghosts are little more than wild guesses and flights of fancy. Separating truth from myth requires actual investigation, not armchair pondering and speculation. Though not well-known outside of Western New York, this case is cited—even among believers—as one of the best-documented and best-researched haunting investigations ever conducted.

On Tuesday, November 11, 2003, our CSI office in Buffalo, New York, received a call from a local woman who believed her house to be haunted and asked us to investigate. Initially there was little interest in the case, but I returned her call. The family had fled the house two weeks earlier and had not been back since. They were staying with her mother, and were desperate for help and answers. I agreed to look into it, and asked her to write down a clear and detailed account of what exactly they experienced and when. I headed down to south Buffalo and Lackawanna. The area is thoroughly blue-collar, and had definitely seen better times. Lackawanna made international news in 2002 when six suspected terrorists from the Muslim community were arrested there, though the area looks much more like a rustbelt town than a terrorist base.

Passing cookie-cutter houses on the right, I made a left turn and found the house, a somewhat rundown but respectable two-story pale blue building (figure 5.1). The houses were close together, separated by little more than a short concrete driveway leading to a tiny back yard. As I gathered my tape recorder, camera, and notebook, a woman in her late twenties poked her head out the door hesitantly. I walked up the steps, where she greeted me and introduced herself as Monica. Her husband Tom, a stocky Hispanic man of about 40, shook my hand and led me through a dimly-lit living room littered with a child's toys. We walked into the small, linoleum-lined kitchen, where I took a seat at a dinette table.

With a pocket tape recorder running, I interviewed them as I scribbled notes. Monica and Tom, with their two-year-old daughter, had lived in the house for about three years. The couple slept in separate bedrooms, both upstairs. Tom suffered from apnea, a sleep disorder, and uses a machine (CPAP) that forces air into his nose while he sleeps. On occasion he felt an unseen force pulling the air tubes from his face. Monica slept in an adjacent room with their daughter. Most of the unnerving events they reported happened at night just as Tom was drifting off to sleep or while he was asleep. Tom was almost always the main person affected, and the first to hear unusual sounds. Sometimes when they were both downstairs, they heard steps on the house's creaky staircase.

The disturbances had begun several months earlier but had recently increased. The wife said, "It got more active when he said to me [on October 27], 'You know, Monica, I hear this, it is pulling my machine [in bed at night],' and I said I hear it too, or I feel it too.' When we admitted it to each other, it got tremendously worse. It started the Monday before Halloween, and then it got really bad." Tom, raised Roman Catholic, called a local priest to perform an exorcism on the house. He did so on October 30 at 8:30 P.M., though Tom felt that the procedure was done just to humor him. The disturbances got worse; later that night they fled the house and were afraid to return. The couple contacted a local psychic who made the problem much worse by "confirming" a ghost in their house.

The house's history is unclear; there are no known reports of any previous problems or strange phenomena there. The pair believe that the house was moved to its present location in connection to the Ford plant nearby. Monica said she was told that the house may have been part of the Underground Railroad (an almost stock statement of old houses in the area), and also that a former resident, a Mr. Hernandez, had died in a rocking chair in the house. Often residents and ghost investigators will try to "explain" hauntings by researching the history of the dwelling or area to find some local death, tragedy, or ghost lore (see, for example, Hauck 2002; Steiger 2001). This is a poor technique, because natural explanation must be ruled out first, and nearly *any* location will have some story of a death some place nearby at some point.

Figure 5.2, a "demonic face" was seen in the bottom left corner of this photo.

Monica and Tom were convinced that some sort of spirit was residing in their house. Monica said, "If somebody had come to me and said that there was a ghost in the house, I would have never believed them until I lived though what I lived through here.... We just want to move back into our home."

As we wrapped up, Tom asked what sort of equipment I was going to use. While glancing in my duffel bag, he apparently didn't see a Negative Ionizer Ghost Containment backpack like the kind Bill Murray wore in *Ghostbusters*. I explained that while some non-scientific ghost investigators use high-tech devices (such as electromagnetic field meters), the problem is that electromagnetic fields are not ghosts, and the devices have never been proven to detect ghosts. I own an EMF meter, but since it's useless for ghost investigations—it finds red herrings instead of spirits—I use it in my lectures and investigation workshops as an example of pseudo-science. My equipment was pretty basic, and proven: two cameras, a tape recorder, notebooks, a tape measure, a flashlight and a few other household items. The most important tools in this or any investigation are a questioning mind and a clear understanding of the scientific process and principles.

Haunting Phenomena

The first step in such investigations is establishing exactly what the witness is experiencing, and under what circumstances. Since it is easy to make a claim—which can be very difficult and costly to investigate—it is essential to find out who experienced what, where, and when. The why and the how are usually the hard parts, but with some luck and detective work, even baffling mysteries can be solved. The family cited about a dozen unexplained phenomena that led them to believe they were being haunted. They reported nearly every classic aspect of a ghost haunting, as well as a few new twists.

1) Tom feels a hard tapping on his feet, near his ankle; he believes it may have been a ghost. This almost always happens at night when he is in bed and going to sleep (or is asleep). "I get a tapping on my feet, not a repetitive tap, a trying-to-wake-you-up tap.... After the tapping, if I don't pay attention to it, then I feel a kick, and I rip my mask off and get up and turn the light on, and come back in the room and see an indentation [on the bed]." Tom interpreted the indentation (round and "as big as a butt") as being from an unseen presence. This happened three or four times. Since then, Tom says, "I won't sleep in this room." Monica claims she felt the tapping once.

2) On several occasions, Tom's bed shook as if from a ghostly kick. At first I thought he meant a violent shaking or levitating (as seen in the film *The Exorcist*, for example), but he said it wasn't quite so dramatic. "If I don't pay attention to it [the tapping], it will kick the bed— it will hit the side of the bed. I feel my whole body move.... Then if I go back to sleep, I start to get a sound sleep, that's when it kicks again."

3) The couple sometimes hears footsteps in the vacant hallway and stairs. The stairs are incredibly creaky and the sound is distinctive. At night, Tom gets up to see if it's his wife, but she is asleep in her room. "After a little while, you'll hear walking up and down the stairs. So I think it's my wife, getting up to go to the bathroom or something, and I don't see any lights on, so I get up to look, and I turn the lights on, and nothing." Monica, who says she doesn't get up much at night, described "constant walking, up and down the stairs all through the night, from midnight until six in the morning."

4) At one point someone suggested to Tom that he take photos of the darkened house's hallways, rooms, and corners. "Somebody told me that if you take pictures in the dark, you should be able to see things," he said while handing me a set of photos. While most of the photographs were very ordinary, Monica and Tom pointed out three or four that seemed to show strange white orbs, strange reflections, and an eerie, de-monic face reflected in a tabletop (figure 5.2). Tom showed the photos to a local radio psychic, who told him that his "house was full of ghosts." I asked to see the whole roll, as well as the negatives, which he provided.

5) They reported hearing faint voices and odd clicking on their cordless phone. (I didn't spend much time on this: odd cordless phone sounds are common. As with the sounds in the night, if we pay a lot of attention to them and give them significance, they will seem strange. But these sorts of events happen every day outside the context of a haunting. As with many paranormal phenomena, our expectations color our perceptions.)

6) The couple sometimes heard faint music, either a piano or heavy metal music around the house. They say they don't leave any radios on, none of their neighbors have pianos, and that heavy metal music is "not likely heard" around the neighborhood because of the elderly neighbors. On October 30, the pair did their own investigating: They put a tape recorder at the top of the stairs to record any ghostly sounds. They waited downstairs and did not hear anything at the time, but upon listening to the tape heard one or more distinct voices (what might be, "Ethan, I'll tell him"), various sounds, and what could be a dog barking. I asked if it could be their dog, but Tom pointed out that theirs is a small breed

(Pomeranian) that sounds different. He also dismissed the suggestion that sounds could be of passersby, saying that people don't walk their dogs in his neighborhood at night. "What I heard on the [audio] tape scared the shit out of me," Tom said, and was the conclusive evidence that convinced Monica's parents that the house was indeed haunted. That night they ran from the house and had not returned overnight since.

7) A family friend, Michelle, said she saw an unexplained, horizontal light on the stairs.

8) Tom claimed that the family pets were afraid to enter his room and sometimes acted strangely. The behaviors were not extreme (such as barking or panic), but the dog or cat would briefly stare at various empty areas of the room as if looking at an unseen presence. The only place where the behavior was marked was Tom's bedroom. "The cat won't come in my bedroom.... He will stay right here [at the doorway], look, and walk right back out."

9) The couple's young daughter is scared to be in the house and told her parents she saw "monsters." Tom says that "my daughter is petrified... you can't get her to do anything but sit in this chair, and she won't move.... And they say children and animals are more vulnerable to seeing spirits..." Monica agreed: "My daughter wouldn't get off the couch...she'd say 'No, Mommy, I'm scared, I see monsters, or I see dogs, or I see frogs.'" Another time, she said, "In the middle of the night she wakes up out of a sound sleep and says 'Mommy, I see monsters.'"

10) The couple complained of strange "cold spots" in the house (in particular the bedrooms), and claimed that the upstairs gave them the chills—literally. "If you go upstairs, it's cold," Monica said. "My room is like the master bedroom of the house, and it's always like there's no heat up there. We always thought heat rises and the upstairs is always warmer than the downstairs." Cold spots, or marked shifts in temperature, are sometimes said to indicate the presence of ghosts (though, like electromagnetic fields, there are perfectly natural reasons for temperature anomalies). When I suggested that poor insulation might be a cause, Tom was skeptical: "No, because this house has—they blew in insulation. And all my upstairs windows are covered in plastic."

Investigating the House

With a daunting list of basic claims established, and far more questions than answers, I began with a tour of their house. My first impression of the house was that, ghost or no, it was a strange and dark place. The structure was not in great shape and had been extensively remodeled; some places had peeling paint, skewed baseboards, and minor cracks in the walls and ceilings. The upstairs in particular had unusual features, such as half-doorways leading to irregularly shaped storage spaces. The stairway was comedically creaky, straight out of a campy haunted house film (I couldn't resist testing the stairs a few times, drawing out the squeak as long as I could). And many of the rooms, especially downstairs, seemed ominously (and mysteriously) dark even with lights on.

We entered Monica's bedroom, and I asked for quiet so I could get a feeling for the house's ambient sounds. There was a mild wind outside, and a few normal snaps and creaks could be heard. As I listened, I heard two eerie, muffled scraping sounds coming from just below us, or just outside the window. Our minds jumped to interpret what it might be. It sounded a little like bloody fingernails on a rusty metal window screen (or something like that). I looked through the window, but it was covered with poorly transparent plastic sheeting: I didn't see any figures moving. I stepped away from the window, and Tom went to look. "There's nobody there," he said soberly; he was clearly spooked. I listened again—it didn't sound human, but it did seem to have a distinct pattern, it wasn't just random. Whatever it was—demonic hellspawn or windblown tree branch—was outside. I rushed out of the room, down the squeaky stairs, through the living room, onto the porch, and into the front yard. Monica and Tom followed behind. I asked them what side of the house we had just been on. Tom pointed to the left side of the house, and I peered back between the houses.

A maroon truck and a black car were parked in the driveway, with a low picket fence just beyond. I didn't see anything move, no tree branches against the roof or siding, nothing that might have made the scraping sound. My pulse quickened as I strained to hear it again. Tom and Monica stayed on the front lawn. As my eyes darted around, suddenly an old woman's head and shoulders popped into view about thirty feet away from behind the car. I then saw a long wooden handle in her hand, and heard the scraping again: she was raking leaves. When our "ghost" noticed me I took a photo (figure 5.3) and gave a polite wave. One mystery solved. It was important to check it out immediately; had we waited, or not gone to investigate, it might have remained a puzzle.

Figure 5.3, investigation reveals the source of spooky sounds.

We went back inside and I told them I'd like to try and experience the haunting, and asked when they would be available to be there after dark. They said I could return later that night. I headed back to my apartment. In the twilight of the unfamiliar neighborhood I missed my turn and went about a block farther than I should have. A few people wandered the sidewalks and streets, including a young man walking a Dalmatian.

The Ghost Investigation

I hadn't planned on spending my Wednesday night investigating a haunted house, and I had laundry to do. With about four hours until I needed to return to the house, I fixed some dinner, watched the nightly news, and washed a load of laundry. I also flipped though a copy of Joe Nickell's book *Missing Pieces*, which contains suggestions for investigating hauntings. I headed back to the house around ten thirty, cold November rain on both my windshield and my stereo. The night was unusually nasty and windy, definitely appropriate for a haunted house investigation. (In fact the windstorms that night knocked out power to many areas of Buffalo and the eastern seaboard.)

Monica and her daughter refused to return, but Tom was there to greet me. In preparation for the haunting noises, I told Tom to do all the things he usually does; turn on or off any lights that are usually on or off, close whatever doors are normally closed, etc. While we waited to hear any noises, I asked him more about his job. He'd been at the same factory job for thirteen years, a forklift driver at a nearby Ford plant. He often works from 3 P.M. until 11 P.M., though that changed around June or July. At that time, he had adopted a new work schedule, 7 A.M. to 3 P.M.. He had occasionally felt tapping on his feet at night but ignored it. "I let it go for so long, and finally I told my wife. I sat in the kitchen, talking to her in the morning. And that's when she said, 'You know, I felt it too, I felt the tapping too.'" I wondered aloud if he had problems shifting work and sleep schedules. He said no, but told me that, "It [the haunting phenomenon] got a lot worse when I got the seven to three shift. ... I thought hallucinations, because of me changing my shift."

I pondered this for a while. The ghostly phenomenon seemed to be linked to Tom's psychological state, especially his sleeping patterns. I remembered that Monica had also said that the ghostly activity "got tremendously worse" when they discussed the situation, compared notes on strange events, and reinforced each other's conviction that their home was possessed. The key seemed to be Tom and Monica's belief in the ghost or spirit, not necessarily independent ghostly activities—though I knew that might be disproven shortly.

Tom seemed to sense what I was thinking. "If I knew it was only me seeing these things, feeling these things, I'd say 'oh, it's my problem.' But Monica, she experiences some of this too." From my training in psychology, I could think of several reasons why this might happen (including a married couple unconsciously influencing each other's perceptions and interpretations), but I didn't want Tom to think I was being dismissive, so I just scribbled my observations in a notebook.

Tom, slumped into his sofa, looked over at me between draws on his cigarette. "Can they [ghosts] follow you?" he asked. I told him that if there was something in the house, I didn't think that it would pursue them anywhere else. If worse comes to worst, I said, his family could just move out. I asked Tom what he thought was going on. "I think there's something going on, a spirit or something—a pissed-off spirit."

I suggested we head upstairs to sit quietly and let the sounds come if they're going to come. "Oh, they will. They usually do," he said. I had a tape recorder ready. Our attention and anticipation magnified everything, and our nerves danced on edge with every faint creak. The minutes and hours crept by. We watched and waited, but nothing happened: no ghostly voices from upstairs, no ghostly footsteps on the creaking stairs, nothing at all. Tom seemed puzzled by the silence but offered no explanation. Finally, at just past one, Tom and I left.

Deciphering Ghostly Voices

I worked on the case over the next few days. Because of the importance they placed on the audiotape as evidence of spirits (it was what ultimately drove the family from their house, "scared the shit" out of Tom, and convinced Monica's parents of the haunting), I spent considerable time analyzing the tape. The tape was essentially what is known in ghost circles as EVP, or electronic voice phenomenon: the voices and sounds of the undead or spirit world supposedly captured on audiotape. Despite years of research and many theories, EVP have never been shown to be proof of anything other than the mind's ability to decipher meaningless, random messages in static (Gaeddert 2005, Levy 2002).

I suspected that the tape recording of the faint music, dog barking, and conversation probably came from somewhere outside the house, not upstairs as Tom and Monica assumed. The couple said that none of their neighbors owned or played pianos, but I pointed out to them that the music was probably recorded. I wasn't sure if a tape recorder could record street sounds (from inside the house on the second story), but it seemed a more likely explanation than ghost voices. If it was a ghost or spirit communicating from beyond the grave, why would it create ordinary background sounds one might hear in a neighborhood? I wasn't expecting a cliché like "Boo!" or the theme to Ghostbusters, but something a little more, well, ghostly.

Tom Flynn, an audio expert with the Center for Inquiry, analyzed the recordings. He concluded that "there's nothing of obviously paranormal origin" (such as recognized voices of the dead). The 30-minute audiotape contained mostly silence but some noises; much of it was hard to distinguish over the sounds of the tape recorder itself. Flynn used equalization to make some of the noises clearer, but could not entirely eliminate the sound of the tape recorder's own transport mechanism because that noise was apparent at every frequency range. Among the sounds were five coughs, four bumps, a dozen or so dog barks, what sounds like some faint music and a conversation, and a train whistle. Most of these were clearly ambient noises from both inside and outside the house. Though I listened carefully, I did not hear the phrase "Ethan, I'll tell him."

I later tried to speak to the woman who lived in the house next door, partly to ask if she had any friends or relatives named Ethan. If she did (if for example, Ethan was a nephew), it would solve the mystery. Unfortunately the woman was not home, or unwilling to speak to me. Even without her information, it seemed likely that the conversation was that of passersby. The couple were disturbed by the fact that they didn't hear the sounds at the time, though that is not surprising given the fact that they were downstairs, through a short hallway, and essentially on the other side of the house.

I struggled with what to tell the couple. I had not seen evidence of any paranormal activity so far, but I knew they were genuinely scared. I suspected that psychological and social processes could explain some of the phenomena, but that didn't necessarily mean that their house wasn't haunted. There was still much to explain and test, including the ghostly voices and the bed kicking. I had an idea for experiments, but they would have to be done on a calm day, devoid of the howling winds that had recently battered Buffalo.

More Experiments and Investigation

I returned to the house on Saturday, arriving early in the afternoon. Earlier that day I had called the couple and asked that one of the witnesses, Michelle, be available, along with at least one of the family pets. I arrived in the area half an hour early and drove around the neighborhood to get a better idea of its layout and community. It was mostly residential, with scattered stores and few parks. A church sat about a block away, offering Sunday morning services in English at 7:30 and Spanish at 9:30. I drove northeast a few blocks and began to see store signs in Arabic script, often with patriotic September 11 memorial signs nearby.

When I arrived at the house, I had an audience. In addition to the family, Monica's mother was there, as were two of her friends. As I went to get my notebook, I noticed something strange about the walls. Even at midday and with drapes open, the rooms were gloomy and dark. After a few seconds I realized why the downstairs interior often seemed spooky: the walls were painted light brown, and absorbed much of the ambient light. I asked Monica why, and she explained that the walls had originally been white, but they showed dirt and imperfections so Tom had re-painted with cans of tan-colored paint he had found in the basement. Until I pointed it out, they hadn't realized just how dark it made the room, even when it was brightly lit.

I met and interviewed Monica's friend Michelle promptly, as she was quite pregnant and queasy and couldn't promise that she wouldn't throw up on me. She said she had seen a small, horizontal light on the fifth step of the stairs. They had all been in the living room together, had heard something on the stairs, and she got up to look. When she saw the light, she screamed and woke up Tom; no one else saw the light, and she couldn't give much detail. I let her go before the heaves set in.

While the family sat around the living room, sometimes watching me curiously, I measured the stairs and unpacked my camera gear. As I finished, Tom's daughter wandered into the room. I said hello, and she smiled shyly. Despite reports by Tom and Monica, she didn't seem terrified at all, and behaved like a normal, happy two-year-old. I didn't doubt that the child was scared when her parents were in a panic about the haunting, but from my observations her fears reflected those of her parents, not necessarily her own experiential terrors. The child had been displaced, moved out of her home, and was clearly aware that her parents were terrified of the house. There had been considerable screaming, yelling, and crying in the family in the previous two weeks, and the child was keenly aware of it.

Both parents told me that one of their concerns was her mention of monsters. I asked the girl about the monsters, careful to avoid leading questions. I asked if there were monsters around now (during the day-time), and she shook her head no. "Are there monsters in the house at night?" I asked. Instead of crying or looking scared, she just she shook her head and said no. Her parents and grandparents seemed reassured that the girl was not seeing spirits or monsters after all.

I suspected that Tom and Monica had assumed that if their daughter was scared at night, or nervous, it was due to an unseen spirit. They might have asked her leading questions like, "You saw a monster, didn't you?" to which the girl probably nodded (a similar process occurs in the creation of false memories about alien abductions and ritual abuse; see Campbell 1998, Ofshe and Watters 1994). I later explained that the fact that she mentioned "monsters" is almost meaningless (consulting my notes, I pointed out that she also mentioned dogs and frogs, neither of which was presumably haunting their home). I explained that a child of her age could mean many things by "monsters," and that she might be saying the word from something as innocent and the children's book *Where the Wild Things Are*, or the films *Toy Story* or even *Monsters, Inc.* They understood and agreed to avoid bringing up monsters or ghosts.

It was now time for an experiment. I asked everyone to leave the house except for Monica, who sat in the living room. I instructed Tom to put his small tape recorder in exactly the same position he did the evening of October 30 (see figure 5.4). I turned it on and we walked down the stairs and out into the driveway below the windows that faced the staircase.

We talked about the weather, and he commented that the conditions were exactly as they had been the night he recorded the audiotape: no wind, very calm. We spoke for about five minutes, then went back up to get the tape. I wanted to see if voices could be recorded from across the staircase, through the plastic-coated windows, and out toward the sidewalk.

I rewound the tape and played it in front of Tom and Monica. I didn't know what it would show—there were a few suspenseful moments as the leader tape spooled—but my hypotheses turned out to be correct. Our conversation was muffled but clearly audible. Tom and Monica were surprised at how much the tape recorder picked up. The sounds and voices they recorded upstairs were almost certainly from beyond the house instead of beyond the grave. The couple agreed that the outside was a likely explanation for that ghostly phenomenon, but Tom reminded me that I hadn't explained the tapping he felt on his foot at night. "And she felt it too. I want to see if you can explain that." I nodded as I scribbled notes. "I'm working on it," I said. "One thing at a time."

For my next experiment I scooped

Figure 5.4, testing a tape recorder that captured "spirit voices."

up Scrappy, the family's pliant orange calico cat, and carried him with me upstairs to Tom's haunted room. Tom (perhaps influenced by the many books on ghosts and hauntings that Monica had recently read) had said that the animals would refuse to go in the room, or act strangely if they did. With a camcorder recording the event, I placed Scrappy in the middle of the room to see if he would hiss, scamper out, or react in any unusual way. Instead, he sat there looking at me with that distinctly feline air of superiority, and soon wandered over to be petted. If he sensed any supernatural spirits, Scrappy didn't show it as he purred and enjoyed a scratch behind the ears (figure 5.5). It's possible that the cat acted strangely at some point, but there may be many reasons why, and at any rate another person might not have interpreted the cat's actions as odd at all. Another mystery evaporated.

As I packed up, I told Tom and Monica that I would be willing to come back that night for one more ghost stakeout. Since I had been told that the steps and squeaking happen constantly throughout the night, it seemed that surely a second night in the haunted house should provide some evidence. Both said they'd like that, so about seven hours later I returned to the house. I arrived just before eleven, and Tom met me at

Figure 5.5, the author interviews Scrappy the ghost-detecting cat.

the door and led me into the living room where their daughter was asleep on a sofa and Monica sat near her. I could see that the family was gradually growing more comfortable in their home. My presence reassured them, there had been no new phenomena, and with each minor mystery I explained they grew in confidence that not everything they had taken as a sign of haunting necessarily was one. I was knowledgeable and credible, taking them seriously and treating them respectfully. Tom had slept there the night before without incident, and this was the first time Monica had been in the house at night in the last two weeks. Both felt comfortable enough downstairs (on the sofa and floor) while I was there, but neither would sleep upstairs. Tom showed me a new light fixture he installed at the base of the stairs, shining a bright light not only up the stairs but also into the hallway. I told him I thought that was a very good idea, as was repainting the walls and contacting a carpenter stop the stairway's noisy squeaks.

I sat on the couch, my camera and tape recorder at the ready. We all listened intently to the normal house sounds: the clock in the kitchen, the songbird clock chime, the fish tank bubbles and chirps. We sat in silence for an hour, until just past midnight. The only ghostly haze I saw was caused by the pair's chain smoking. We made quiet small talk and discussed if the creaking stairway and footsteps could just be the house settling, normal noises, or imagination. I explained that I hadn't seen evidence of anything else. I didn't doubt that Tom and Monica heard what they claimed (actual footsteps and not just creaks), but for the second night I went to the house in the hours before and after midnight (when it "constantly" occurs), and nothing happened while I was there. They admitted that I had explained—or not found evidence of—most of the ghostly phenomena, with two major exceptions: the demonic ghost face photograph and the ghost kicking his bed.

"Did you look at the photos?" Tom asked. "What do you think?"

"Well, the photographs you took in the house don't show anything unusual or paranormal, at least not to me. There were a few anomalies, such as a few white specks and dots, but nothing I haven't seen before." I explained that they were clearly common artifacts of the photography (such as flash reflections) and processing (such as specks of dirt). It is important to note that the camera was not of good quality, the photographer was amateur, and the developing adequate but unprofessional. Some non-scientific ghost hunters try to claim that the "orbs" are images

Figure 5.6, a mysterious light's origin on a "haunted staircase" is revealed.

of ghosts, but this is due to photographic inexperience (see Nickell 1994). I've seen hundreds of orbs, caused by everything from tiny debris in spider webs to a flash reflecting raindrops to flying insects to dust on a lens. Not one was convincing proof of the spirit world.

I explained that if a person takes enough photographs, eventually he or she will usually find a few that seem to show odd lights or reflections. "Look," I told Tom, "You shot a whole roll all around your house. Out of twenty-four pictures, if you look close enough and long enough, you'll find two or three that maybe have a weird reflection or something you can't identify." I went though his ghost photos, one by one. Some were obviously reflections from a mirror; others were flash reflections (figure 5.6). Tom nodded in agreement; I got the impression that Monica had made much more of the photographs than he had. "But what about the face?"

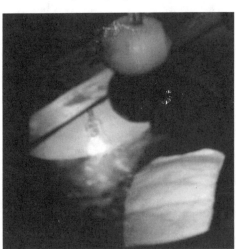

Figure 5.7, the demon's face (between the diaper and the pumpkin) is actually a reflection from a lampshade in a glass tabletop.

I had taken the negatives to be reprinted, and paid special attention to the demonic face. I asked the technicians to print all the way to the edge of the negative (negatives contain information not visible in prints), to get as much of the face as possible. I handed Tom an enlargement of his photo, and he could see that the face was simply the reflection of a table lamp on a glass tabletop (figure 5.7). "The demonic face is what we call a simulacra. It's basically an image that the mind tries to make sense of. People see faces like that and images in everything from stains to dirty windows to clouds. You remember the woman who had the image of Jesus in a tortilla? Sort of like that."

Tom looked a little defensive. "You mean we made it up?"

"No, no," I said. "It's just the way your brains—everybody's brains—work. They look for faces, look for patterns. In fact there's even a part of the brain specialized for recognizing faces. We all do it."

"That could make sense," he admitted. "But I want you to make sense of the tapping I felt.... Everything else you can find an explanation for, but you're not going to find out about the tapping. You're not gonna find out the kick in my bed." Monica pulled a blanket over herself sleepily. I told them that I wasn't done yet, but that as far as I was concerned, they should not be worried about staying in the house. Though the incidents had been alarming and scary, no one had been harmed and they apparently did not feel threatened.

I walked to the top of the stairs and sat at the top landing in the dark, waiting for something unusual or paranormal to happen. After about fifteen minutes, the only thing I was feeling was chilly. Not the spine-shivering, soul-chilling fear one might expect when in the presence of a spectre from beyond the grave, but an actual, annoying chill. I realized that there was indeed a cold spot near the top of the stairs, and I could feel cold air drifting past my waist. I announced I was coming down (so as not to startle them with the squeaky stairway sounds) and asked if they had any incense. Tom got up off the floor and brought me a lit vanilla stick from the kitchen. I took it upstairs and held the incense at the bottom of the doorways. I shined my flashlight on the smoke stream, which bent from vertical to a 45 degree angle as a draft pushed it down the stairs. It was clear that the cold was not a "cold spot" at all but instead simply a cold draft coming from the poorly-insulated bedrooms. I then asked Tom to join me, and showed him my findings. Though Tom and Monica expected the upstairs to be warmer than below because heat rises, it's also the upstairs that will lose the most heat for the same reason. When I examined the attic (where neither of them had looked before), I saw that it was poorly insulated. Especially in a house that looks somewhat haphazardly built or remodeled, it would not be surprising at all to find uneven heating and insulation. I stayed at the top of the stairs, in the dark, while Tom lay quietly on his bed nearby.

At one point, I left my chair at the top of the steps to retrieve a camera tripod. When I returned, Tom said he heard tapping right after I left. "A tap [on the wall] like letting you know, 'Yeah, I'm here.'" I had purposely left my tape recorder on while I was gone, but when we listened to it, we didn't hear anything strange or unusual. Yet even if it had recorded taps, the sound could be anything; other than Morse Code, I'm not sure what would distinguish a "regular" tapping sound from one that seemed to be a message indicating, "Yeah, I'm here." Tom's mind was clearly interpreting ordinary sounds in extraordinary ways.

Tom and I discussed the nighttime tapping and kicking. I told him that the tapping on his feet was most likely his imagination, a medical condition, or both. The fact that it invariably happens when he is going to sleep —or, by Tom's own account, actually asleep—is very significant. This might be considered a hypnagogic hallucination (a sensory illusion that occurs in the transition to sleep), a fairly common phenomenon that can easily lead to misperceptions (see Baker 1988). Monica did report feeling the same thing once, but that can be explained by suggestion and what psychologists term *Folie à deux*, when one person (often a spouse) takes on the symptoms of another. The person hears about a certain, usually minor, sensation—such as an itch, or ache, or tapping—their partner is experiencing and begins to share the symptoms.

Tom's sleep disorder, combined with a dramatic shift in work schedules, probably induced occasional waking dreams or misperceptions. It's not that the creaks and taps are not occurring, just that they are normal and made all the more significant and noticeable at night when trying to sleep. I reassured Tom that I wasn't suggesting he and Monica were making it up; on the contrary, I believed that they probably experienced more or less what they said they did. But they—like many people—might have misinterpreted those experiences.

The ghostly bed kicking was harder to explain, but I found a clue when I remembered that Tom slept alone. I examined the bed he slept in, which was a single-person, metal-framed twin. It was actually fairly lightweight (Tom had carried it into his wife's room by himself). Significantly, the bed only jerked at night when Tom is in the bed and going to sleep or sleeping. Several days into my investigation I had discussed the case with a police officer, who mentioned that often when he is drifting off to sleep, his arm or leg will twitch or jerk. In fact his wife told me that just the previous evening, her husband's leg had twitched as he was going to sleep and had not only shaken the king-size bed but woken her up. It is not unusual for people to do that in bed; I have done it myself. It seems likely that Tom, as he was going to sleep, had simply twitched or jerked, causing the bed he was on to jostle or shake. Tom would probably be unaware of this, and interpret it as a ghostly kick or unexplained bed shake. Tom, at over 250 pounds, was a big man and a leg twitch or spasm could easily shake the lightweight bed. The fact that Tom has sleep apnea further supports this explanation; restless legs (Restless Leg Syndrome; see Lakshminarayanan et al. 2005) is actually one of the most common symptoms of apnea. As for the round spot he saw on the bed, it may simply have been a normal indentation in the blanket.

I waited another hour or so, finally leaving after one in the morning. I had been ready and willing to experience and record the self-squeaking staircase, the footsteps, or any other ghostly goings-on, but once again the ghost activity had failed to show up. Perhaps the spirits were just shy with a scientific investigator around, but without any evidence there was little I could do. With mother and daughter asleep in the house for the first time in weeks, I packed up my gear and headed out. I told Tom I'd meet with them the following week, and that I thought everything would be fine. As I left, Tom said that maybe the spirits had gone (or were never there), that it was over. I agreed, and suggested that if they did hear anything they should just try to ignore it. If something—demonic, angelic, or otherwise—was there at one point, it certainly didn't seem to be around anymore. I followed up a week later, and the family was back home for Thanksgiving.

References

Baker, Robert A. 1996. *Hidden Memories: Voices and Visions from Within*. Prometheus Books.

Campbell, Terence. 1998. *Smoke and Mirrors: The Devastating Effect of False Sexual Abuse Claims*. New York, New York: Plenum.

Gaeddert, John. 2005. Peering Through the Static of White Noise. *Skeptical Briefs*, March, p. 3.

Hauck, Dennis. 2002. *Haunted Places: The National Directory.* New York, New York: Penguin.

B. Lakshminarayanan, S., K.D. Paramasivan, A.S. Walters, M.L. Wagner, S. Patel, and V. Passi. 2005. Clinically significant but unsuspected Restless Legs Syndrome in patients with sleep apnea. *Movement Disorders* 20(4): 501-503.

Levy, Joel. 2002. *The K.I.S.S. Guide to the Unexplained.* New York, New York: DK Books, p. 110.

Nickell, Joe. 1994. *Camera Clues: A Handbook for Photographic Investigation.* University Press of Kentucky.

Ofshe, Richard, and Ethan Watters. 1994. *Making Monsters: False Memories, Psychotherapy, and Sexual Hysteria.* New York, New York: Scribners.

Steiger, Brad. 2001. *Out of the Dark: The Complete Guide to Beings from Beyond.* New York, New York: Kensington.

Commentary and Follow-up

Though I used one method to "remove" the resident ghost, there are many techniques. In his book *Missing Pieces,* Joe Nickell describes how he and a partner used loud music to scare away ghosts from some haunted houses: "On several occasions, as soon as we were informed of the whereabouts of said wraith, we assembled several loudspeakers and stroboscopes and went to work. Our procedure is somewhat analogous to fumigating, except our purgatives are light and sound rather than toxic gases. To ensure maximum results, all of the haunted family members must be present for the first few minutes of the de-haunting procedure."

The haunting activity did not coincide with any family deaths or trauma, but instead with a change in Tom's work (and therefore sleep) schedule. The strange events were infrequent and minor until Tom told his wife about what he had been experiencing. "When we admitted it to each other, it got tremendously worse," Monica said. With my background in psychology, this struck me as very strong evidence for a psychological explanation. It seems a classic case of each person reinforcing the other's expectations and interpretations of strange events. The fact that all this occurred right before Halloween might also be significant; it is the season when ghosts, spooks, witches, and spirits are in the public's mind.

Ironically, this case study helps illustrate how people, not ghosts, can haunt houses. People misunderstand and misperceive things all the time; it doesn't mean that they are stupid or crazy, just that they do not necessarily know what to look for. Much of this case was simply a collection of unrelated and mundane phenomena that, taken together and in the context of a possible haunting, seemed to be evidence for supernatural activity. This case serves as an excellent example of why a skeptical, science-based investigator is needed. The family first turned to a well-known local psychic—who, without doing a shred of actual investigation or even setting foot in the home, lied to the family and reinforced their fears. Monica's research into ghost lore actually helped create their haunted house. After experiencing some of the strange phenomena, she went to libraries and bookstores, collecting ghost hunting books that described classic haunting symptoms (cold spots, orb photos, etc.). Armed with this mental set of expectations, she and her husband then reinterpreted—and misinterpreted—what they were seeing into the context of a haunting. A poorly-insulated area of the house became evidence of a ghostly "cold spot"; three or four photos out of a roll seemed to show "spirit orbs"; a comment about monsters by their two-year-old became evidence that she could sense the unseen spirits.

Monica and Tom tried their best to understand and explain what was happening. When that failed, they tried to record the events—but misinterpreted their findings. Normal ambient noise became mysterious ghostly voices; normal photographic glitches and artifacts became unexplained lights and faces. The mistake they made was not in the tools they used, but in the scientific methods they didn't use, and in this way their investigation was typical of most ghost investigators. Piece by piece the mystery unraveled, turning what at first seemed to be a strong, classic haunting case (complete with ghost photographs, EVP audiotapes, and unexplained phenomena) into a series of smaller, solved mysteries. In this case, the house of ghosts, like a house of cards, fell apart when the evidence failed to support it.

The family was desperate for answers, and they turned to popular books, television shows, and a local psychic—all of which made the problem worse. In a Halloween 2007 interview on ABC's *Nightline*, Grant Wilson of the TV show *Ghost Hunters* said, "I don't care at all what the skeptics think of what we're doing because they don't need help in their homes. Who's helping them? Are the skeptics going to help them? No!"

In fact, skeptical scientific investigators such as myself often help families who are scared by misinformation from "experts" such as the T.A.P.S. crew, Ryan Buell, Hans Holzer, Brad Steiger, and others. Good scientific paranormal investigation, not mystery-mongering, made a difference in this family's life.

CHAPTER 6
The Psychic
and the
Serial Killer

Parsippany, New Jersey

A mie Hoffman, an 18-year-old cheerleader at Parsippany Hills High
School in Parsippany Township, New Jersey, left her part-time job at
a local mall on the evening of November 23, 1982. She had worked a double shift and was heading home for Thanksgiving holiday with her parents.

Unfortunately, she never arrived. Hoffman's worried mother later
went to the mall, where she found Amie's car in the parking lot. The
keys were in the ignition, her purse and sweater in the front seat. There
was no evidence of a struggle; it seemed Amie had simply vanished.

She was found floating face down in four feet of water in a concrete
water tank at the Mendham Borough Reservoir on November 25 by a couple walking their dog. Hoffman had been stabbed several times in the chest
and other areas with a sharp knife. The killing set the community on edge,
partly because it was only the latest in a string of recent, unsolved murders.
A $5,000 reward was offered for any information about Hoffman's killer,
and within a week, the FBI was involved in the investigation. Several eyewitnesses came forward with a description of a man and his vehicle last
seen with Hoffman, though as time passed the case stalled.

Finally one detective working on the periphery of the case, Capt. Jim Moore, contacted a local psychic of his acquaintance named Nancy Weber. Moore soon brought in a second detective, Bill Hughes. Weber told both police officers details about Hoffman's death that apparently even the police did not know at the time, helping convince them of her credibility (more on that later; see Note 1).

After a few initial meetings, the three of them drove together to the crime scene, and Weber gave the police information about Hoffman's killer. Weber (2008) told them, "The man who did this, his first name is James, his last name is Polish, multiple syllables, beginning with a K and ending in an 'ish.' He came up from Florida where he had been imprisoned for murder. He lived in the area... [and] his brother owned or worked at a gas station."

Moore and Hughes took down her information, but were unable to locate the killer. They tried to arrange a meeting with the prosecutor's office to formally introduce Weber into the investigation, but the District Attorney was not interested in listening to a psychic. The community grew restless, and police urged the killer to turn himself in. Amie Hoffman's killer murdered a second woman, Dierdre O'Brien, nearly two weeks later on December 5. Like Hoffman, she had been abducted and repeatedly stabbed. She was rescued by a driver at a truck stop and briefly described her attacker to him, but she bled to death in his arms. On December 10, Morris County police released a sketch of the suspected murderer; three of Hoffman's coworkers had seen the man and his Chevrolet at the mall. This turned up no new leads, and the investigation continued. (Note 2)

The serial killer was not arrested until six weeks later, in the early morning hours of January 17, 1983. He had called the Morristown police from his home to report that he had been attacked by an unknown assailant. It turned out to be a false report, but while at his home, an observant police officer noticed that his car matched the description of the suspect's car, a turquoise Chevrolet, and arrested him on the spot. The tread on his right rear tire matched a track left at the scene of O'Brien's murder, and fibers found in his car matched those from the clothing of one of his victims. The reign of terror that had gripped Morris County

Missing cheerleader found dead

By LORRAINE ORLANDI
Staff Writer

RANDOLPH TWP. — An 18-year-old Parsippany Hills High School cheerleader, missing since Tuesday, was found dead yesterday, floating face down in a concrete water tank at the Mendham Borough Reservoir.

Amie Hoffman, who was to have cheered at yesterday's homecoming game against Mount Olive, was stabbed several times in the chest and other parts of the body with a sharp instrument. She died some time Tuesday night, Randolph Township police said.

Her body was found at 12:15 p.m., in one of three, 3-foot-deep water holding tanks at the reservoir, by nearby residents walking their dog. Police would not identify the couple. The site is about 10 to 15 miles from the Morris County Mall in Cedar Knolls, Hanover Township, where her car was found parked in the lot with the keys in the ignition and her pocketbook inside. She was a part-time saleswoman at the Surprise Store in the mall.

Detective Capt. Paul McKenna, head of Morris County's Major

McKenna said there does not appear to be a link between Hoffman's murder and the shooting death of Christopher Thomas at the Rockaway Townsquare mall, Rockaway Township, last month.

About 15 Randolph and Hanover Township police officers, officials from the county sheriff's office and the county prosecutor's office yesterday went to the reservoir, in a densely wooded sparsely populated area along Combs Hollow Road near the Mendham Township border.

Florence Hoffman, mother of the

Amie Hoffman

Morris County Sheriff's Department Sgt. Robert Reder, left, and officer Jeff Endean search for clues with police dogs near the Mendham Reservoir. Amie Hoffman's body was found nearby.

Staff Photo By JOHN BELL

Retailers merry about shopping

since Thanksgiving finally eased. Police identified the suspect as James Koedatich, a 34-year old man who lived nearby in Morristown. He had served ten years in a Dade County, Florida, prison for robbery and second-degree murder, and was released August 18, 1982. He was of Polish heritage, and his brother worked at a gas station.

Nancy Weber's psychic information about Hoffman's killer (apparently) turned out to have been true in nearly every detail. Even Moore and Hughes, interviewed years later, were impressed by the amazingly specific and accurate details. Nancy Weber and others have touted this case many times, including in her self-published book *Psychic Detective*, on her Web site, and most famously on a 2006 episode of the Biography Channel's TV show *Psychic Investigators*. Weber also appeared on the Court TV "reality" show *Psychic Detectives*.

The Skeptiko Psychic Detective Challenge

I first heard about the case in mid-2008, when I was a guest on a podcast called Skeptiko (the tagline is "Science at the tipping point"). During an interview about testing psychics, host Alex Tsakiris made several comments about the various missing persons and criminal cases that psychics had solved over the years. Having investigated psychic detectives for about a decade, I gently corrected Tsakiris, saying that while there were many claims made, I didn't know of a single case that had actually been solved by a psychic. He assured me there were many solid cases, but didn't elaborate.

On his show Tsakiris also repeatedly accused skeptical investigators of purposely choosing the weakest cases. According to Tsakiris, skeptics steer away from the "best cases," and instead choose the most dubious ones, the equivalent of a professional boxer intentionally choosing unworthy opponents ("tomato cans") to inflate their apparent success rate. Tsakiris (2008 a) asked me, "Why don't you ever investigate very good cases?"

That wasn't true of me or any other skeptics I knew—as an investigator, I don't want to waste my time on poor evidence. Time and again, a skeptical investigator will spend days, weeks, or months carefully investigating and solving a case, only to have the proponents shift the emphasis: "Okay, maybe *that* one turned out to be a hoax or misunderstanding, but what about this case over *here?*" Then the investigator is expected to do more unpaid, hard work on that case. If and when that case is solved, the process then repeats. For this reason, many skeptics will often tackle only cases which are well supported by strong evidence.

James Koedatich

Nancy Weber
Psychic

So I challenged Alex Tsakiris to find his best case for psychic detectives: "You find the best case you can. Look through all the psychics you want, pick the one case you think is airtight." He could choose any case from any time, anywhere in the world, that presented the gold standard for evidence of psychic detectives. He would then present it to me, and I agreed to investigate it. This challenge turned into one of the most in-depth and thorough examinations ever conducted of a psychic detective's claims.

A few weeks later, Tsakiris contacted me with the Amie Hoffman murder case. I had never heard of it, nor Nancy Weber. Here, finally, I was being offered the rock-solid proof—one of, if not the best, cases in the world, according to Tsakiris. All other cases, in his opinion at least, were no better than this one. If I could solve this mystery, not only could Tsakiris no longer claim that skeptics avoid the best cases, but if this "best case" was found to be flawed, then by definition all other cases have even less evidence for them.

Tsakiris referred to Weber's information in this case as "amazing" and "off-the-charts extraordinary." People who posted on Skeptiko's Web site were also impressed. "Appears to be a slam dunk," wrote a man named Rod McKenzie; another wrote, "That was a lot of very specific information she gave." A New Zealand blogger named John Baylis (2007) who had seen the TV show on the case wrote, "Brilliant psychic detective converts hardcore skeptiscs [sic]. We watched on a recent TV documentary how brilliant psychic Nancy Weber solved a crime for the New Jersey State Police.... Nancy Weber, during the course of her psychic investigation came up with clues the police did NOT have at any time. Remember homing in on critical events means that the gifted psychic medium can tune in to the frequency and vibrations of afterlife physics. It cannot be explained in any other way... All of her clues were 100% correct!"

Interestingly, everyone involved—including Weber—admitted that her information did not solve the case. According to New Jersey reporter Abbot Koloff (2006), "Law enforcement authorities who were in charge of the Koedatich case say Weber had no role in the investigation... They say Koedatich was caught by old fashioned police work, a combination of his own mistakes, and an examination of the evidence. 'She played absolutely no role,' said Lee Trumbull, the Morris County prosecutor at the time.....

Russell Vanderbush, in charge of homicide investigations for the prosecutor's office at the time, said Weber's information 'wasn't credible'."

Still, Weber and her supporters believe that the information she gave regarding Koedatich was so amazingly accurate and specific that psychic ability is the only plausible explanation. Before examining the specifics of this intriguing and complex case, a short background on psychic detective claims and methods is helpful.

Psychic Detective Methods

Psychics (and psychic detectives in particular) impress people by creating the illusion of accuracy and specificity. They make predictions that appear to be amazingly accurate, when instead they are general and vague. For example, psychic detectives will often say that a body will be found "near water." This seems very impressive until you realize that the bodies of most missing persons are found near some sort of water—a pond, a river, a reservoir, a ditch, a lake, an ocean, a swamp, a drainage or water pipe, and so on. (Of course, "near" is a relative term, and could be interpreted to mean any distance from inches to miles.)

The criterion for "success" is very simple: psychic information that specifically leads police to missing person. This is not to be confused with what psychic detectives do, which is not prediction but "postdiction," also known as retrofitting. This is where information may seem accurate only in retrospect, after the fact, after the body has been found or the killer has been captured. In psychology this is called the Barnum Effect, in which individuals will give high accuracy ratings to descriptions of their personality that supposedly were created specifically for them, but are in fact general enough to apply to a wide range of people. The same principle occurs with astrological horoscopes, where vague lists of characteristics or descriptors can seem very specific.

The irony is that even if psychic detectives were correct—even if they had the powers they claim—their information is worthless. It doesn't at all help police or the families of the missing to basically say, "Well, I can't lead you to the body, but when you find it, it might be near some rocks..." or "I can't lead you to the killer, but if you find him, he might be Polish."

The Burden of Proof

In this case, there are several people making claims for Weber's abilities. The basic claim (made by Nancy Weber and echoed by Tsakiris and the *Psychic Investigators* TV show) is that she gave amazingly accurate information about Amie Hoffman's killer to police before his identity was known. Though skeptics often end up disproving claims, it is important to remember that the burden of proof is on the claimant. In law, if a person claims a suspect committed a crime, the claimant must provide evidence of the crime. The burden of proof is not on me as a skeptical investigator to prove that Weber did not provide the "amazingly accurate" psychic information she claims; it is on Weber to prove she did. Tsakiris (despite his alleged expertise in the field) repeatedly failed to grasp or accept this fundamental principle, stating at the conclusion of the case that "the notion that somehow the burden of proof is greater on me than it is on you, I do not accept that at all."

And what evidence was produced to support this extraordinary claim? Virtually none. As I researched the case, I kept expecting Weber or Tsakiris to present me with some hard evidence that supported her claims. The only evidence Weber offered are the two police detectives who worked the Hoffman case.

I interviewed Sgt. Bill Hughes and Captain Jim Moore several times. Both said they took notes at the time, but had long since discarded them. There are no other witnesses or written records of what Weber said about Hoffman's killer. None of Weber's information appears in the police file.

Tsakiris (2008) told me, "These detectives have no reason to lie.... And it just doesn't seem very likely they're mis-remembering these specific facts—cops get this kind of stuff right! Let's face it, you're going to have to get Moore and Hughes to change their recollection of things. I don't see that happening."

The burden of proof in this case lies squarely with Weber (and by extension Tsakiris), and by any reasonable measure they failed to meet that standard from the outset. Two people's quarter-century-old memories are simply not adequate to establish proof of psychic powers. I wasn't there when Weber gave her information to the police, nor was Tsakiris. All we can go by is what Moore and Hughes say that Weber told them back in 1982. This amounts to third-hand information. In legal terms, I was being expected to accept what amounts to hearsay evidence. If this were a legal issue with Weber and Tsakiris presenting their case, they would be laughed out of court.

I considered simply pointing out to Tsakiris and his Skeptiko listeners that I had won by default, since Weber had completely failed to meet the burden of proof. But that would have been unsatisfying, since the issue would have come down to an obstinate argument, with me pointing out to Tsakiris that Weber did not prove her case, and Tsakiris telling me that the police officers' support of Weber claims was all he needed to accept her extraordinary claims. That discussion would have clearly illustrated the very different standards of evidence that skeptics and believers have for proof of the paranormal, but it would not bring us any closer to understanding what really happened in the Amie Hoffman mystery. Despite the weak evidence offered, was Weber's information really as inexplicable as it seemed? Did the police really support her claims? I wanted this "best case" to end up with something conclusive, coming as close as possible to either proving or disproving Weber's psychic claims.

I chose to try and prove Weber's powers; good scientists and investigators try to disprove their own theories, and I decided to try to disprove my suspicion there was far less to this case than met the eye.

Eyewitness Testimony and Memory

Tsakiris's confidence in the reliability of human memory—even the memory of police officers—is belied by the overwhelming weight of decades of research (see, for example, Sabbagh 2009 and Loftus 1996). People like to believe that they accurately experience, remember, and understand what they see and hear. Yet, as any psychologist or police detective can tell you, our experiences are impressionable and fragile, subject to moods, drugs, expectations, assumptions, and beliefs. We often see what we wish or expect to see; this is not a sign of a foolish or dull mind but a profoundly human one.

Both Moore and Hughes were struck by Weber's apparent sincerity. In my discussions with her, she seemed sincere as well. But in my investigations, I have encountered many cases where a believable, sincere person reported a first-hand eyewitness account of something that simply never occurred (see, for example, Radford 2009). In one case ("The White Witch of Rose Hall," Chapter 12) a famous psychic medium who claimed to relay information from a dying victim (as Weber did with Hoffman) unconsciously fabricated those details, since the "victim" turned out to be fictional.

When police officers are called to give sworn testimony in court cases, they always consult written notes taken at the time. This is standard procedure, since officers and detectives may be involved in several investigations at once, and hundreds over the course of a career. A typical homicide investigation may involve interviewing dozens of witnesses and suspects, and because it is impossible to remember important details given by each one, police officers and detectives are required to take written, contemporaneous notes.

While I agree with Tsakiris that police officers have more credibility than, say, a used car salesman or the average person off the street, police officers are only human. They sometimes forget and misremember things; everyone does. That doesn't make them any less professional, it just means that people do not magically develop superhuman powers of memory when they choose a career in law enforcement.

Examining the Psychic Detective Claims

Because this case was complex and multifaceted, Tsakiris and I agreed to limit our investigation specifically to the information Nancy Weber gave regarding Hoffman's killer (and not, for example, any information she gave about Dierdre O'Brien's murder). Tsakiris (2008) noted, "I want to focus on and verify whether Nancy provided the investigators the first name of the perpetrator, when that name was not known to them; whether she provided information regarding the last name, that it had three syllables; was of Polish descent, ended in an 'itch' sound. I want to verify whether she provided information about him being a convicted murderer who had left Florida and returned to New Jersey, that he was originally from New Jersey."

On the *Psychic Investigators* TV show, Weber described her experience when Moore and Hughes accompanied her to the site of Hoffman's murder: "I felt almost as if Amie was waiting for me there on the ground. So I got down on the ground on my knees, I could feel no separation between the memory of what Amie went through and myself at that point." In a later interview, Weber elaborated: "I walked over to an area and I got down on the ground and I thought I would just fall apart, because I could feel her pain. It was very fresh... [Amie's spirit] was sharing with me everything that happened, and I was re-experiencing it for them" (Weber 2009). (Note 3)

"I began to speak words I believed were the last words where she was begging, 'Please don't kill me.' I believe she knew that that's what he was about by then. She had already been raped, she has already been badly cut. I believe that she understood that he was enjoying this and she did not know how to get through to him. She had no idea how to get through to this person who seemed bent on destroying her. Went back in the car and kept reviewing. Now, I'm going over all the film [in her mind], again and again like an editor, attempting to be as detailed as possible. Pop; he's from Polish descent, he grew up in Morristown. He was in Florida, he was in jail there for murder. I'm telling Jimmy and Billy, I get it, 'in the car driving, they let him out, early parole. His name kept coming to me, the man who was with her, James. I don't know if she knew his name. I knew *I* know it. So when I got the last name beginning with a K [and ending with] an 'ich' sound."

Tsakiris writes, "All three [Weber, Moore, and Hughes] agree that Weber provided information on the most important aspects of the incident. All three agree she provided: the first name, James; the last name, begins with a hard K; Polish/Eastern European descent, with an 'itch' sound on the end; [he was] from New Jersey; and was serving time in a Florida jail for murder." Indeed, the TV show from which Tsakiris drew much of his information suggests that Moore and Hughes support all of Weber's claims.

A Closer Look

Both police officers generally endorse Weber's claim that she contributed accurate, seemingly psychic information about Amie Hoffman's killer. To Weber and Tsakiris, that is proof enough: Weber says she gave specific information about the killer that the police didn't know, and two detectives back up her story. Case closed; it's a slam-dunk.

Yet, as in most investigations into supposedly paranormal phenomenon, the devil is in the details. Claims that seem amazing and unexplainable at first glance are often far less impressive upon closer inspection. Because this case rests entirely on the memories of the three participants, in order to judge the validity of the information we need to look closely at what each says.

I consulted transcripts from both the *Psychic Investigators* TV show and the Skeptiko podcasts, and interviewed all the principals at least once. As I reviewed the information from Sgt. Bill Hughes and Cpt. Jim Moore, it became clear that—despite claims made on the TV show and by Alex Tsakiris—their accounts are very different than those of Nancy Weber. I will examine each claim in turn. (Note 4)

1) Weber claims she specified that Hoffman's killer had served prison time in Florida: "He came up from Florida where he had been imprisoned for murder."

Moore agrees with Weber on this account, though Sgt. Hughes disputes this, telling me that Weber merely stated the killer "had served prison time in the *south*... I don't recall her specifically saying that he'd done time in Florida, just that he'd done time in the south." In a later interview Hughes changed his mind and stated that Weber *had* in fact specified Florida. (Note 5)

Of course, "the south" can be interpreted in several different ways. It might mean the part of the United States thought of as "the South" and the original southern colonies, including Louisiana, Mississippi, Alabama, Florida, Georgia, Tennessee, Texas, Arkansas, North Carolina, South Carolina, Virginia, Delaware, and Maryland. Or, the psychic might say, "No, I meant south of *here*"; in that case, south of New Jersey would include about 40 states, or the vast majority of the country. The psychic, of course, benefits from as broad an interpretation as possible. Regarding the claim that Hoffman's killer had spent time in prison, Moore stated, "I didn't think we had enough to narrow it down."

2) Weber claims that she specified of Hoffman's killer that "his last name... begins with a K."

Unfortunately for Nancy Weber, Moore and Hughes do not corroborate her story. Sgt. Hughes said, "I don't specifically recall her coming up with the 'K'." Cpt. Moore remembers Weber telling him that the killer had "a hard 'K' in his name" —not that the killer's name *begins* with a K, but instead that there's a "hard K" *somewhere* in the name.

Three different people provided three different recollections. Which do we believe? Did Weber specify that the killer's last name began with a K, as she claims? Or did she not tell the police that detail, as Hughes remembers it? Or did she tell only Moore that there was a "hard K" somewhere in the name, as Moore recollects?

3) Weber claims that she specified that Hoffman's killer's "last name... ends in an 'ish'" (or "itch" or "ish").

Neither Hughes nor Moore support Weber's claim. According to Sgt. Hughes, "I don't specifically recall her coming up with the 'ich'" [in the name]. Moore agrees: "To be honest with you, I don't remember [Weber saying the killer's last name] ends with 'ich'."

4) Weber claims that she specified that Hoffman's killer was of Polish descent, and that "his last name is Polish."

Both Moore and Hughes dispute Weber's claim that she told them the serial killer was Polish. Instead, Hughes (2009) says, Weber said the killer "was of Eastern European descent." Moore corroborates Hughes's recollection: "Eastern European. That is exactly what she said to me." Interestingly, Hughes's story changed: in Weber's 1995 book he stated that "She... said he was Czech or Polish" (p. 166).

Hughes told me that the information was far too vague to be of use: "Eastern European descent—maybe Slovak, or Russian, or Romanian. Again, you're talking about thousands of names. Where do you begin?...

[she] narrowed it down from 275 million people in the United States to maybe 30 million."

Both police agree that Weber said that the killer was of Eastern European heritage, though the pool of nationalities is far broader than only Poland, including Czechoslovakia, Romania, Ukraine, Croatia, Serbia, Austria, Hungary, Belarus, Latvia, Lithuania, Moldova, and Bulgaria. If it is true that Weber said the killer was Eastern European—and there exists no independent confirmation of this or any other statement—then Weber correctly targeted the killer's (general) heritage. However, New Jersey is one of the most ethnically diverse states in the country, with the third-highest percentage of foreign-born residents. Polish residents make up the largest Eastern European population by far, comprising 7% of New Jersey residents. A given man of Eastern European descent is far more likely to be found in New Jersey than in many other parts of the country.

5) Weber claims that she specified that "the man who did this, his first name is James."

In this case, Moore's memory agrees with Weber. But Weber and Moore are contradicted by Sgt. Hughes, who stated, "She didn't have complete names for us... I do not remember the first name at all." Which is it? Did Weber provide the first name "James" or didn't she? Is it likely that Hughes would have forgotten such a specific, complete name? Or did Weber give that information only to Moore, who inexplicably failed to tell his partner that the man they were looking for was named James?

6) Weber claims that she specified that the killer's brother "owned or worked at a gas station."

Both Hughes and Moore say that Weber was not as specific as she claims. Hughes stated that she instead told them said that the killer himself—not his brother—"was associated with a mechanic; either he was a mechanic himself, or associated with a mechanic." Moore's recollection of Weber's information is even more vague and general: "either he [the killer] or a member of his family had a gas station or worked at a gas station;" or merely had "something to do with a gas station," (Moore 2009) or "Something to do with the gas station work, whether the brother

owned it or he worked at it or something, she couldn't be specific."
Hughes (2009) echoed Moore's frustration with the vagueness of Weber's
information: "a mechanic or related to a mechanic—but where do you
go from there?"

If what the police say is true, the scenario Weber described suddenly
jumps from one specific circumstance to dozens or hundreds. The killer
(or a family member, or someone associated with him) might have
worked at either a gas station or as a mechanic. It could have been later
interpreted as anyone who had recently visited a mechanic, or knew a
mechanic, or lived near a mechanic or visited a gas station.

In stark contrast to Tsakiris's confident statement that "All three agree
that Weber provided information on the most important aspects of the
incident," the two police officers contradict virtually every specific claim
she made. Remarkably, Tsakiris—even after being presented with quotes,
transcripts, and live interviews—refused to admit that the three eyewitnesses' stories were anything but rock solid: "This is silly," he told me.
"None of these things are inconsistent. They do not refute what she was
saying..... This is just meaningless minutia that gets in the way of really
looking at the big picture."

This is a statement that could have only been made by a non-investi-
gator; to reduce the significance of several important, bald contradictions
to "meaningless minutia" betrays a stunning indifference to critical thinking and logic. It is the psychic's word against the police, and since we
have no record of what Weber told them, there is no way to be certain
who is accurate (though of course the police are far more credible than
the psychic).

Catching the Killer

Tsakiris was adamant that the police and the psychic were saying the
same thing—a situation that reminded me of a person in a swimming
pool treading water while insisting he is not wet.

I decided to approach the case from another angle: If Weber is telling
the truth, and the police are misremembering and were in fact given
about a half dozen specific, identifying details about the killer, why

weren't they able to arrest him before he killed again?

Out of all Weber's "amazingly specific" information, Hughes said, "the only specific thing we had to follow up on was that he was upset with a police officer." All the other information provided by Weber—the killer having served prison time somewhere in the south; being a mechanic (or related or associated with a mechanic); being of Eastern European descent; having been arrested for a petty offense, and so on—was far too general and vague to be of any use. Moore agreed that the information Weber provided was not specific enough to be useful. Weber, for her part, blamed the District Attorney's office for not accepting the information that she gave to Moore and Hughes.

A final nail in the coffin for this "best case" comes from an even stronger piece of evidence proving that the information Nancy Weber gave police in 1982 was not as specific as she now claims. Weber claimed that Hoffman's killer lived nearby in the Morris area; that his first name was James; that his last name began with a K and ended with the suffix "ich," and that he had served prison time in Florida for murder. If the police were given even that limited information, as Weber claims, the case should have been solved within days.

I know this because I tracked down the serial killer using Weber's information. With the help of Joyce Leuchten, an assistant living in the

Authorities arrest suspect

MORRISTOWN, N.J. (AP) — A 34-year-old man released this summer from a Florida prison after serving time for a murder conviction was charged Tuesday with killing one of three Morris County women slain in recent weeks.

James Koedatich, a resident of this community, was arraigned before Warren County Superior Court Judge John Kingfield on a murder charge and was ordered held at the Warren County Jail in Belvidere in lieu of $250,000 bail. He did not enter a plea.

He was charged with the Dec. 5 murder of Deirdre O'Brien, of Mendham Township, a waitress and one of three Morris County women killed in a six-week period. Miss O'Brien, 25, was driving to her parents' home when her car

about statements," Lt. Joseph Kobus, a state police spokesman, said at a news conference here that also was attended by Warren County authorities.

Koedatich was described as being 5-feet-11, weighing 180 pounds, with curly brownish-blond hair. Authorities said he had worked as a supervisor in recent weeks at an apartment complex in Wharton. They said he was living with his mother and stepfather.

Vernon Bradford, a spokesman for the Florida Department of Corrections, said Koedatich was sentenced in Dade County to two concurrent 30-year prison terms on convictions of second-degree murder and robbery.

He began serving his sentence on Oct. 27, 1971 and was released last Aug. 18, Bradford said.

JAMES KOEDATICH

area, I obtained a copy of the New Jersey Bell phone book for the Morris area, from July 1982. I went through all the last names that began with K and ended in "ich," and whose first initial was J. It took about twenty minutes, and I found a grand total of four names (from two families) that fit the criterion. On page 252, in the middle of the second column, are listings for Koedatich—the serial killer's brother Joseph, and their father; see figure 6.1.

If Weber's claim that she told the police that the killer's brother worked at (or owned) a gas station is true, then the police could have confirmed the validity of this lead with one question. Weber's information would have led Moore and Hughes directly to Koedatich's door (or at least to his family's door).

So what happened? Either Moore and Hughes are so incompetent that they couldn't look in the local phone book to see if Weber's information matched anyone local, or the information they had at the time was not as accurate and specific as it is now being made out to be. Tsakiris repeatedly made the point that the detectives were smart, intelligent, capable officers, and I have no reason to doubt that.

Furthermore, according to Morris County homicide investigator Russell Vanderbush, Koedatich's name had been circulating among police officers and detectives at the time (Koloff 2006). Though Koedatich was not officially named a suspect in either the Hoffman or the O'Brien murder until

Figure 6.1, the author located the serial killer in a phone book using information that psychic Nancy Weber claimed she told police in 1982, yet the detectives were unable to find him.

after he was arrested, he was indeed known to the police because of his criminal history. If the claims of Weber's accurate information are true, this makes Moore and Hughes's inability to zero in on Koedatich all the more puzzling. Even if all they knew was that he was a local parolee who had done time in a Florida prison for murder, one phone call to the local parole board could have solved the case. One wonders why Nancy Weber herself, if she was so concerned about stopping the serial killer and confident of her psychic information, didn't spend a few minutes looking in the phone book to save a young woman's life.

The principle of Occam's Razor prompts us to ask: Is it more likely that the police detectives had the "amazingly specific" information Weber claims but were not smart enough to use to find the serial killer, or that the information Weber gave at the time was not as accurate or specific as she remembers it, nearly three decades later?

Fuzzy Memories

Alex Tsakiris, like many proponents of paranormal phenomena from Bigfoot to UFOs to ghosts, places a high value on the accuracy of eyewitness testimony and memory—and especially that of police officers. Both Moore and Hughes were very sincere and forthcoming, freely admitting when they could not remember. In our final interview, Hughes (2009c) discussed the difficulty in accurately remembering the specific details upon which the case hinges: "We have discussed this so many times and have done so many shows over and over a period of time. I have heard Jimmy Moore says, well, he remembers this, and Nancy says I remember that, and sometimes it's hard to separate what I specifically remember of the incident when we were there, and what I just remember hearing from all of the interview that we have done."

Hughes's honest admission provides keen psychological insight into the problem. When people remember events, they actually reconstruct it each time. Decades of psychology studies show that human memory is remarkably fallible. Memories change over time—especially if, as in this case, the three have repeated the stories and heard each other tell their versions. If anything, it's remarkable that their accounts are not more similar.

With three different recollections, and without corroborating evidence, it's impossible to know who to believe. Obviously psychic detective Nancy Weber has a strong personal and financial interest in making her information seem as amazing and accurate as possible. Logic suggests that the police officers (despite being friends of Weber) have less to gain and more to lose from biasing their information.

In some cases, we have three different stories, three different memories of what was said. In each case, Weber's memory is that she gave very accurate, specific information. Moore and Hughes agree on some details, but disagree on many others. One can't just cherry pick whichever evidence supports a preconceived answer, nor arbitrarily choose whose memory to believe.

In fact, there are only two pieces of information that all three of them unequivocally remember and agree on: 1) that Hoffman's killer had done time in prison for murder (whether in Florida or in "the south"); and 2) that he lived nearby.

Again, we have no independent confirmation of this, but assuming that Weber did make these claims, they are far less impressive than they first appear. News reports of the day reported the savagery of the attack on Hoffman. The November 26 front page of the local *Daily Record* stated that Hoffman "was stabbed several times in the chest and other parts of the body with a sharp instrument" (Orlandi 1982). The next day, the *Record* reported, "Police said [the stab wounds] were made by a blade eight to nine inches long, perhaps a large hunting knife or bayonet. One of the stab wounds reached almost through her body... There were also cuts on Hoffman's neck as if someone held a knife to her throat, police said. The autopsy also revealed three fingers on Hoffman's right hand had been cut as if warding off knife thrusts" (Harpster 1982).

Does it take psychic powers to guess that a person who slashes and stabs a young woman multiple times with a large knife in such a vicious attack might have killed before? It is of course *possible* that this was the killer's first victim, but correctly guessing that it is not is hardly remarkable. The same goes for the killer's location; most homicides are committed by locals, not by people from other states or countries. Weber's psychic information that the killer was from somewhere in the Morris County, New Jersey area—instead of, say, from San Diego or Istanbul—is unremarkable.

I asked Sgt. Hughes specifically if he believed that the information Weber gave was useful in this case. His answer was both emphatic and negative: "No information she gave led to his arrest... The case was solved by good police work—a police officer being at the right place at the right time, not any information she gave us." Still, he said, he found her information "astounding."

Interestingly, Weber (2009) acknowledged that Hughes did not recall her specifying that the killer's first name was James, that he came from Florida ("Yes, he does not recall it but... If he said he does not recall, it does not mean I did not say it, it means he does not recall it"), that neither Hughes nor Moore remember her specifying that the killer's last name ended with "ich," or that he was Polish. So on at least four of the five main issues, Weber herself admits that one or both of the police officers contradict her story.

Weber and Tsakiris argued that the police officers' failure to recall Weber telling them information does not mean that she did not tell them that information—just that they do not recall it. Tsakiris apparently wants us to believe that Moore and Hughes (his only witnesses, whose memory Tsakiris repeatedly claimed was excellent) both somehow forgot virtually all the specific information Weber told them about Hoffman's killer.

Not only does this explanation beggar belief, it also ignores the fact that Moore and Hughes did not simply say they didn't remember Weber giving them specific information: indeed, they *did* recall Weber giving them information which was far less specific than she claimed. For example, Weber insists she told the police the killer was Polish. Hughes and Moore say that is not true: "Eastern European is exactly what she told me," said Moore. Note that Moore did *not* say, "Weber might have said Polish, I don't remember." Instead, Moore directly contradicted Weber, stating categorically that she did not say Polish, instead "Eastern European." These two statements cannot be reconciled; either Weber is wrong, or both Moore and Hughes are wrong.

Weber's Psychic Insights

Aside from investigating Weber's claims, I was curious to determine what had convinced Moore and Hughes to listen to Weber in the first place. Weber's "amazingly accurate" information about Koedatich could not have impressed them in November and December 1982, since he had not yet been arrested, and there was no way to know if the information she had given them about the killer was dead-on or completely wrong. There must have been some earlier case or incident, some reason why the two officers felt that Weber had credibility.

I asked Sgt. Hughes what had made them confident enough in her powers to approach the District Attorney with her information. "Based on the fact that she knew details about the murder that nobody else could have known," Hughes said, "such as that Hoffman had been sexually assaulted—even the authorities didn't know that at the time.... This gave credibility to everything she was telling us" (Hughes 2009b). This "inexplicable" element was also emphasized in the TV show *Psychic Investigators*: Weber (2005) claimed that newspaper accounts of the crime reported two incorrect facts about Hoffman's death that she psychically knew were not true.

Hoffman's Cause of Death

The first is that Hoffman's body had "no obvious wounds." In her book *Psychic Detective*, Weber (1995) states, "The next day I went out to my driveway to pick up my newspaper, and read, 'Body of Amy [sic] Hoffman found in a water tank in a wooded area of Randolph.' As I read the account it went on to say the body was fully clothed and there was no indication of rape or any marks on the body." Weber (2009) repeated the statement in my interview with her: "I read the local newspaper... where they said her body was found and they could not determine the cause. And I thought, that is a pack of lies." In an interview on the Skeptiko podcast, Weber told Alex Tsakiris (2008b), "I knew the newspapers reported Amie's body was found clothed and they couldn't determine death. That's the truth."

Actually, that's *not* the truth. A search of newspaper archives reveals that the day after Hoffman's body was found, November 26, the press did indeed report that she had obvious wounds that caused her death: *The New York Times* ("Missing" 1982) quoted a Detective Lieut. James McLagan as saying "She was stabbed to death," adding that Hoffman had several wounds; and the front page of the *Daily Record* (a newspaper Weber read and which she reprints in her book; see figure 6.2) stated that Hoffman had "been stabbed several times in the chest and other parts of the body" (Orlandi 1982).

Amie Hoffman, who was to have cheered at yesterday's homecoming game against Mount Olive, was stabbed several times in the chest and other parts of the body with a sharp instrument. She died some time Tuesday night, Randolph Township police said.

Her body was found at 12:13 p.m., in one of three, 5-foot-deep water holding tanks at the reservoir, by nearby residents walking their dog. Police would not identify the couple. The site is about 10 to 12 miles from the Morris County Mall in Cedar Knolls, Hanover Township, where her car was found parked in

Figure 6.2, Information about Amie Hoffman's murder was published in the local newspaper, yet Nancy Weber says she knew it from her psychic powers.

Weber claims to have had psychic details about Amie Hoffman's murder that were unknown and not reported in the press, when in fact those details had been widely reported on the front page of the local newspaper and in the *New York Times*. I had caught "psychic" Nancy Weber claiming to have gotten accurate details of Hoffman's death from her psychic abilities, when in fact she read it in the local newspaper.

Hoffman's Sexual Assault

Weber claims to have known another detail about Hoffman's death that turned out to be accurate: that she had been sexually assaulted (despite the police and press claims otherwise). A check of newspaper reports reveal that in this case Weber is correct: The police did tell the press that Hoffman had not been sexually assaulted, when in fact she had been. It is not uncommon for police to withhold or change some details about an ongoing investigation through the news media; doing so helps weed out false confessions and focus on suspects with intimate, unreported specifics of a crime.

How likely is it that Weber could have come up with this specific, accurate detail in this case? Moore and Hughes were apparently impressed, and

Tsakiris (2008) expressed his amazement at Weber's powers: "Is that information that Nancy brings forward, that Hoffman was sexually assaulted and has been raped, is that remarkable? Yes, that is quite remarkable."

But a closer look at Hoffman's disappearance reveals that Weber's conclusion is quite the opposite of "remarkable," it is in fact distinctly unremarkable, logical, and rather obvious given the circumstances of the case. If a young woman is last seen in the presence of an unknown male and is soon found dead, there are very few likely scenarios.

If he had intended to rob her, he would not have left her car and purse untouched, so robbery is ruled out; if he had intended to kill her, he could have simply done so on the spot that night at the mall, so random homicide is ruled out; if he had intended to kidnap her for money, there would have been a ransom demand (and she would not have been found dead); so that too is ruled out as very unlikely. Obviously her abductor wanted to take her alive, do something with or to her, and then kill her. That leads to one very likely and obvious conclusion: Hoffman was probably sexually assaulted before she was killed. In fact, statistically it would be remarkable if Hoffman had *not* been sexually assaulted under these circumstances.

Weber and her advocates try to play up her guess as a remarkable piece of information, but I suspect most people would come to the same conclusion if you described the scenario under which Hoffman was abducted: "A young cheerleader was abducted from a mall by a male stranger, and later found dead. If you were to guess, how likely do you think it is that she had been raped?"

And what of the claim that even the police didn't know that Hoffman had been sexually assaulted? When Hughes states that "even the authorities didn't know that at the time," he does not mean that the Morris County detectives were shocked to discover that fact; as he said in interviews, he simply means that the results from the forensics lab had not been completed. Logic and experience told the police that Hoffman had *probably* been sexually assaulted, but Hoffman's autopsy took several days, and that fact had not yet been conclusively proven through medical testing. Weber's "remarkable psychic knowledge" that Hoffman had been raped is little more than an obvious and intuitive logical conclusion.

Psychology Solves the Case

Weber's claim is typical of how psychic detectives use a technique called retrofitting to make their predictions appear amazingly accurate. Once the answer, or the specifics of the case are known, the psychic retroactively refines the original predictions. Once Hoffman's killer was arrested, pieces of his biography and past were picked through in a search for any information that matched Weber's predictions. It turns out Koedatich had spent time in a Florida prison, so Weber remembers that she had told the police that fact earlier, when instead she had told them he had done time in "the south."

Koedatich, like many in the Morris County area, turned out to be of Polish descent, so Weber remembers that she told the police exactly that; only they say that her information was much more general, that he was of Eastern European descent. Once Koedatich was arrested, Weber, Moore, and Hughes all were amazed at the pieces that seemed to fit, and Weber especially remembered the information as being far more specific than it had been. There are no liars or hoaxers in this case, just people with fallible human memories.

In example after example we find that the amazingly specific details that made this a "best case" are only claimed by Weber, and only years after the fact. It's like shooting an arrow into a stack of hay, then drawing a bullseye around it and claiming amazing accuracy.

I doubt that Nancy Weber consciously changed her story to make her psychic information seem more accurate than it was. Instead, it is more likely that she and the police were so convinced of her powers that they simply fell prey to a common psychological mistake called confirmation bias. We all do it: we seek out information that confirms our beliefs, and we tend to remember the hits (the things we get right) and ignore the misses (the things we get wrong). The times when we find out that we were right about something are far more easily remembered than the times when we find out we were wrong. (Note 6)

100% Accuracy?

In fact, we have proof in this case that Weber, Hughes, and Moore are remembering the information that Weber claims was correct, and conveniently forgetting Weber's incorrect information. All three claimed in interviews that all the details Weber provided were completely accurate (Tsakiris 2009). Yet in her self-published book *Psychic Detective*, Weber (1995, p. 119) gave the following information: "I see a small brown car with a hatchback. In the car I see a man who is extremely wild-looking... I see a woman with pigtails, sitting there terrified...[she is] running out of the car and losing a shoe..." The description goes on, but apparently Weber's visions were wrong, and had nothing to do with Amie Hoffman or James Koedatich. As Sgt. Hughes admits on page 167 of Weber's book, "Nothing was ever found out about this. No one was ever reported missing." (Note 7)

It seems that Weber, Hughes, and Moore all forgot about the information she gave that was completely wrong. Indeed, they "remembered the hits and forgot the misses" —exactly the memory errors that psychic detectives rely on to make them seem "amazingly accurate." While it is possible that Weber's information was 100% on target, it is far more likely that the detectives simply didn't remember the parts she got wrong. Hughes (2009) describes exactly this process: "She gave very specific details that when we went back and looked, when [Koedatich] was arrested and we looked at him, me and Jimmy were just astounded with what she had given us. I mean, again, a lot of what she gave us was stuff that really could not be tracked."

Specificity

Frustrated that the police officers were not supporting Weber's claims, Tsakiris tried to explain away the discrepancies as minor and inconsequential. He claimed that there was no substantive difference between "Florida" and "the south," or "Polish" and "Eastern European." But accepting answers that are less specific than claimed is exactly the trap that psychic detectives (and indeed psychics in general) wish to play. Once we start accepting answers other than the correct one, the criteria for accuracy shifts heavily in favor of the psychic, so that almost any answer can, with some mental and logical gymnastics, be considered correct. If "the South" is deemed to be just as accurate as "Florida," should we accept "the United States"? Or "North America"? If Tsakiris accepted "Eastern European" as just as valid or specific a response as "Polish," why not accept "European," or even "White"? (This issue also appears in Chapter 10.) For information to be useful it must be falsifiable; there must be some pre-determined criteria for what answer is correct, what level of specificity is required.

The fact that two police officers were impressed by Weber is interesting, but means little. I have interviewed several police officers who were impressed by psychics who clearly failed. Gary Posner discussed a case that aired in 2005 on Court TV's *Psychic Detectives* show, about the role of a psychic named John Monti who claimed to have helped solve a murder case. While at least one police chief seemed to endorse Monti's role in finding a body, other police chiefs disputed that. Posner writes, "The Court TV documentary was so inaccurate, according to [Police Chief Mark] DeJackome, that 'While I was watching it, I was going, 'Are we talking about the same incident?'" (Posner 2005).

The police officers' notes are long gone, Moore having thrown his away around 2002. The Amie Hoffman case file is not available (Note 8), and there are no other records of Nancy Weber's information, as she inexplicably refuses to keep notes about her information. It is of course possible that the written notes Moore and Hughes took at the time and disposed of years ago might prove Weber's case. It could be that the notes, forever buried in a landfill somewhere, completely vindicate Weber, and state in writing that her recollection is correct, and both police officers are wrong.

Conclusion

This investigation began with my specific request for the "best case" for psychic detectives, a phrase which became a sore point for Tsakiris, saying "This is a great case, there is no such thing as the best cases, no such thing as a perfect case." Best case or not, Tsakiris was convinced that I was being unreasonable and obstinate. "There is no holy grail in terms of evidence here that would satisfy you," he told me. "If they had the notes, you would not be satisfied." Of course, if we had the notes, this case would be very different, because we would have an objective, independent record whose content is not error-prone and has not changed in twenty-seven years.

This was a fascinating case on many levels, and took about a year of research and investigation. It was an interesting intellectual challenge to tackle the "best case" for psychic detectives (and one which, at first glance anyway, was corroborated by police officers). Seeing Tsakiris's obstinate refusal to acknowledge the gaping holes in his case was very instructive. Skeptics and believers can look at the exact same evidence and testimony, yet approach the topic from very different points of view. (Note 9)

Tsakiris stated that "sometimes the claims that skeptics make can really test the limits of common sense and reason." In this case—the "best case" for psychic detectives—it seems that common sense and reason are on the side of skeptical investigation.

Acknowledgements

My research into this case was aided by Joyce Leuchten, who provided important library research; and Blake Smith, who offered suggestions and organized audio segments and transcripts.

Notes

1. Weber's credibility was called into question when I read the following statement on the back cover of her book, "In 1972 she studied psychotherapy at the Center For Feelings and Creativity." An Internet search turned up only one reference to a "Center For Feelings and Creativity," a workshop given in 1978. If Weber "studied psychotherapy" there in 1972, it seems odd that the only reference to it doesn't appear until 1978, six years later. If the center is a legitimate school, college, or learning institution, it seems that no one else attended, studied, worked, taught, or graduated from it. I suspect that the Center is either a diploma mill or some friend's made-up "college." If Nancy Weber wants to be considered a credible source who doesn't exaggerate or fabricate her abilities or accomplishments, this does not help.

2. Amie Hoffman was only one of many unsolved homicides in the area at the time; in fact the Morris County Prosecutor's Office was dealing with a half-dozen other unsolved murders (Sperling 1982). If psychic Nancy Weber's information was as amazingly accurate as is now claimed, it seems odd that she was

not asked to help in those other investigations.

3. Weber's description is interesting, and quite typical of people who believe that they are communicating with the dead (or otherworldly entities). Often they report that they feel sympathetic experiences, for example re-living the murdered person's terror, misery and fear. It seems far more likely that they are simply succumbing to the power of suggestion; for another example, see chapter 12.

4. Readers can listen to audio excerpts of the interviews, prepared by Blake Smith and myself. The audio files are available at www.radfordbooks.com/psychicdetectiveinterviews.html

5. Weber repeatedly claimed that Koedatich had been "wrongly released" from a Florida prison, yet newspaper accounts state that he was paroled as normal process; there was no mistake, loophole, or glitch that mistakenly released the killer. In 1971, Koedatich had been sentenced in Dade County, Florida, to two concurrent twenty-year prison terms for robbery and second-degree murder; he was released on parole August 18, 1981. It seems that Weber was wrong about that detail too.

6. This can easily be demonstrated with a short experiment. Try this yourself: List any prizes or awards that you have received over your lifetime. Then make a list of any prizes and awards that you competed for, or were in the running for, but that you did not get. Most of us remember our successes far more easily than our failures.

7. Interestingly, this information was elicited during hypnosis by an anonymous psychotherapist friend of Weber's. According to Weber, the session was taped, and Sgt. Hughes was in attendance. If this is true, it would provide some evidence of what information Weber gave at the time (though of course they are no substitute for police notes). I requested a copy of the tapes, though they were not made available—perhaps, because, as Hughes admitted— they provided evidence of her incorrect information.

8. I tried unsuccessfully to obtain the public record police files on the Hoffman case from the Morris County Prosecutor's Office. I reached a dead end when I read the first line: "The terms 'public record' and 'government record' in New Jersey do not include criminal investigatory records or victim's records." I would not have access to the files, nor could the police provide them to me. Though the records would have been very useful in determining the accuracy of Weber's claims, Moore stated that none of Weber's information was entered into the official police file on Amie Hoffman.

9. Part of what confused Tsakiris and Skeptiko listeners was a loose use of language. They would use terms like "she knew" and "she said" interchangeably,

as in "she knew that the killer was Polish." Yet it is more correct to say "she said that the killer was Polish," since knowing implies certain factual knowledge. Instead, it might simply be a guess. If a guess turns out to be correct, it is still a guess; its accuracy does not imply true foreknowledge of an event. Compare "I said the Buffalo Bills were going to lose the game," to "I knew the Buffalo Bills were going to lose the game." If the Bills do indeed lose, saying you "knew" it would happen doesn't mean you had supernatural precognitive powers; it just means you thought it was very likely. So when a police officer is seen on television saying the Nancy Weber "knew" a fact before it had been officially confirmed, it misleads the audience by suggesting she had factual certainty.

References

"Authorities arrest suspect in one of three slayings." 1983. AP story in the *Daily Intelligencer*, January 19.

Bayliss, John. 2007. Brilliant psychic detective converts hard core skeptics. November 16. Blog post at http://www.victorzammit.com/archives/June2006.html.

Biography Channel. 2006. *Psychic Investigators* television show. Season 1, episode 2, air date March 17.

Granville, Kevin. 1982. "Disappearance stuns cheerleader's friends." *Daily Record*, November 25.

Hambling, David. 2008. Re-making memories. *Fortean Times* 243, December, p.14.

Harpster, Richard. 1982. "Suitor theory pursued." *Daily Record*, November 27, p. 3.

Harpster, Richard. 1982. "Cops sketch Amie suspect." *Daily Record*, December 10.

Hughes, Bill. 2008a. Quoted in Tsakiris 2008a.

Hughes, Bill. 2009b. Interview with Benjamin Radford, February 18.

Hughes, Bill. 2009c. Quoted in Tsakiris 2009.

Koloff, Abbott. 2006. "A killer, a psychic, and conflicted memories." Daily Record, June 3.

Moore, James. 2008a. Quoted in Tsakiris 2008a.

Moore, James. 2008b. Interview with Benjamin Radford, February 17.

Moore, James. 2009. Quoted in Tsakiris 2009.

"Missing Jersey cheerleader is found stabbed to death." 1982. *The New York Times*, November 26.

New Jersey Bell. 1982. Morris Area telephone book, July.

Norman, Michael. 1982. Suitor clue is reported in Jersey slaying. *The New York Times*, November 27.

Orlandi, Lorraine. 1982. "Missing cheerleader found dead." *Daily Record*, November 26, A-1.

Posner, Gary. 2005. Police chief misleads viewers on Psychic Detectives. *Skeptical Inquirer* November/December 29(6).

Radford, Benjamin. 2008. The White Witch of Rose Hall. *Fortean Times*, September, Issue 239.

Radford, Benjamin. 2009. Ghosts, doughnuts, and A Christmas Carol. *Skeptical Inquirer*, May/June 33(3): 45.

Sperling, Ed. 1982. Unsolved crimes plague prosecutor. *Daily Record*, November 28, B-1.

Tsakiris, Alex. 2008a. Skeptiko transcript 58: Psychics and police, November 23.

Tsakiris, Alex. 2008b. Skeptiko transcript 77: Nancy Weber, February 17.

Tsakiris, Alex. 2009. Interview with Benjamin Radford, Nancy Weber, Jimmy Moore, and Bill Hughes. Skeptiko transcript 69: Psychic Detective Smackdown, Ben Radford. March 18, available at www.skeptiko.com/transcript-69-psychic-detective/#more-133\.

Weber, Nancy O. 1995. *Psychic Detective: The True Story of Psychic Detective Nancy Orlen Weber*. Self-published by The Unlimited Mind Publications, Denville NJ.

Weber, Nancy Orlen. 2008. Quoted in Tsakiris 2008b.

Weber, Nancy Orlen. 2009. Quoted in Tsakiris 2009.

Commentary and Follow-up

The Nancy Weber / Amie Hoffman case turned out to be one of my more lengthy and contentious investigations, conducted sporadically over the course of nearly a year. For a while I appeared on Skeptiko's boards, responding at length to questions that Tsakiris and the podcast listeners had, and correcting misunderstandings and logical errors made by posters there. Interestingly, many Skeptiko listeners eventually expressed doubts about the case, and criticized Tsakiris's handling of it. They were not necessarily completely swayed by the skeptical arguments and evidence I had presented, but they were clearly troubled by the many unanswered questions and contradictions.

I posted lists of questions that Tsakiris had ignored and could not or would not answer about the case (see, for example, http://forum.mindenergy.net/skeptiko-podcast/863-questions-alex-cant-wont-answer-about-nancy-weber.html). Eventually Tsakiris requested that I return for a follow-up interview on Skeptiko. Weary of his obstinate refusal to acknowledge the many problems in his case, I asked him if he had anything new to discuss, as I had already made my case several times in several different ways and had nothing more to add. It was clear that he had no new evidence to present, would continue to ignore the questions asked of him, and simply wanted to re-hash our arguments in the hope that he would come off better to his listeners. Having neither cause nor time nor interest, I declined.

Tsakiris then banned me from posting on the Skeptiko boards. Apparently he didn't like the information I was posting, had no response to the questions I'd asked, and decided that the best way to handle the issue was to silence his critics. Tsakiris offered to reinstate my ability to comment on his boards if I agreed to another interview, but by that time I had moved on to other projects and had grown tired of his tirades and insults (he accused me of "intellectual dishonesty," among other things). Another poster on the Skeptiko boards compared me to a Holocaust denier, and, invoking Godwin's Law, I decided I'd taken enough abuse trying to explain this mystery to those who would not listen.

Because the case was exhaustively researched, I had hoped that this could be used as a textbook example of how to investigate psychic detective claims. As it turned out, it was. As the case wound down in May 2009, I was contacted by John Farquhar, a professor at Western Washington University, who said that he had been following the Weber case on the Skeptiko podcasts. He wanted to use my investigation as a case study in a course on skepticism he was teaching in the fall, as an example of how to investigate and analyze unusual claims. "The Nancy Weber case that you recently completed would be an excellent case for this purpose due to its complexity and the availability of rich resources," he said, and asked me to share my research files with him for his university students. I provided copies of all the original files, transcripts, and sources, and the material presented in this chapter was used to teach college students about scientific paranormal investigation.

The exposure of Weber's claims has had little or no impact on her popularity as a psychic. As often happens, psychics simply ignore skeptical challenges to their claims, (correctly) assuming that the skeptics' voices won't be heard by their clientele anyway. As of this writing, Alex Tsakiris continues his podcast and Nancy Weber continues her business as a psychic, charging $225 per hour for her services. Their reputations in this case remain largely unblemished. The true victims are Amie Hoffman's family, with her death served up as entertainment fodder for a television show and as a "success story" advertisement for Nancy Weber.

CHAPTER 7
Riddle of the Crop Circles

Iona, Ontario, Canada

Who—or what—would create patterns in wheat fields? And why?

There are many ideas about what create crop circles, from message-bearing aliens to mysterious vortices to wind patterns, but all the theories lack one important element: good evidence. Though many people believe that crop circles have been reported for centuries, in fact they only date back about thirty years. The mysterious circles first appeared in the British countryside, and their origin remained a mystery until September 1991, when two men, Doug Bower and Dave Chorley, confessed that they had created the patterns for decades as a prank to make people think UFOs had landed. Several crop circle "experts" had pronounced their work as unexplainable, and were soon embarrassed when Bower and Chorley proved they created the circles (Clark 1993). They never claimed to have made all the circles—many were copycat pranks done by others—but their hoax was responsible for launching the crop circle phenomena.

It's generally accepted that many, perhaps most, crop circles are man-made. But, crop circle believers argue, not all of them are: at least some are too difficult or complex for hoaxers to create. In August 2003, some mysterious entity (aliens, hoaxers, or unknown forces) was considerate enough to make a crop circle in southern Ontario, not far from the CSI offices in Buffalo, New York. Joe Nickell and I were asked by Marissa Nelson, a reporter for the *The London* (Ontario) *Free Press*, to investigate the strange formation found in a local farmer's field of "hard red" variety wheat in Iona, near Wallacetown.

Nelson sent us information on the crop circle in advance of our investigation, which Joe and I examined before we left and reviewed on the drive to London. The design had been found on the morning of August 12, ten days earlier. During that time it had become something of a regional tourist point, with groups of curiosity seekers, "croppies" (crop circle enthusiasts), and media stopping by to marvel at their local mystery. The "crop circle" was actually two circles connected by a straight path, creating a rough dumbbell formation.

In fact, it was not the first crop circle that had appeared in Ontario recently. About sixty miles north of Wallacetown, in the small town of Hensall, a mysterious pattern was found in crops about two weeks earlier. According to the August 2, 2003, *Winnipeg Free Press*, "Hundreds of people are flocking to a southern Ontario farm to inspect something they've only seen in movies—crop circles.... Erv Willert says the elaborate geometric designs appeared in his sixteen-hectare wheat field on Wednesday evening, and he doesn't think anybody in the area is responsible" (*Winnipeg* 2003; see figure 7.1). The news story quoted local croppies apparently vouching for the authenticity of the crop circles: "According to those who study crop circles, the ones in Hensall are as legitimate as they come." On this, the crop circle buffs were surely correct: the Ontario crop circles were no less—and no more—credible than any others. No one has ever been able to demonstrate the differences between a "genuine" crop circle and a hoaxed one.

And there had been another formation as well; the Iona crop pattern was in fact the third crop circle in the area. All three crop circles might have the same origin, or perhaps the later ones were copycat hoaxes. It has been proven that many crop circles have been created by hoaxers, and indeed as Joe Nickell and John F. Fischer (1992) note, the escalation in frequency and complexity of the designs is strong evidence for a "copycat effect." Three crop patterns occurring within a few weeks of each other (and within about an hour's drive of each other) by itself doesn't prove that copycat hoaxers are at work, but if one or more can be revealed as a likely hoax, it is strongly suggestive evidence. As we approached the farming regions outside London, Joe and I discussed what we might expect to find once we examined the crop circle.

A year earlier, Joe and I, along with public relations director Kevin Christopher, had conducted field experiments in crop-circle making. Joe, prescient about the public's interest in crop circles with the impending release of the Mel Gibson film *Signs*, arranged for the three of us to create circles in a farmer's field in Steuben county, New York, south of Rochester.

Armed with "stalk stompers" (wooden boards attached to rope; see figure 7.2) modeled after those used by hoaxers Bower and Chorley, the three

Crop circle mania

HENSALL, Ont. — Hundreds of people are flocking to a southern Ontario farm to inspect something they've only seen in the movies — crop circles.

Erv Willert says the elaborate geometric signs appeared in his 16-hectare wheat field on Wednesday evening, and he doesn't think anybody in the area is responsible.

According to those who study crop circles, the ones in Hensall are as legitimate as they come.

Willert has no theories about the origin of the circles.

Figure 7.1, the *Winnipeg Free Press* reported mysterious crop circles in an Ontario farm.

Figure 7.2, Kevin Christopher, Benjamin Radford, and Joe Nickell practice creating crop circles.

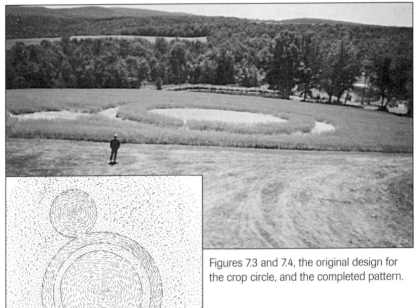

Figures 7.3 and 7.4, the original design for the crop circle, and the completed pattern.

of us had set about learning the crop circle making business.

I brought along a crop circle design for us to attempt to create (see figure 7.3), and armed with little more than a rope, tape measure, and the stalk stompers, we created an impressive design 110 feet long and 80 feet wide (see figure 7.4).

The process took only a few hours from start to finish, including breaks to photograph our results. The process was easier and faster than we expected, and with practice our crop circle making trio could have finished a similar circle in half the time. The main impediment was the heat; it's little wonder that most crop circles appear during the cool of the evening instead of in the company of mad dogs and Englishmen. The first-hand experience of actually going into the field (literally) and making crop circles was invaluable, and gave us insights into the process.

Thus Joe and I knew what we might expect to find if the Iona crop circles were hoaxed. For one thing, we would be able to tell from the stalk patterns which circle was made first. I further predicted that—if it was the work of hoaxers—the circle nearest the road or access point would be made first. That would be much easier for hoaxers to do than beginning with the farthest circle and working back toward the road. Furthermore, creating the nearest circle first would help the hoaxers avoid leaving evidence of their presence in the form of damaged stalks leading to the farthest circle. If the work was done by hoaxers, we also expected to find that the wheat in the line connecting the two would be laying down from the first circle toward the second, and that circle's wheat pattern would itself overlay the wheat pattern coming in from the connecting line. In short, there would be distinct stages of the

The author investigating patterns in an Ontario crop circle.

circle's development that we would be able to identify upon close inspection.

We first met with Marisa Nelson at her newspaper office, then the three of us headed to the farm. When I saw the crop circle I was surprised at how close to the road it was, only about 130 feet. We began by talking to the farmer who discovered the circle, Lawrence Holland, and his wife Grace. He confirmed some of the details we'd read in news reports, and added others. Having brought his stalk stomper, Joe demonstrated the technique for Nelson and the Hollands, who were intrigued and bemused by the whole event.

Joe and I then set about measuring the formation. The larger circle was 70 feet in diameter, the smaller circle 42 feet wide. The path connecting the two circles was 58 feet long and 4.5 feet wide (this measurement is, probably not coincidentally, about the optimal width of a stalk stomper). The center points of the circles were misaligned, with the center of the path about six feet off from the center of the larger circle.

As we examined the circles, we found telltale signs of hoaxing, and soon every element of our prediction was proven correct. The larger circle nearest the road was indeed made first, leading to the connecting line, then leading to the smaller circle, in exactly the pattern we predicted.

From all the evidence, it matched our profile of a hoax, and there was nothing to suggest anything other than a hoax. Still, we were challenged by a few locals who overheard our discussions with the reporter and the Hollands. They were obviously crop circle believers, and had read some of the comments by local crop circle experts about the pattern that made it seem inexplicable. One woman challenged us to explain the fact that the formation faced north. It was true that the formation was aligned north (or south, depending on how you looked at it), and to her this apparently made the crop circle's origin all the more mysterious.

Joe, with patience and good humor developed through years of such challenges, simply pulled a compass from his ever-present, multi-pocketed investigation vest and held it out for all to see. The needle bobbed for a few moments and settled parallel to the crop circle. Actually, he noted, the connecting bar on the pattern was aligned to *magnetic* north, not *true* north. The implication was clear: whatever made the pattern—whether hoaxers or aliens—used a compass.

The woman, clearly unhappy that her mystery was getting a reality check from intrusive American skeptics, then challenged us to explain, if hoaxers were responsible, how the pattern could be made in the dark of night. Actually, Joe noted, it hadn't been: Mr. Holland said that the "formation appeared on a clear night around the full moon" (Nelson 2003). Consulting an almanac, we later confirmed that the night of August 12 was in fact a full moon—perfect conditions for a little nocturnal cereal mischief. The woman, annoyed at having the mystery solved (or perhaps at having been misled by mystery-mongering croppies), wandered off.

A little later as I stood between the crops circle and the road scribbling in a notebook, another bystander approached me, a housewife in her thirties, there with her husband and children. "I heard you all are investigators?" she asked. I nodded, and she continued. "Well, I heard what you said about the orientation due north and all that, but there's no tracks at all, no footprints or traces. What about that?"

The lack of footprints around crop circles has been claimed in many cases as evidence that hoaxers could not have created the patterns. Unlike many bits of misinformation about crop circles, this assertion is often true, including for this circle.

"Look at the ground you're standing on," I said, pointing to her feet with my pen. She looked down, then back up at me quizzically.

"You're not leaving tracks either. There must have been dozens, maybe hundreds, of people walking around here since the news got out about this crop circle two weeks ago. No one is leaving tracks, so why would the hoaxers?" I kicked at the hard-packed dirt with my heel, to little effect. "This ground is hard-baked clay. It's not wet, and it's not dusty. Nothing short of an elephant is going to leave tracks in this stuff. Unless it rained that night, there would be no tracks."

The woman looked at me for a second, then back down at the ground. She kind of smiled and walked away, apparently satisfied. The hoaxers had indeed left strong evidence of their presence—not in obvious footprints or cigarette butts, but in clues and recognizable patterns invisible to those who had not studied the phenomena or experienced in making the circles.

Joe and I soon finished our interviews with the reporter. Mr. Holland thanked us for explaining the mystery, and we headed back to the office via the side roads of Ontario's farming community. We didn't conclusively prove that the Iona crop circle was the work of hoaxers; short of a confession or hard evidence like catching them in the act, obtaining absolute proof in a case like this is impossible. But all the evidence points to only one conclusion: it was a hoax. All the questions were answered, all the mysteries were cleared up. If aliens (or some unknown, mysterious force) created the crop pattern, they did an amazing job of exactly duplicating a hoaxer's procedure.

References

Christopher, Kevin. 2002. CSICOP Field Investigations: 2002 Crop Circle Experiments. *Skeptical Briefs*, September, p. 3-5.

Clark, Jerome. 1993. Crop circles, in *Unexplained! 347 Strange Sights, Incredible Occurrences, and Puzzling Physical Phenomenon*. Detroit, Michigan: Visible Ink Press, p. 88.

Michell, John, and Bob Rickard. 2000. *Unexplained Phenomena, A Rough Guide Special: Mysteries and Curiosities of Science, Folklore, and Superstition*. New York, New York: Penguin Putnam, p. 188.

Nelson, Marissa. 2003. Mystery or myth? *The London Free Press*, August 23.

Nickell, Joe, and John F. Fischer. 1992. The crop circle phenomenon. In *Mysterious Realms: Probing Paranormal, Historical, and Forensic Enigmas*. Amherst, NY: Prometheus Books, p. 177.

Nickell, Joe. 2004. Crop circle capers. *Skeptical Briefs*, March, pp. 9-10.

Nickell, Joe. 2004. Circular reasoning, Chapter 14 in *The Mystery Chronicles: More Real-Life X-Files*. Lexington, Kentucky: University Press of Kentucky.

Winnipeg Free Press. 2003. Crop circle mania. August 2, p. 4.

Commentary and Follow-Up

This case is a good example of how experience and knowledge gained in one investigation can reap great benefits when applied to another. Joe and I already had good background knowledge of crop circles, but we would have been much less prepared to investigate the Iona crop circle if we hadn't spent time understanding how crop circles could be made and practicing it ourselves. It's easy (for both skeptics and believers) to offer armchair theories and explanations, but there's no substitute for personal experience. It guides the investigation by helping you know what to look for and what questions to ask.

Because of my research into crop circles, in 2005 I was asked to be a consultant on one of a series of children's books. An editor for Capstone Press sent me about three typed pages of material to look at (it was a short book with a lot of room for photos and art). She was perhaps expecting I would offer a few comments and corrections; instead she got back a four-page e-mail detailing over a dozen factual mistakes, logical errors, misleading statements, and unsupported claims made by the writer. My explanation of all the things wrong with the book was longer than the book itself. I suspect the editor's discussion with the author about this was somewhat awkward.

In one place the book referenced "scientific" studies into supposedly anomalous crop circle characteristics by a man named Levengood that I knew had been recently discredited by Italian researchers. The book also claimed—without evidence—that watches and cameras don't work in crop circles, and I noted that this statement appeared directly above a photograph *taken inside a crop circle*!

In another place, the author claimed that, "Many people think crop circles started appearing just in the last few years. In fact, they have been reported as far back as the 1600s. One famous account is from the summer of 1678. It describes a crop circle that appeared in a field of oats. No one could explain where it came from."

I hadn't heard this story before, and if true it would seriously undermine the most likely explanation, hoaxers. Intrigued by this information, I did a bit of research and discovered that this "account" was actually a "mowing devil" legend from 1678 in which an English farmer told a worker with whom he was feuding that he "would rather pay the Devil himself" to cut his oat field than pay the fee demanded. "That night a fiery light was seen in the field and the following morning revealed the crop cut, with supernatural exactness, into 'round circles'" (Michell and Rickard, 2000).

This story is obviously folklore, though the book's original text made it seem like historical evidence of an early crop circle. I showed my research to the editor, and the published version completely contradicts the original: "Researchers do not believe this legend is proof of an ancient crop circle. They point out that the legend says the crops were cut down. But plants in crop circle fields are bent." Score one for good research.

The author had clearly done a typical paranormal book cut-and-paste job, simply copying bits of information on crop circles from various sources without doing any independent research or investigation. It seemed that any crop circle information (whether true report or mythical legend) that filled the pages was good enough. As an investigator and consultant—especially for a children's book—it was important to me that the information be factual and not mystery-mongering.

The book was published in 2006 under the title *Crop Circles*. Other titles in the series included alien abductions, Bigfoot, ghosts, ESP, and the Loch Ness monster. I don't know if any of the other books in the series were reviewed by knowledgeable, science-based experts, but I hope so. The book editor, Katy Kudela, deserves a lot of credit for seeking out a skeptical consultant to fact-check her book. I wish more book, magazine, and television editors would take the time to make sure their facts are right.

CHAPTER 8
Ogopogo, the Bloodthirsty Lake Monster

Kelowna, British Columbia, Canada

I t's out there in the lake," Arlene Gaal tells me. "I'm sure of it." Arlene
is a resident of Kelowna, a city on the shores of Canada's Lake Okanagan, and by "it," Arlene means Ogopogo, the region's famous resident
lake monster. Arlene has lived in British Columbia most of her life, and
has been collecting sighting reports for decades. On her kitchen table
she proudly displays dozens of photographs, sketches, and tourist trin-
kets, all featuring the dark, long, elusive beast.

Okanagan is three times longer than Scotland's Loch Ness, and the
monster said to dwell within is Canada's best known lake creature. The
City of Kelowna's coat of arms, adopted in 1955, features a seahorse,
which, according to a city brochure, "in heraldry is the closest approxima-
tion of our Ogopogo." (As with Memphre, the lake monster of Mem-
phremagog, Quebec, there is something of a turf war between neighboring
towns as to who can reap the revenues generated by being the "home of
the lake monster." Two towns, Kelowna and Penticton, have laid claim to
that title. The victor, in recent years anyway, seems to be Kelowna.)

For monster-hunters like John Kirk of the British Columbia Scientific
Cryptozoology Club (BCSCC), Okanagan's Ogopogo is the most likely
and best-documented of all lake monsters, far more so than Loch Ness's

denizen. Ness is a high-profile money pit, swallowing hundreds of thousands of dollars and countless hours of effort over the last three-quarters of a century, yet yielding precious little in return. According to Kirk, "The catalogue of films and video of Ogopogo are more numerous and of better quality than anything I have personally seen at Loch Ness and I believe that several of them are very persuasive that a large, living, unknown creature inhabits the lake" (Kirk 2005). Jerome Clark and Nancy Pear, in their book *Strange and Unexplained Happenings*, also suggest that "Despite its silly name, Ogopogo is one of the most credible of the world's lake monsters" (Clark and Pear 1995, 440).

I had been contacted by producers for National Geographic Television, interested in the Ogopogo monster. They had seen the work Joe Nickell and I had done on Lake Champlain, and wanted us to conduct a science-based investigation. We did so on a chilly and blustery week in March 2005. Joe and I (along with John Kirk) joined the television crew to search for Ogopogo. We explored the lake by boat, car, and airplane, using binoculars, video cameras, side-scanning sonar, and professional divers. We examined dozens of original photographs and videotapes, interviewed eyewitnesses, and conducted field experiments. Our investigation constituted the largest single effort to find the lake monster to date.

Before setting out, we extensively researched the monster's history. Our experience in folklore was helpful in the first phase of the investigation. As with many lake monsters, native Indian tales have been used to suggest historical precedence for the creatures. Some monsters, such as Loch Ness's Nessie and Lake Champlain's Champ, are depicted as mysterious but fundamentally friendly beasties, playful and elusive. Not Ogopogo, or at least not the Indian stories upon which it is supposedly based: that of the fearsome N'ha-a-itk (Note 1). The N'ha-a-itk / Ogopogo link is firmly cemented in the creature's history and lore, more closely tied to native myths than any other lake monster. Virtually all writers on the subject lump the two together, and in fact most use the terms interchangeably— and erroneously, as we shall see. Scientific investigation demands clarity in distinctions, and the failure to be clear about which monster we are talking about—and thus searching for—has stymied many researchers.

Figure 8.1, Lake Okanagan's Rattlesnake Island, reputed home of Ogopogo.

N'ha-a-itk (various translations include "water god" and "lake demon") would demand a toll from travelers for safe passage near its reputed home of Rattlesnake Island (also known as Monster Island), a small rocky clot in Lake Okanagan (see figure 8.1).

The fee was not just a bit of gold or tobacco, but a live sacrifice. Hundreds of years ago, whenever Indians would venture into the lake, they brought chickens or other small animals to drop into the water. The drowned fowl would sink into the lake's depths and assure its owners a protected journey. The island's rocky shore was said to be littered with the gory remnants of passersby who did not make the sacrifices.

Joe and I were mindful that skeptical investigators have traditionally not fared well when it comes to Ogopogo. "'Let the paleface tremble at the mention of N'ha-a-itk's name!' Such would have been the fate of skeptics in an earlier day," Arlene Gaal wrote in her book *In Search of Ogopogo*. Indian traditions speak of Timbasket, the chief of a visiting tribe who paid a terrible price for challenging N'ha-a-itk. Historian Frank Buckland tells the story:

> Timbasket, the Indian cynic... declared his disbelief in the existence of the lake demon. He was told that the Westbank Indians intended to sacrifice a live dog to the water god as

they passed Squally Point, but he was quite unimpressed. He knew too much to concern himself with outmoded customs.... [Later when crossing the lake] Timbasket defiantly chose to travel close to the rocky headland. Suddenly, the lake demon arose from his lair and whipped up the surface of the lake with his long tail. Timbasket, his family and his canoe were sucked under by a great swirl of angry water (Quoted in Moon 1977, 25).

This was *modus operandi* for N'ha-a-itk: it would use its mighty tail to lash the lake's waters into a fierce storm that would drown its victims. According to Mary Moon, author of *Ogopogo* (1977), "The Indians... looked on it as a superhuman [supernatural] entity." Other writers agree, including W. Haden Blackman, who points out that the Sushwap and Okanakane Indians "believed that it was an evil supernatural entity with great power and ill intent" (Blackman 1998, 71). N'ha-a-itk's paranormal connection to the elements is perhaps the strongest of any lake monster. Not only does N'ha-a-itk seem to have supernatural control over the lake's waters, it also commands aerial forces as well: "the Indians said no boat could possibly land [on Rattlesnake Island], for the monster would cause a strong wind to blow and baffle the attempt.... the monster was something more than an amphibian. It was always in some way connected with high winds...." (Moon 1977, 32).

Such stories and descriptions suggest that, to First Nations peoples, N'ha-a-itk was a disincarnate force of nature, not a corporeal creature actually living and eating, breathing and breeding, in the cold waters of Lake Okanagan. Researchers must be careful about accepting native stories and legends as true accounts of actual creatures. Just because a given culture has a name for, tells stories about, or depicts a strange or mysterious beast—be it Sasquatch or Ogopogo, dragon or leprechaun—doesn't necessarily mean that those references were meant to reflect reality. This highlights a problem that folklorist Michel Meurger points out in his book *Lake Monster Traditions*. Meurger suggests that claiming native evidence for unknown creatures is an "old gimmick of portraying the sighter as a kind of 'noble savage,'" a process he aptly names "the scien-

Statue of Ogopogo, the reputed monster in Canada's Lake Okanagan.

tification of folklore" (Meurger 1988, 13). In our book *Lake Monster Mysteries* I refer to this as the Bangles Fallacy, after the 1980s rock group that hit the charts with "Walk Like an Egyptian." The song playfully assumes that Egyptians walked exactly as depicted in ancient artwork.

The Investigation

Despite sporadic efforts by a handful of individuals including John Kirk, there had not yet been a thorough, sustained scientific search of the lake. This is more a result of limited finances than a snubbing by the scientific community. As with all searches for mysterious animals, the quest comes down to time and expense. Given the lack of tractable evidence from Loch Ness over the past 75 years, institutions are understandably not eager to invest substantial amounts of money in what is likely to be an 80-mile-long money pit. Those who do have the time and interest in pursuing the creatures often don't have the resources. Much of what passes for scientific investigation comes about in the process of filming documentaries about the monster. The most famous, and the most thorough, was a 1991 expedition financed by Nippon Television. In cooperation with the BCSCC, the Japanese film crew provided many high-tech devices, including a remotely-operated vehicle and Deep Rover, a miniature

━━━━ OKANAGAN ━━━━   A4

THE DAILY COURIER, WEDNESDAY, FEBRUARY 2, 2005

National Geographic to investigate Ogopogo

By Daily Courier Staff

A film crew from the National Geographic Society arrive in Kelowna today to shoot material for a new television series.

Behind the Mysteries looks at strange phenomena and attempts to prove or disprove the existence of the subject being investigated.

Producers Noel Dockstader and Brook Hoiston will interview locals who say they have seen the lake creature, review existing film footage and do some searching themselves on a sonar-

equipped houseboat.

"I have spent the past 10 days putting together the witnesses, providing a boat, deciding on the material to be used, etc.," said local Ogopogo expert Arlene Gaal.

She said the producers will also bring the so-called Skeptical Inquirer, Ben Radford, from New York to critique the evidence.

John Kirk, Vancouver president of the B.C. Cryptozoologist Club, will also work with Gaal as a consultant.

"I have had a number of interesting e-mail con-

versations with Ben Radford, who appears to be quite fair in his assessments," said Gaal.

The John Casorso video, which generated a stir in Kelowna when it was first reported in The Daily Courier, will be reviewed by the skeptics and experts.

Footage Gaal calls the Folden Film will provide another look at the creature, and that encounter is to be recreated by the film crew.

Radford intends to scientifically examine the Folden Film, which was shot north of Peachland in 1968.

submarine. The pilot took the vehicle to a depth of 840 feet along the lake bottom at the deepest part of the lake, but no Ogopogos were sighted, nor were any of the creatures' carcasses or bones discovered. Hard evidence, alas, is still lacking.

Almost fifteen years after that effort, we plunged into the mystery afresh. Despite the fact that our well-known lake monster had a well-known grudge against skeptics, we pressed on, conducting a multifaceted field investigation. The evening of our arrival Joe and I met the National Geographic crew to discuss filming, boating, and investigation logistics. Producer Noel Dockstader was in charge of the shoot, aided by a producer from Georgia named Brooke and a camera / sound duo. A boat had been hired to take us out on the lake, and I discussed with Glenn Kohaly the boat captain and a scuba diver, DJ Swanson, whether I would be diving to seek the monster. I had told Noel I would be willing to do it, though I was starting to have my doubts. My concern wasn't so much becoming Ogopogo bait, but instead something else that literally sent shivers down my spine: the frigid cold. I am a certified open water diver, but I had never done a dive outside of the tropics, and steel-grey Lake Okanagan in March was about as far from the tropics as I could imagine. I had done my diving in the warm, crystal Caribbean waters, usually amid pina coladas and skimpy swimsuits. I knew this was going to be a very different experience.

Joe and I were up at five the next morning, taking photos of the town and making lists of places to visit and questions to ask. While Joe hit the library and conducted interviews, I spent the afternoon at the Kelowna Museum, trying to find information on Ogopogo. When I asked at the front desk, I was told politely but coolly, "Ogopogo is a myth, and we don't have myths in our museum." This seemed like a sensible (if not especially tourist-friendly) answer, and after I explained that I was looking for an expert to interview, I was given directions a few blocks down the street to another nearby museum to see a woman named Celeste Ganassin. I asked Ganassin, an attractive, 30-ish curator of education at the Kelowna Museum, about the oft-repeated link between N'ha-a-itk and Ogopogo: Were they the same creature? She explained that for many First Nations peoples the distinction between reality and myth in their traditions was not particularly important, and writers tread shaky ground when they conscript Indian myths of N'ha-a-itk into evidence for a modern Ogopogo's reality: "People pick and choose parts of the First Nations myths to fit their needs, to support whatever argument they are trying to make. To those people who crossed that body of water, it was a real phenomena," Ganassin (2005) told me. She also pointed out that Lake Okanagan is hardly unique in its native stories of terrifying creatures inhabiting the depths. "You can't look at a First Nations group anywhere without finding a tradition of some sort of entity in a lake they had to respect or fear." In fact, the stories of N'ha-a-itk are virtually identical to those in many other North American lakes, including Ontario and Superior. (For a fuller discussion, see chapter 3 in Michel Meurger's *Lake Monster Traditions*.)

I also tried, unsuccessfully, to locate ancient Indian petroglyphs, or rock art, said to depict N'ha-a-itk. Yet the link between petroglyphs and N'ha-a-itk (and therefore Ogopogo) is dubious at best. The petroglyph most often cited is in fact not from the Okanagan Valley at all, but instead from Sproat Lake, on Vancouver Island (Kirk 2005). Writer Karl Shuker suggests that petroglyphs dating from around 1700 BC might be evidence for lake monsters. One particular drawing, Shuker writes, "is a strikingly accurate depiction of the vertically undulating, elongate water monsters frequently reported from the lakes and seas of Canada—so much so that it could easily be taken to be a sketch made by one of these beasts' twentieth century eyewitnesses" (Shuker 1995, 112). Yet the petroglyph Shuker describes was found not on the shore of Lake Okanagan, nor in British Columbia, nor even in the western half of Canada, but instead over 2,000 miles away, near Peterborough, just outside of Toronto. It may represent a monster, but its location does not suggest Ogopogo. "There is no true academic evidence that specifically states that First Nations people ever put down in petroglyphs the shape of N'ha-a-itk," Ganassin said. "The pictures didn't come with captions."

After leaving Ganassin, I rushed to meet with a local land surveying

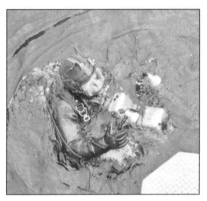

company to discuss their assistance in some scientific experiments I had planned. I then headed to a local dive center, where DJ familiarized me with the diving equipment to be used in the underwater monster search. Not only the large camera, but also the diving gear I would don. I expected the wetsuit, but I grew incredulous he applied more and more hoods and vests and masks and gear, all of which I was not used to and found very hot, uncomfortable, unwieldy, and restricting. From deep inside my neoprene and metal sarcophagus, I asked DJ if all this was really necessary. Actually, I think the phrase I used was, "Are you serious"?

He grinned as he tightened yet another clasp around my head and said that many warm-water divers are amazed at how different and difficult cold water dives are. Colder temperatures means more insulation, more gear, different physiological responses, and a higher breathing rate. I did several fully-suited practice pool dives with him, though more than once I had difficulties: a leaking mask, ears that wouldn't clear, and an air supply that DJ had apparently forgotten to turn on. Now, as you might have guessed, I don't believe in bad omens, but I was beginning to wonder if I'd really be up for the dive. Following my exhumation and some equipment reviews and safety rehearsals, I returned to the hotel where Joe was already enjoying some expense-accounted beers with our affable Scot-bred monster man John Kirk.

I'd exchanged e-mails with the lanky Canadian on many occasions, but never had the pleasure of meeting him. Though in some ways John and I were on opposite sides of many issues relating to mysterious creatures (I'm skeptical, he's more of a believer), we got on very well. Some people (probably including the National Geographic producers) expected sparks to fly when Joe, John, and I got together, but we instead had considerable respect for each other's work, ideas, and opinions. We had a few pointed moments, but on the whole we all recognized

Figure 8.2, using sonar to search for the monster

that we were gathered in a unifying mission to try and find—or at least better understand—this modern mystery. John recognized that we weren't the closed-minded debunkers many might assume, and we realized that John wasn't the blind believer some skeptics might have assumed.

Joe and I rented a car and staked out the lake on several occasions, positioning ourselves at good vantage points overlooking sighting-rich areas. We later chartered a small plane and surveyed the lake by air, as any large, long, dark creature at the surface (or just under it) should be very easy to spot from above. An aerial search should also eliminate the problem of mistaking oblique waves for moving humps— a recurring problem, as we would later find out. The flight was useful for getting a sense of the Okaganan Valley, and despite watchful eyes and ready cameras, no trace of Ogopogo could be seen. Noel had sent his cameraman Ian with us, and the poor man and his large camera were awkwardly cramped into the seat next to the pilot, getting some aerial views but often trained on Joe or myself as we scanned the waters below. I kept wondering if a stray knee or heel from Ian would bump one of the black

An ultralight wreck.

or red control knobs and send us spiraling into the lake—perhaps food for Ogopogo after all. At least, I thought, they'd get some compelling footage that would make the final cut.

Our surface searches came up empty, but we held out hope that by going into the lake itself we might find the creatures— or at least their remains. We boarded a sonar-equipped boat (see figure 8.2) to scan both the lake's surface and its depths.

The creatures are naturally elusive, yet no matter how hard the live ones are to find at any given time, there must be dead specimens that can't so easily elude searchers. Given the supposedly long history of creatures in the lake, and the number of them that must exist to have remained in the lake for centuries, there should be dozens of Ogopogo skeletons littering the lake or washing up on shore. A sighting would be exciting, but a forensic find like that would be a first in history.

With piles of huge black cases of tripods, blank videotapes, batteries, microphones, and monitors on every available surface, the boat was standing room only as we headed out. While one man monitored the sonar screen inside the boat, another stood on the aft and took instructions by radio, raising and lowering the sonar as needed. With eyes on the video screen, we searched the sighting-heavy area south of Kelowna, and again as we approached Rattlesnake Island. Divers with cameras were on hand to be dispatched on short notice. Nothing unusual was spotted, though we recorded the sonar scans for later analysis.

Darryl Bondura, who was in charge of the sonar, showed us an interesting image he had picked up earlier along the lake bottom: not a monster, but the wreckage of a crashed ultralight airplane (see above).

Research later showed that most ultralights of that configuration have a wingspan of about 30 feet (Ultralight 2002), which is considerably smaller than the reported length of many Ogopogo sightings. Ultralight frames are necessarily thin, and it seems reasonable to assume they might be about the same size as Ogopogo bones. So the question arises: If sonar can detect (and get a clear image of) the thin frame of an ultralight at a depth of nearly 100 feet, where are the Ogopogo bones that should litter the lake bottom? I asked Darryl if, in all his years of scanning the lake's bottom and sides, he had ever found anything that he thought might have been a lake monster. He said no. "What about any bones? Have you ever seen any large bones, or ones that might be laid out like a giant snake?" He scratched his stubbled cheek and shook his head.

Having seen nothing so far, we raised the sonar to speed the boat and make better time. As we bounced though the chop and scanned the waters, I was still undecided about whether I would dive. I knew Noel would like a shot of me diving in, and though I would be the only investigator diving, I wasn't sure. I felt my presence would be better spent on board instead of bound up in unfamiliar gear in the frigid waters. I told DJ and Noel of my decision. Soon we approached the monster's reputed lair of Rattlesnake Island. John, Joe, and myself stood on the bow, cameras and binoculars at the ready. We went a little past the island to a rock outcropping called Squally Point, where we dispatched the divers to search for Ogopogo and its cavernous lair.

While the divers were gone, we continued sonar scanning, with brief visits to a table laden with cooling coffee and cookies. Still nothing unusual appeared. Twenty minutes later the divers surfaced. The water was very cold, they said, and the currents were forcing them to burn through their air faster than expected. "It's nasty down there," DJ told me, "and not much to see. It's bare as the surface of the moon in places." I was quietly relieved that I hadn't gotten all suited up and dived, especially given the poor visibility and wretched conditions I'd have faced. No monsters were sighted, but DJ reported that Ogopogo's reputed "cave" wasn't big enough to hold a monster, and in fact wasn't really a cave at all but instead a shallow concave cliff. Our first-hand investigation demolished a myth. I surveyed the eerie, light green-tinted underwater footage he shot, in case they had filmed the beast without knowing it. Once again, Ogopogo was a no-show. No sightings, no video, no bones. Like all investigations previous to ours, the methodical search for Ogopogo creatures came up empty.

Before we left the area, Joe, John, and I clamored onto the small, rocky island for an on-camera interview. I searched in vain for any evidence of the lake monster, but (literally) stumbled across something almost as bizarre on Monster Island: the crumbling remains of a miniature golf course. Years ago, a rich Lebanese man, Eddy Haymour, tried to turn the island into a tourist theme park. The plan failed and was eventually abandoned; all that remains are a handful of windswept concrete slabs and cinderblocks. We soon headed to port, and then to a nearby German restaurant for a much-deserved dinner.

Evaluating Ogopogo Sightings

We didn't see Ogopogo, but apparently many people had. While sightings are interesting and should be examined, they are essentially anecdotes, and anecdotes are not evidence. This is why scientists test and retest claims to see if they are really true. When physicists Stanley Pons and Martin Fleishmann announced to the world that they had found evidence of cold fusion in 1989, it was essentially an exciting and interesting anecdote, which was refuted by later testing and research. The same is true for any unusual personal experience, whether with ghosts, monsters, psychics, or anything out of the ordinary.

But what did they see? Though the supernatural N'ha-a-itk of the Okanagan Valley Indians is long gone, it has been replaced by a decidedly less fearsome—and more biological—beast whose exact form is a matter of opinion and debate. This Ogopogo is supported not by Indian myths but by photographs, sonar readings, and eyewitness reports. This creature is often described as dark and multi-humped. Some writers (e.g., Jerome Clark) claim that the descriptions of Ogopogo are "strikingly similar"; Roy Mackal, in reviewing hundreds of descriptive reports, was "struck by repetitive consistency of the descriptions, almost to the point of boredom." Mackal continues: "The skin is described as dark green to green-black or brown to black and dark brown... [or] gray to blue-black or even a golden brown. Most often the skin is smooth with no scales, although the body must possess a few plates, scales, or similar structures observed by close-up viewers.... Most of the back is smooth, although a portion is saw-toothed, ragged-edged, or serrated. Sparse hair or hair-bristle structures are reported around the head, and in a few cases a mane or comb-like structure has been observed at the back of the neck" (Mackal 1980, 231). Furthermore, the head is said to look like that of a snake, or a sheep, or a horse, or a seal, or an alligator. Or a bulldog. Sometimes it has ears or horns; other times it doesn't. Many sightings simply refer to a featureless "log" that came alive. It seems that the chameleonesque Ogopogo takes on an incredible variety of forms, making analysis difficult and reports hard to reconcile.

The vast majority of Ogopogo sightings are brief, ambiguous, and from an unknown distance. Though very rare, there are a few up-close eyewitness descriptions. Ideally, these should provide the very best eyewitness evidence: close-up and first-hand. One man, Ernest A. Lording, reported that "he came so close to me I could have touched him....He was within three feet of me and it wasn't my imagination. He was definitely scaly and greenish...like a sturgeon's scales. He's [got] stabilizing fins or flippers" (Moon, 81). On the other hand, Ed Fletcher and his wife Diane, claim they saw Ogopogo twice, also "quite close up." The skin, they reported, "seemed smooth and brownish. There were no scales; it was rather like a whale's skin. The back was ridged" (Moon 95). Frustratingly, the lengthy, close-up, detailed descriptions are just as contradictory as the far-away glimpses. One person unmistakably sees a scaly, greenish creature with flippers; another, just as certain, clearly sees a brownish beast without scales or flippers but instead with a ridged back.

The wildly divergent descriptions pose a significant problem for searchers and those who believe the monsters exist. Logically, there are only two possible explanations: 1) the eyewitnesses are inaccurately reporting what they saw; or 2) the eyewitnesses are accurately reporting many different types of physically different lake monsters. Neither serves as strong support for Ogopogo. Even given normal species variation (and sexual dimorphism), surely the smooth, log-like Ogopogo is not also the horse-headed, ridge-backed Ogopogo. The creature is Okanagan's Rorschach ink blot: different people see different things. This is one reason why eyewitness testimony is so unreliable, a fact that psychologists and police detectives know well.

The sporadic pattern of Ogopogo sightings is also curious. As with many lake monsters, the beast is most often seen in clusters: many sightings will occur over the course of a few weeks or months, then nothing for months. Many years went by with few sightings—or none at all. While the late 1920s had a plethora of reports, there were very few in the twenty years between 1930 and 1950. In 1973 there was only one sighting; the number doubled the following year. (Note 2)

Assuming that the number of people on the lake (and thus the number of potential witnesses) did not plummet during these many lean years, how do we explain this pattern? After all, if there has been a sizeable group of these Ogopogos in the lake for centuries (biology dictates there must be at least a dozen to maintain a breeding population), logically they should be seen not only much more frequently, but much more regularly. This is true even if the creatures migrate in and out of the lake seasonally, as some have claimed.

Individual eyewitness descriptions do not add up. Instead of a coherent mosaic of Ogopogo, we have bits and pieces of dozens of different creatures, often with features that cannot biologically coexist. Since it seems arbitrary to give one description more credence than another, we are left with contradictory information about a creature never even proven to exist.

Ogopogo does have several characteristics that distinguish it from other monsters. For example, the beast has an uncommonly large number of sightings that report high speed movement, at times even creating a spray. This observation is hard to reconcile with many mundane explanations, such as a floating tree, fish, or a swimming otter or beaver. One eyewitness said that Ogopogo was "tearing madly along in circles about 200 feet in diameter, and kicking up a tremendous spray" (Moon, 55).

Said another, "the lake creature was simply too fast-moving for their motorboats to keep up with."

There are almost as many accounts of Ogopogo chasing boaters. In her book *Ogopogo*, Mary Moon mentions at least three incidents. Needless to say, the lake monster never caught up with its prey, but here again eyewitness descriptions conflict with scientific analysis and with each other: If the creature actually can move in the water "faster than any motorboat could achieve" then why was it apparently unable to catch rowboats and speedboats it chased? Logic suggests that either the eyewitness accounts of chasing are wrong, the eyewitness accounts of the "tremendous speed" are wrong, or both are wrong.

Even the most skeptical of cryptozoologists admit that many, perhaps the majority, of sightings are mistakes. But, they insist, there must be *some* that we cannot explain, a few that cannot be chalked up to illusions or mistakes. But conclusions must follow evidence, not the other way around. As with monsters in other lakes, supposition about the Ogo-

The author and Joe Nickell review photographic evidence of the Ogopogo lake monster with local expert Arlene Gaal.

pogo creatures—what they are, where they live, what they eat, how they behave—has far outpaced actual evidence about them. Without hard evidence upon which to proceed (or really base an inquiry), such speculation amounts to little more than an amusing but fruitless parlor game.

Film and video evidence

Our primary source for images of Ogopogo was Arlene Gaal, an invaluable resource and a tireless researcher. We met the camera crew at Gaal's home in a Kelowna suburb. She has collected photographs, videos, and sighting reports since she moved to Kelowna in 1968. She shared her photos and videos with us, explaining picture by picture what each image suggested to her.

In 2004, several Ogopogo films were professionally analyzed for the SciFi Channel show *Proof Positive*. Though it was the most thorough and sophisticated computer analysis done to date, each film failed to provide good evidence for the monster. In one case the investigator concluded that dark humps that appeared to be moving in fact weren't, when the image was stabilized and compared to fixed objects in the background. In another, the Ogopogo humps were misaligned in the water, and therefore couldn't all be from the same creature— suggesting waves and several small animals (perhaps beaver or otter) instead of one large monster. One video was interesting because what one eyewitness described as "three very distinct humps" another saw quite plainly as waves created by "something pushing the water up." Is the object a wave or a creature's hump? Two eyewitnesses can't agree, despite seeing the same thing at the same time—and capturing it on videotape.

One widely-seen Ogopogo video shot by a man named Ken Chaplin became a local joke, with viewers pointing out that the "mystery creature" was obviously a beaver swimming with its head raised out of the water—the telltale tail slapping the water was one clue. John Kirk said he was "flabbergasted at how Chaplin could possibly have thought he captured the Ogopogo on tape. He had categorically stated that the animal was between nine and twelve feet long, but what we were seeing on the screen was obviously nowhere near that size" (Kirk 1998 p. 88). Here again we have an eyewitness problem—is it more likely that Chaplin videotaped a lake monster or a nine to twelve foot beaver, or that he was expecting to see a monster and overestimated a beaver's size in his excitement?

One Kelowna resident told me that many local folks were embarrassed when the film was broadcast, as it made them look like they didn't know a beaver when they saw one. (I pointed out that it was probably an honest mistake, and besides, it was an American TV show, Unsolved Mysteries, that paid $30,000 for the most expensive beaver footage in history!)

Most films, of course, are more ambiguous, and some such misidentifications are to be expected. The majority of Ogopogo images are of too poor quality to yield much information, but a few were offered as the "cream of the crop." None had been thoroughly examined, and Gaal was pleased to have the expertise of ourselves and the National Geographic crew available. I will highlight our scientific analyses of the best Ogopogo film.

The Folden Film

The best evidence of Ogopogo, according to Gaal and other writers, is about a minute of footage shot in 1968 by a man named Arthur Folden. On a sunny day in August of that year, Folden and his wife were driving on Highway 97 south of Peachland when Folden noticed "something large and lifelike" out on the calm water. They immediately pulled over, on a nearby bluff overlooking the lake, which, according to Arlene Gaal, "at this point runs fairly high above the lake and about three hundred yards from the shore." Folden, an 8mm movie buff, pulled out his camera and captured the object in the water. Concerned that he was near the end of his tape, he stopped and started the segment several times, turning the camera off when the object submerged and starting again when he saw it resurface.

Though we were unable to see the entire, unedited footage, we did our best with what was available. I was sent a video clip containing about 45 seconds of footage. The object was estimated at seventy feet in length, according to Folden and his wife. Though the quality is mediocre at best (it is fuzzy and scratched) Folden was professional enough to hold the camera steady most of the time. Thankfully, the film begins with a wide angle shot,

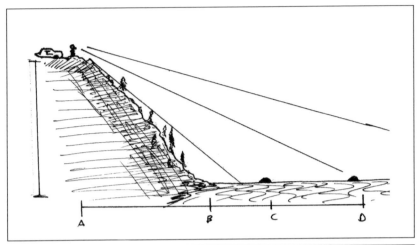

Standing where the most famous footage of the Ogopogo lake monster was filmed, a surveyor calculates distances to various points on the lake.

allowing us to roughly estimate Folden's distance down to the shore.

The object Folden filmed was estimated at another 200 yards out in the lake. If the camera was about 300 yards from the lake shore, then the object, whatever it was, was seen at 500 yards, or about 1,500 feet. If this estimate—a third of a mile— is correct, the object would have to be truly monstrous to be seen with the naked eye from the highway.

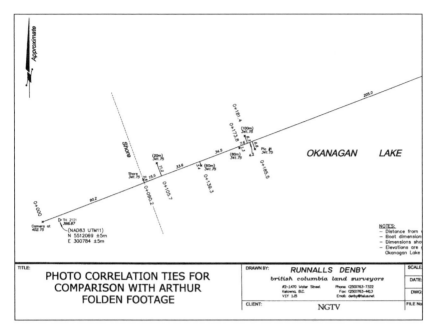

Figure 8.4, a surveyor's map used to calculate the size of the creature that Arthur Folden filmed at British Columbia's Lake Okanagan in 1968.

According to Loren Coleman, author of the *Field Guide to Lake Monsters, Sea Serpents, and Other Mystery Denizens of the Deep*, "The short footage shows a large creature diving and reappearing, until it finally takes off, churning up waves and leaving a heavy wake, before making its last dive. Based on the size of pine trees onshore, about twenty-five feet tall, the creature was estimated to be about sixty to seventy feet long." The film begins by showing what appears to be a noticeable disturbance in the water. Since it's not clear how far out onto the lake the disturbance is, there's no way to tell how large an area it covers. Within a few seconds, the object begins moving to the right of the screen. A tree in the foreground provides a basis for comparison— not necessarily of the creature's size, but of its horizontal journey. The object picks up speed as it moves away from the tree, even creating a noticeable crest as it parts the water. The object then slows somewhat, and the film ends.

It is important to remember that, though the footage itself lasts about 45 seconds, Folden reported the whole sighting as lasting two to three minutes. From an analytical perspective, distance is crucial, because an object moving across a film frame can either be a massive object covering a great distance, or a much smaller object covering a much lesser distance depending on how far away it is. Without something of known scale near the object, it can be difficult or impossible to distinguish between the two possibilities.

Though we knew that many specifics would be impossible to establish nearly forty years after the fact (and with Mr. Folden unavailable to help), we were able to set some parameters and answer a few basic questions. For example, how large must an object or animal be for Mr. Folden to see it and film it from his position along the highway? Are small or medium-sized animals discernable from his position, or merely imperceptible dots?

Having previously conducted scientific field experiments at Lake Champlain to reconcile lake monster sightings with information from photographs (discussed in detail in *Lake Monster Mysteries*), I was asked to bring my knowledge and experience to bear on the Folden film. With input from Joe Nickell and John Kirk, I designed and arranged a set of experiments to see what information we could glean from Folden's film, despite the nearly four-decade time lapse. Our experiment was filmed for National Geographic and broadcast in August 2005. We located a site along Highway 97 that all of us agreed was either the original site or very near it.

For the experiments we took photographs of the Folden site and placed a survey boat out on the lake at set distance intervals. Runnals Denby, a professional land surveying firm located in downtown Kelowna (and less than a block from the city's famed Ogopogo statue) was contracted to help with the tasks. The resulting surveyor's map (see figure 8.4) shows the distance from the eyewitness's position to various plotted points out on the lake.

We took photos and measurements at various distances from shore, including at the distance Folden estimated. With the chilly wind whipping at us, we conducted the experiments in under three hours. As the crew interviewed Joe, John, and myself, I could see Noel's knees shivering out of the corner of my eye. He was off-camera to my left, pitching questions to us, and the poor man was freezing. Still, everyone was professional and we all got out of the cold as quickly as we could. As the experiment progressed, it was immediately clear to all of us that Folden had dramatically overestimated how far away the creature was. Because of this, we can also conclude that the creature's speed has been overestimated. It was nearer to the camera, and thus covered a relatively short distance (perhaps 100 yards) during its two or three minute journey.

We all agreed on several conclusions: 1) we had located the original site of the Folden film, or very near it, a feat never before accomplished; 2) the object in the water was indeed a living creature of some sort; and most importantly, 3) that creature's distance from the camera was greatly overestimated, therefore the creature is much smaller than previously thought. Beaver or otters are real possibilities, though we will never know exactly what Arthur Folden filmed.

Explanations

What are eyewitnesses seeing? As with all lake monsters, there is no one specific candidate that accounts for all sightings. There are the usual suspects, objects and phenomena that are known to mimic lake monsters. Mary Moon offers up about a half dozen Ogopogo candidates: sturgeon, oarfish, manatee, prehistoric reptiles, sea lions, ducks in a row, and geological activity. Joe Nickell (2003) has made a strong case for otters as monster doppelgangers, and I have previously demonstrated how submerged logs can resemble (and act like) lake beasties (Radford 2004).

Some of these explanations, of course, are more likely than others. For example, it is unlikely that sturgeon are mistaken for Ogopogo, since none have been caught in Lake Okanagan. Oarfish and manatees are remote possibilities, while large fish and small fauna are more likely. Biologist Roy Mackal has strongly argued that Ogopogo is a zeuglodon, a type of prehistoric whale, basing his analysis largely on eyewitness descriptions. Zeuglodons are believed to have died out millennia ago, and far more mundane explanations must be ruled out before reaching for such an answer. There are other phenomena which mimic Ogopogo and are especially characteristic of Lake Okanagan.

Wave Patterns

According to many locals I interviewed, Lake Okanagan's geological features create unusual waves that can look exactly like the monster, down to Ogopogo's signature series of humps. One woman at the Kelowna Museum told me she had recently seen some footage shot locally of a series of dark humps moving through the water, thought to be Ogopogo. "My husband and I see that out on the lake sometimes when we're out walking," she told me. "It's not a monster. It's a wave, no question about it. It looks just like moving humps in the water...."

Many others, experts and laypeople alike, offer the same observation. Canadian fisheries expert David Stirling suggested the same explanation: "My theory is that Ogopogo is an optical illusion produced when an observer views obliquely a bow wave moving across flat water under certain lighting conditions" (Moon 135). In 1989, John Kirk, while surveying the lake, noted "many optical illusions which appeared to resemble a lake monster....A variety of standing, reflected, and refracted waves produced artificial humps, and at times strongly resembled a head just above the surface" (Kirk 1989, 77). During our expedition on the lake, longtime boat captain Glenn Kohaly told me "I think I know what 90% of the people who saw Ogopogo saw....I don't know if there's a name for it, but I call it the 'phantom wave.' It can be calm, with no boats or obvious wakes, and this wave will come from nowhere. It looks just like humps... exactly like humps. It can look forty to fifty feet long, and like it's moving. People see the waves and they say, 'That is Ogopogo, there's no other explanation.'" Indeed, several prominent Ogopogo videos have been analyzed and deemed to be waves.

Logs and Trees

At least some Ogopogo sightings are almost certainly floating logs. This has been a staple explanation for many lake monster sightings, and is easy to dismiss until you actually read what eyewitness after eyewitness describes as "a living log." Take, for example, the following accounts: "I saw something that looked like a huge tree trunk or log floating in the lake" or "It looked just like the trunk of a huge pine, but I saw neither head nor tail; it was not a bit like the serpent since seen by others." Or they saw "what they thought was a log, six feet long, floating on the water" or "It was like a great moving log, but alive, moving up and down a little in the water." (Quotes from Moon, p. 33, 40, 56, etc.) In fact, a survey of sighting reports collected by Mary Moon and Arlene Gaal reveals that there may be more accounts of Ogopogo describing it as "log-like" than any other single characteristic.

This explanation is supported by the fact that there are thousands of truly massive logs in the lake; logging companies use the Okanagan Valley waterways to transport timber through the area. During a survey of the lake, Joe Nickell and I came across several log booms easily a quarter-mile wide.

These were not man-size pieces of wood: some of the larger specimens reached sixty feet. When these stray logs get loose and become waterlogged, they can bob at or just under the waterline. In choppy water or waves, it is not hard to imagine how they could double for Ogopogo: something dark, smooth, low to the water, and glimpsed between waves. (For an explanation of how waterlogged timber can behave like a monster, sinking, rising, and sinking again, see page 61 in *Lake Monster Mysteries*.)

When currents and strong winds blow across the water, the ripples and wave patterns can give stationary objects the illusion of movement.

Thousands of logs and trees float in Lake Okanagan; perhaps a few are monsters.

I've seen this first-hand, observing rocks and logs that were not moving but appeared to be, when compared to all the waves rushing past it. Many commuters experience this effect on trains, when one car pulls past another on parallel tracks. It can be confusing for a moment, trying to figure out which car is actually in motion. Many Ogopogo sightings exactly fit this description (e.g., "he saw a big log going against the waves").

As Mary Moon mentions, there are mundane explanations for some of the Ogopogo-related phenomena. One writer commented on the monster's unusually foul flatulence: "[Several eyewitnesses] experienced an offensive smell coming from the water below, while encountering what appeared to be Ogopogo. The creature may have been expelling gas or perhaps emitting a natural scent due to its activity at the time. Most who encounter Ogopogo can be thankful this does not happen very often" (Gaal 2001, 114).

The lake's geological activity offers a more likely explanation than lake monster farts: While investigating the lake in 1991, John Kirk noted "two large patches of foaming bubbles not far from my vantage point on the east side of the lake. The duration of the bubbling led me to conclude that the source was natural gas escaping through a fissure on the lake bottom. These bubbles have obviously been mistaken in the past for signs of Ogopogo's presence or activity by witnesses who were unaware that the Okanagan Valley is dotted with thermal vents, the vestiges of its former position as the center of volcanic activity" (Kirk 1991, 73).

Ogopogo Found

After several days on the lake, it became clear that Ogopogo was as elusive as ever. Whether we searched above the lake, on the lake, or in the lake, Ogopogo was nowhere to be found. Still, it wouldn't be quite accurate to say that we didn't find Ogopogo; indeed, the beast's presence in the Okanagan Valley is as unmistakable and remarkable as its absence is in Okanagan Lake. Like Bigfoot, Ogopogo's cultural impact seems inversely correlated to the amount of hard evidence for its existence.

Ogopogo does exist, as a regional mascot, hero, and tourist attraction. Long gone are the echoes of live sacrifices, drowning deaths, and bone-

strewn beaches. This is N'ha-a-itk and Ogopogo updated for modern Canada and presented by a savvy public relations department. Nicknamed Ogie, this public-friendly Ogopogo can be found peering down from shelves in tourist hovels, next to snow globes and plush beavers in little red Mounties uniforms. This Ogopogo is devoid of nasty scales or slimy skin, sheathed instead in a fuzzy and lovable countenance. This scrubbed-up, reformed beast can be found in many children's books, including *With Love We Can All Find Ogopogo* by Brock Tully, *Ogopogo: The Misunderstood Lake Monster*, by Don Levers (in which the beast heroically saves several buses of schoolchildren from drowning), and *The Legend of L'il Ogie* by Garfield Fromm.

"Ogopogo has mellowed with the passing of time," Arlene Gaal explains. "Of recent years, he frolics in the water with almost impish delight, flips a flirtatious tail, and, with a sly wink, disappears into the froth to return from whence he came." This mellowing occurred rather suddenly in the 1920s, perhaps coinciding with a popular music hall song called "The Ogopogo: The Funny Fox-Trot" (Shuker 1995). Hayden Blackman notes that at the time "reported Ogopogo attacks had ceased completely, and the peoples living on the lake were beginning to view the monster in a much kinder light" (Blackman 1998, 71).

Unless lake pollution over the past centuries has had a sedative effect on the beast, this marked change in its (their) behavior is very curious. It seems that the public's perception of Ogopogo— independent of its actions— influenced reports of the monster's behavior. Part of this transformation is surely an effort to capitalize on tourism; what tourists are going to fly in from across Canada and around the globe to seek out a murderous leviathan that may demand a blood tithe, or the family puppy?

As with N'ha-a-itk, the real question is not what Ogopogo means in some absolute or biological sense, but what Ogopogo means to the culture and age embracing it. The First Nations peoples have N'ha-a-itk; the cryptozoologists and eyewitnesses have Ogopogo; and the tourists and Okanagan Valley children have Ogie. N'ha-a-itk and Ogopogo are fundamentally amorphous, while with Ogie we finally have captured the beast, in its cultural, if not its actual, form.

On the last day of the investigation, the National Geographic crew asked Joe, John, and myself to reflect on our expedition. From one perspective, we failed (as a friend of mine once told me, "You know, if you were any good at this investigating stuff, you'd find the monster"). From another perspective, though, we succeeded: We made a scientific, sincere effort to find hard evidence for the beast. We may have come up empty, but we still did one of the most thorough investigations ever. We simply found a fictional Ogopogo instead of a biological one.

Notes

1. Though the spelling *Naitaka* is very common, I have chosen to use the more authentic spelling *N'ha-a-itk* throughout this piece, except in quotations.

2. Note that the increases in Ogopogo sightings were strongly linked to publicity and not other sightings. The most likely explanation for the increased sightings is that people were more aware of the creature, were expecting to see it, and were interpreting ambiguous lake phenomena as Ogopogo even in the monster's absence. A similar spike occurred in 1981 at Lake Champlain following the publicity surrounding Sandra Mansi's photo of Champ.

References

Blackman, W. Haden. 1998. *The Field Guide to North American Monsters*. New York: Random House.

Clark, Jerome, and Nancy Pear. 1995. *Strange and Unexplained Happenings: When Nature Breaks the Rules of Science.* Detroit: Gale Research Inc.

Coleman, Loren, and Patrick Huyghe. 2003. *The Field Guide to Lake Monsters, Sea Serpents, and Other Mystery Denizens of the Deep.* New York: Tarcher.

Gaal, Arlene. 2005. Personal correspondence, January 24.

Gaal, Arlene. 1986. *Ogopogo: The True Story of the Okanagan Lake Million Dollar Monster.* Surrey, B.C.: Hancock House.

Gaal, Arlene. 2001. *In Search of Ogopogo.* Surrey, B.C.: Hancock House.

Kirk, John. 1998. *In the Domain of the Lake Monsters.* Toronto, Canada: Key Porter Books Ltd.

Mackal, Roy P. 1980. *Searching For Hidden Animals.* London: Cadogan Books.

Moon, Mary. 1977. *Ogopogo.* North Vancouver, Canada: J.J. Douglas Ltd.

Meurger, Michel, and Claude Gagnon. 1989. *Lake Monster Traditions: A Cross-Cultural Analysis.* London: Fortean Tomes.

Nickell, Joe. 2003. Legend of the Lake Champlain Monster. *Skeptical Inquirer* July/August.

Ogopogo. 2004. *Proof Positive: Evidence of the Paranormal.* Episode 9. The Sci Fi Channel, airdate December 1.

Radford, Benjamin. 2004. The Lady and the Champ. *Fortean Times* 182, April, 44.

Shuker, Karl. 1995. *In Search of Prehistoric Survivors.* London: Blandford Books.

Tully, Brock. 1982. *With Hope We Can All Find Ogopogo.* Vancouver: Intermedia Press Ltd.

Ultralight Flying! 2002. The Magazine of the U.S. Ultralight Association. January, Issue 309.

Commentary and Follow-Up

The Ogopogo investigation, like many that Joe and I did for television shows, was the result of discussions with the shows' producers. Instead of having one of us as a talking head expert discussing lake monsters, it seemed a better idea to actually go out and do an investigation. This not only made the shows more interesting and innovative, but also allowed us to take advantage of doing an investigation on National Geographic's dime. In other cases (for example, our investigation of Champ at Lake Champlain) we re-created for the Discovery Channel experiments we had done several years earlier. Returning to the site allowed us to do some follow-up investigation as well.

As with many cases of solved mysteries, the new information is very slow to make it into mainstream books on the topic. In 2009 I examined recent books to see if they had any mention of the work that Joe and I did on Ogopogo, Champ, or any of the other lake monsters years earlier. Sadly (and predictably), the authors of books such as *Mysteries of the World* (2007) and *The Element Encyclopedia of Magical Creatures* (2008) made no reference at all to any skeptical investigations. This is a frustrating problem for many scientific paranormal investigators—doing solid research that is generally ignored by later authors on the subjects, either due to poor scholarship or intentional mystery-mongering. This, in turn, perpetuates the public's idea that such phenomena have not been plausibly explained. Unless people actively seek skeptical or scientific materials, they are unlikely to find it.

CHAPTER 9
The Mysterious Santa Fe Courthouse Ghost

Santa Fe, New Mexico

Very few New Mexican ghosts have ever been photographed, and none as clearly as the mysterious, glowing white blob that was captured on videotape in 2007. Early on the otherwise mundane Friday morning of June 15, 2007—at 7:27 and eleven seconds, to be exact—Santa Fe deputy Alfred Arana saw a ghost.

He had been reviewing surveillance video from the previous evening at the First Judicial District courthouse on Catron street when he saw a mysterious, glowing white spot of light (see figure 9.1). The entity seemed to come out the courthouse's back door at the top right hand corner of the frame, cross in front of a parked police car, and then move diagonally offscreen, covering the distance in about ten seconds.

Arana walked to the side door to see if the bizarre object was still there. Instead of a glowing ghost, he saw only an empty area and a few bleary-eyed commuters heading to work or the nearest coffee shop. He waited until Sgt. Vanessa Pacheco arrived. "I've got something you should see," he said. "I can't explain it, I don't know what it is." The pair rewound the video and watched it together. As more court personnel showed up, the observers and theories multiplied.

It was soon dubbed the "Courthouse Ghost," and what started out as a minor local curiosity soon took on a life of its own as a full-blown mystery when state, national, and finally international press reports carried the story. The "ghost video" was eventually seen in various versions nearly 100,000 times on YouTube.com (at http://www.youtube.com/watch?v=ZBR6wD6rzPg).

A courthouse in Santa Fe, New Mexico, where a ghost was captured on video.

The Theories

Theories about the entity circulated outside the courtrooms, in downtown cafes, and on the Web site of the *Santa Fe New Mexican* newspaper. Some skeptical Santa Feans suggested earthbound explanations, such as a video glitch, a hoax, an insect, cottonwood tree fluff, or a reflection from a passing car. "Generally, most people who have seen the video believe it is some type of spirit or ghost," Sgt. Pacheco told the *Santa Fe New Mexican*. She added, "I don't believe in ghosts, so I don't think that's what it is."

Several people noted that the object seemed to be trailed by a shadow as it moved. Others saw odd faces in the blurry images; one woman,

Marylou Parna, saw a male's face in the image of the police car: two eyes, a nose, and lips. One anonymous woman who posted to the *New Mexican's* Web site claimed to be a spiritual reader, said that the video was clearly of a ghost. In fact, she saw five separate spirits in the video—including a man near the tree, a child, and a woman with a hat.

Santa Fe New Mexican journalist Jason Auslander noted reactions among courthouse staff:

> "To me, it looks like a person walking, but I don't know why they have this neon light on their head," said Steve Aarons, a lawyer. The light looked a bit like a crab and seemed to crawl like a bug, though Pacheco and others who regularly look at the video said they've seen bugs on the lens before, and they don't look like Friday's image [the ghost image].
>
> Perhaps the most bizarre aspect of the image is that it appears to cast shadows that look a bit like the movements of the invisible movie monster in the 1987 Arnold Schwarzenegger film, Predator. Many who watched the video said the shadows looked like legs. Mary Marlowe, another lawyer, said she saw hands in the image. Courthouse employees debated whether it might have been a reflection. However, the angle of the sun didn't fit with the image, and a large tree outside the door shaded most of the area from above.
>
> "It looks like a reflection of something but the angle of the sun is all wrong," said Juanita Sena-Shannon, a court clerk. District Judge Michael Vigil said he, too, thought it was a reflection at first, perhaps from a passing car. But when he looked closer, he realized a reflection would have moved in a straight line, which the light did not. "It doesn't make sense," the judge said. "It is bizarre." Arana said the footage was clearer when he first watched it than when it was replayed over and over Friday. During that first viewing, he said, it looked as if the light had stars in the shape of a diamond that were each spinning clockwise. Arana said he had no idea what the cameras might have captured."

One deputy suggested the ghost was perhaps that of a convict who had been killed at that very courthouse in 1985. (This specific spectral speculation was scuttled within days after the widow of the murdered man allegedly threatened to sue any courthouse personnel who repeated the

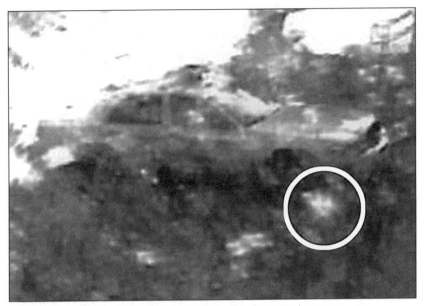

Figure 9.1, a mysterious object (circled) was captured on security camera.

story.) One woman said she believed the ghost was the spirit of a lost little girl; another woman noted that a nearby area was being excavated for a new convention center and suggested that perhaps an Indian burial ground was being disturbed. Yet another asked if a local psychic had been asked to contact the ghost and help put it to rest.

Jude Torres, employed as a courthouse janitor for four years, said that sometimes he encounters spooky sounds at night, phantom footsteps or doors closing apparently on their own accord. Despite his potentially spooky experiences, he thought that the ghost was in fact a spider. Public defender Earl Rhoads was similarly skeptical, suggesting a piece of cottonwood fluff was the culprit.

Hundreds of people posted their comments on the video at YouTube.com, swapping ideas and discrediting each other's theories. A sampling:

"It's a piece of plant matter, like a dandelion seed."

"It's a bug, a spider or something."

"The problem with the bug supposition is that it

doesn't account for the translucent shape that moves along underneath it. If it was a bug crawling across the lens it would be far blurrier and it also wouldn't appear to give off light. As the light ball passes in front of the cruiser, you can see right through it."

"In the original article it's clearly stated that the people who view the surveillance footage regularly know what bugs look like when they crawl across, and that it does not look like a bug of any sort. They would have known if it was any kind of bug or spider."

"It's obviously a ghost. Of a spider. That is haunting that parking lot. Where it met its untimely death the day before, when it got ran over."

"It's a hoax! None of the pixels in the image change in the slightest except the moving light. It's a still image with the light photoshopped into each frame."

"It's Bigfoot!"

"A mirror reflecting sunlight or a flashlight."

And so on. Dozens of theories and guesses, but no answers. Yet.

The Investigation

I was asked by Auslander from the *Santa Fe New Mexican* to look into the case. This was certainly mysterious, and I was intrigued. I examined the video, and sent Auslander the following quick-and-dirty analysis:

Having investigated haunted places and ghost sightings for years, I've seen dozens of "ghost" videos and images very similar to this. Usually they're simply misperceptions, camera or image glitches, or common objects like dust or insects. It just depends on the specific case, there isn't one blanket explanation for all ghost images.

The quality of the image is often inversely proportional to

the belief that the object is a ghost; the fuzzier and more ambiguous the form, the more likely it is that someone will suggest a ghost as an explanation. In cases like this, however, you
have to eliminate all alternative explanations, and for now a
ghost is way down on the list of likely candidates.

In the case of the courthouse ghost, nothing in the video
is in sharp focus, and it's hard to know how far away the object is from the camera; is it a half-inch fluff of floating cotton
hitting sunlight near the camera, or is it a two-foot glowing
ball farther away? At this point it's difficult to know which it
is, but logic suggests that people walking and driving by on
the street nearby would have noticed a giant glowing ball near
the courthouse.

Some people see a shadow following the object, which certainly makes the video more mysterious. There does seem to
be a slightly darker patch that follows underneath the glowing
object, but a closer inspection suggests that the "shadow" is
simply an artifact of the video image, not being cast by the object itself. As the video progresses, other parts of the scene
lighten and darken slightly, even though they are not near the
object.

I'm open to other possibilities, but my best guess at this
point is that it's a small floating object near the camera lens,
probably a fluff of cotton from the cottonwoods nearby, or
an insect or something like that. I plan to do more investigation and experiments to test my theory.

I quickly found that many of the "rational" explanations simply did
not fit the facts: If it was a prank, why would a hoaxer choose such an
odd, easily-missed phenomena to create—not to mention doing so on a
courthouse surveillance camera with police watching? If it was a reflection from a passing car, where was the car and why was the sun in the
wrong place to cause a reflection? If it was an insect on the camera lens,
why didn't it look like a bug, and why was it glowing? If it was a piece of
fluff from cottonwood trees, why did the object glow and seem to move

with intent? If it was a video glitch or artifact instead of a physical object, why did it seem to cast a shadow? Nothing seemed plausible; it was a puzzling case indeed.

Video Analyses

I spent several hours examining the video. The first question was about the shadow: was it real, or an optical illusion? There did seem to be a slightly darker patch following underneath the object as it moved, but a closer inspection revealed that the "shadow" closely followed the movements of the object on the video screen—not the texture of the terrain beneath it, as a shadow would do. It seemed the shadow was on the lens, not on the ground.

Amiran White/The New Mexican

A surveillance camera caught a mysterious light floating around the First Judicial District courthouse downtown early Friday.

'GHOST' KEEPS PEOPLE GUESSING

Image captured on courthouse camera has viewers baffled

By Jason Auslander
The New Mexican

Apparition or reflection, that is the question. A surveillance camera at the First Judicial District courthouse downtown captured

ON THE WEB a strange image Friday morning that left sheriff's deputies, lawyers,
♦ See the foot- clerks and judges scratching their

A second clue came from the angle of the sun; at one point the "shadow" appeared to be directly beneath the object, yet the video was shot at 7:28 in the morning, not midday when the sun is high overhead. Furthermore—and most obviously, in retrospect—if the object was giving off its own light, it would not cast its own shadow. Based on this analysis, I realized that the object was reflecting, not emitting, light. It was something the sun was hitting; not a video artifact, not itself a reflection, and not a glowing ghost.

The next question was of size. Since nothing in the video is in focus (you'd think a bottle of Windex would be in the court's budget), it's hard to know how far away the object was from the camera. Was it a tiny object near the lens, or a large object farther away? Logic suggested that people living in the apartments across the street and walking nearby would have noticed a large glowing ball near the courthouse. So it was instead small, and probably close to the camera. But what?

The Experiments

The two most likely explanations that fit the facts were a piece of floating tree debris or an insect of some sort. I needed to eliminate these remaining explanations before entertaining the ghost hypothesis. Could they have created the ghost image? Possibly, but without further tests I couldn't make any assumptions about how either would appear on camera.

I headed up Interstate 25 to Santa Fe and began an investigation at the courthouse, starting by taking measurements of the area. The camera was mounted 12 feet above the ground, 35 feet from the street, and about 48 feet from the police car seen in the video image.

A few courthouse employees watched me curiously as they (and I) went into work. "Are you looking for our ghost?" one woman asked as she passed by on the sidewalk. I nodded and told her I'd show her when I found it—preferably in a small box. A local television station had heard about my investigation and dispatched a reporter and cameraman.

Normally I'm not keen on having news media around when I'm doing an investigation; they tend to get in the way and expect quick, easy, TV-friendly answers to what can sometimes be difficult and complex mysteries. Definitive answers aren't always possible, and investigations are often solved by tedious trial and error. If they edit footage of the investigation the wrong way, you look like a fool. But the reporter seemed genuinely interested, so I cooperated and explained what I was trying to do.

My first experiment tested the floating cotton hypothesis. I wanted to have cotton drift past the surveillance camera to see if it later resembled the "ghost" on videotape. This was easier said than done, as the camera was far too high to reach. I searched the area and on the streetcorner found a few tree branches bundled for the garbage collector. I grabbed the longest one, sheared some extraneous twigs with a knife from my investigation kit, and attached a long plastic tube to it with some bits of wire. I then gently poked some cotton fluff into the top of the tube, hoisted it near the camera, and puffed. Two bits of cotton popped out and rather unconvincingly wafted back to the ground.

I probably looked a bit silly, a serious investigator blowing cotton fluff through a makeshift periscope tube, but the reporter remained interested. After all, while plenty of "watercooler investigators" and armchair theorists were idly guessing about what the ghost was, I was the only person on the scene actively investigating the case.

After a few attempts, we went inside the courthouse to review the resulting video with the court's deputies. The results were not encouraging: The cotton did make a fluffy ball, but it did not glow, nor did it move as the ghostly image had. A piece of wind-blown cotton seemed less likely than I had first expected. Even though the experiment "failed" it was valuable, since any valid experiment is a good one, helping eliminate possibilities.

The reporter left with a tentative explanation. Out of ideas and needing a green chile refuel, I headed over for a burrito lunch and ghosthunting analysis. It was pretty clear to me that the entity was something floating or moving close to the camera, but actually proving it to my satisfaction seemed very difficult. I felt tantalizingly close to solving the case, but despaired of finding a conclusive answer to the mystery that thousands of people were discussing and watching on YouTube at that very moment.

The cotton was unlikely, leaving insects as a possible solution. But I had no idea how to arrange an experiment with insects. I couldn't just buy a box of spiders, aphids, or trained fleas at Trader Joe's; even if I could, how would I get them onto the camera and crossing the lens in exactly the same way, in the same light?

That evening, I reviewed the video footage once again. The object looked more like an insect than ever, steeling my resolve to test it. The only insects I could think of that I could buy in quantity and on short notice were ladybug beetles (family *Coccinella*). I rushed to a nearby greenhouse just before it closed and purchased a bag of 1,750 ladybugs, with a few smaller incidental insects included as well (see figure 9.2). (It's a business expense, though I expected itemizing "Ladybugs for ghost investigation" would trigger an audit.)

Say Hello to My Little Friends

The next morning, an hour before sunrise, I returned to Santa Fe for a final attempt. It was important that the experiment conditions be as close

Figure 9.2, a bag of ladybugs used for an experiment to catch a ghost. The ladybugs were dumped into a plastic bottle and attached to a long pole.

to the original as possible. I arrived just before 7 AM, cut out the top of a plastic liter bottle and attached it to a collapsible aluminum pole designed for cleaning pools. As a few amused office workers stood by, I dumped a few hundred sleepy (or chilly) ladybugs into the makeshift cup and then onto the top of the camera (see figure 9.3). I noted the time to synchronize with the video's time code, took photos of the bugs, and waited for them to crawl around. Many tumbled off immediately. Some flew away, but a few lingered. I could only hope that they were feeling cooperative and would dutifully crawl across the lens.

As I watched, I realized with a wry irony that after all my preparation, . video analysis, and research, the definitive success or failure of my ghost investigation might come down to which direction, if any, some bugs decided to walk. So much for the glamour of ghost hunting; *X-Files* this ain't.

I repeated the process two more times, in ten-minute intervals. By 7:30 AM, I had run out of both time and ladybugs. This was it: Either I had found my ghost or I hadn't. I couldn't invest any more time on the case. A deputy came out to watch me, and we went inside to check the videotape.

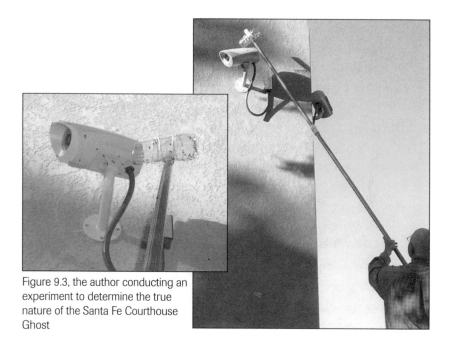

Figure 9.3, the author conducting an experiment to determine the true nature of the Santa Fe Courthouse Ghost

Let's Go to the Tape

The deputies rewound the video to replay the past fifteen minutes. For a few boring minutes, three police officers and I stared blankly at the videoscreen watching nothing unusual. It was getting slightly embarrassing for me, but finally a large ladybug crawled across the screen, and my heart sank. It did not match our ghost at all. It looked just like a ladybug, was dark instead of light, and was far too large. A few minutes later, a second insect also crossed the screen; it too was not a match. I sighed and began thinking of ways to put the best face on the case when, at 7:26 A.M., the ghost appeared.

"There it is!" I nearly shouted, pointing at the video monitor in vindication. "That's it!" Sure enough, the "Courthouse Ghost" moved across the video monitor. Everyone agreed that the image was exactly the same as the original ghost in every respect, including size, shape, color, and movement. "You got it," Deputy John Lucero said. "I'm convinced it was a bug." (A short clip can be seen at http://www.youtube.com/watch?v=9OhjYOhhMPc.)

The mystery was solved: The Santa Fe Courthouse Ghost was a bug. While I can't identify the exact species, there is no doubt that it was the unwitting YouTube star. It would be a pretty remarkable coincidence if the ghost just happened to reappear at exactly the same time as my test insects crawled across the lens.

The insect or spider explanation fit all the facts. The object was purposely moving, not floating; the object was blurry because it was close to the security camera's lens; it was glowing because direct morning sunlight hit the lens from a low angle; and the shadow it cast was on the glass of the camera casing. Plus, it appeared at almost exactly the same time of day, under the same conditions.

One lesson I learned from this case is how hard it is to definitively prove a particular solution. Some people suspected that the ghost was a bug or insect, but actually proving that took considerable time, effort, and luck. Speculation and conjecture are easy, requiring little or no effort. As always, the best way to find the truth behind a mystery is scientific, first-hand investigation.

Anyone could have been fooled by such an image, and the larger lesson is that just because something seems mysterious doesn't mean there isn't a good scientific explanation if you look hard enough. Labeling an odd phenomenon as "unexplained" is often simply laziness, the default result of giving up too easily.

After tests, the so-called Santa Fe Courthouse Ghost is revealed to be a bug

ALBUQUERQUE, N.M. (AP) — Jeepers, it was just one of those creepers.

An investigator specializing in all things bizarre has debugged the mystery of the Santa Fe Courthouse Ghost — a specter captured on a blurry surveillance videotape.

"In the end, it was in fact a bug or insect of some sort that was on the lens of the surveillance camera," said Benjamin Radford, a paranormal investigator and managing editor of Skeptical Inquirer magazine.

The image — a glowing spot drifting in front of a patrol car parked beneath some trees — generated more than 132,000 hits on YouTube since Santa Fe County Deputy Alfred Arana first noticed the image June 15.

"There were a wide variety of theories on what it was," said Radford. "Some said it was a ghost.

Some said it was drifting cottonwood fluff. Some said it was a prank."

But the one that stuck was a ghost.

Radford drove to Santa Fe to watch the original video, ruling out a couple of theories.

"If it was a reflection, what would be reflecting and why was the sun in the wrong place?" he said. "And why would someone conduct a prank on courthouse surveillance with deputies with guns watching? That didn't make sense."

After various tests, Radford shelled out $9 for 1,750 ladybugs and put the bugs on the camera casing. "Sure enough, we got the ghost," he said.

Radford said it's a rare definitive answer in his line of work investigating haunted houses, crop circles, psychics or Big Foot.

"This case was solved through logic, scientific analysis and methodology," he said.

That the Santa Fe Courthouse Ghost turned out to be an insect doesn't take away from its role as a ghost... in fact, the one thing that most skeptical investigators agree on is that many, many things can be mistaken for a ghost. Since no one knows for certain what a ghost is, it helps to have cases like these that have been conclusively solved, for it tells us what non-ghost phenomena have been interpreted as ghosts.

References

Auslander, Jason. 2007. Video: What was it at the courthouse? June 15. *Santa Fe New Mexican*, also at http://www.freenewmexican.com/news/63222.html.

Auslander, Jason. 2007. Ruling on courthouse ghost: Not likely. *The Santa Fe New Mexican*. June 21, also online at http://www.freenewmexican.com/news/63539.html.

Radford, Benjamin. 2007a. Capturing the Santa Fe 'Courthouse Ghost' *Fortean Times*, November.

Radford, Benjamin. 2007b. Santa Fe 'Courthouse Ghost' Mystery Solved. *Skeptical Inquirer*, 31(5), September/October.

Radford, Benjamin. 2007c. Catching the Courthouse Spirit. *Weekly Alibi* newspaper, 16 (43), October 25-31.

Commentary and Follow-up

This case eventually became of my best-known investigations to date, appearing on CNN, in the *Albuquerque Journal*, and even spawning its own Wikipedia entry. It's somewhat ironic since I briefly considered giving up the night before I solved the case. At the time it just seemed like a lot of work, but my perseverance paid off.

This case also involves one of my most devastating losses in terms of evidence: The videotape of my bug experiment was erased by the courthouse staff. I had been told that in order to get a copy of the tape I would need a judge's permission, so a few days later I wrote to the judge. Weeks went by, and I never heard back so I sent a follow-up letter. I finally got permission to get a copy of the tape about two months later—only to find out that the video had been erased and taped over within a few days of my investigation, as part of routine procedure. All my experiments were lost. Even though everyone at the courthouse saw the tape along with me and agreed that the images caused by the ghost and the bug were identical, I wanted to have something as compelling as the original video to prove that I had re-created the ghost. Fortunately, at the time I watched it I had with me a digital camera, and with it I took a very short video clip of the TV monitor as the tape replayed. I never expected to need or use it, since I was sure that I'd get a copy of the tape, but in the end it was all I had. Though the quality isn't great, it is video proof of the success of my investigation; it can be seen at http://www.youtube.com/watch?v=9OhjY-OhhMPc. Lesson learned; next time I'll make sure to get a copy of the evidence then and there.

This case is one of several in which my original theory turned out to be wrong. My experiments showed that cottonwood fluff was unlikely to create the ghost effect, and instead of trying to make the facts fit my first theory, I looked for better alternatives. It's important to always be open to better evidence, and try to disprove your favored explanation.

CHAPTER 10
The Amazing Lee B., Remote Viewer

Albuquerque, New Mexico

A fter publishing a column about psychics in December 2007, I got an e-mail from a man who claimed to have ESP abilities. Lee B. claimed to be a "remote viewer" and wrote, "The problem with your article is that you group psychics with anyone who claims to be psychic. I can describe hidden objects or photos better than you (keeping it simple so it's verifiable). Every time. Find an impartial party that can judge (and we both agree on) and $100 per round and you and I will play until you believe or go broke. Want an accurate prediction? I predict you won't take me up on this."

Lee's prediction turned out to be wrong, as I accepted his challenge— and it was not his last wrong prediction. I first asked Lee to explain, in detail, what exactly he could do and under what conditions. Lee replied, "Testing me is easy. Set something out on your kitchen table for me to look at, mark it some way with an 8 digit number via tape or tag. I'll check it out when I get a chance and let you know what I see. If you'd like to try this, let me know when the object is in place."

It seemed fair enough. I was familiar with the ways that he might try to weasel out of a wrong prediction, but I was willing to give it a shot. If he could really do what he claimed, that would indeed impress me, and perhaps warrant further investigation.

I searched my house for a good test object. I didn't want to make it too easy to guess what it might be. Although in theory I could have chosen nearly any object in the world, by specifying the place (home kitchen table), Lee had already greatly reduced the pool of likely target objects I might choose to use. It would have to be small enough to fit on a kitchen table, thus ruling out things such as a sofa or exercise machine. Instead, it would likely be something I could easily handle, and that would leave space on my kitchen table for its use as a table during the experiment. Whatever I chose would not be anything that would damage my kitchen table or harm me or others (such as a pool of acid), and it would not be something terribly exotic (such as a container of plutonium). Whatever was to sit on my kitchen table for a few days or a week would also probably not be something disgusting (like a bloody dog carcass) or perishable (such as a gallon of ice cream), and so on. It was, therefore, very likely to be an ordinary household object. This reduces the pool of likely targets from potentially millions of possible objects to a few dozen or so likely ones. (Check this yourself by cataloguing all the things in your home, from books to appliances to dishes, etc.)

I don't think Lee was purposely guiding the target selection in this way; he probably didn't realize how much his (quite reasonable) parameters narrowed the likely field—perhaps unduly impressing him with the

Figure 10.1, a remote viewer's sketches during a psychic experiment.

accuracy of his tests. This is where a good grasp of probability and statistics comes in handy. Even with the greatly narrowed target pool, I decided I could make a fair test of it. After all, if Lee correctly uniquely and correctly identified the target, the one-in-a hundred chance would still be impressive. I was game.

I chose an object and replied to him. "Is it really that simple? I have placed an object on my kitchen table, and attached to it is a piece of tape with the following 8 digits written on it: 21389512. I'll leave it on the table until Sunday, and take a digital photo of it and send it to you when you tell me what it is. How's that sound? I'm happy to think about the object, if that will help..."

Lee replied, "You don't need to, I'm going to look at it right where it is. I'll do it as soon as I can." I wrote back, "No problem, take as long as you like. I already took the photo of the object, in fact it's on my computer desktop, the file name says RVtarget.jpg. I guess you can't really remote view an electronic image ("I see ones and zeroes!"), but in case it helps..."

A few days later Lee wrote back, "Remember, remote viewing is more like a sport than anything else. Think of it as playing golf. We don't always hit a hole in one but we try to get close!" He directed me to a Web site where he had written out the information he had remote viewed, (http://www.dojopsi.com/tkr/goview.cfm?ID=136193&P=PE73QM2B7 D). He wrote, "recurring elements of wood, grass, earth, water and rock. Primarily wood; visuals look like deer antlers or tree branches and porcupine quills, deer; pin cushion; porcupine quills; wood slats; forest; lush green field; straw; coffee cup; empty bucket; something round, but in a cluster of at least two or more; this is likely an ornamental tree or plant in a clay pot."

In his e-mail he wrote, "Beginning to see more water in the target. Also, something corkscrews around as it goes up. Sort of like one of those old barber shop displays or a candy cane." He also included sketches of what he saw (see figure 10.1).

I looked them over and replied: "You have a lot of responses here, the most specific one is 'likely an ornamental tree or plant in a clay pot.' Do you want to go with that? Obviously the more guesses / attempts you put out, the more likely it is that one or more will match, so to be fair I think you should narrow it down to one or two images you feel strongest about."

Lee wrote back, "Well, I'm going to go with an extra small Christmas tree due to recurring images of quills and nettles, combined with a spiraling image which could be maybe garland or ribbon along with spherical objects which may be ornaments and water dripping. If you will allow me two, my second choice would be holly plant."

The fact that all this happened a few weeks before Christmas was interesting, and likely influenced his expectations about what might be on my kitchen table. I replied to him, attaching a photo of the target (see figure 10.2). "Okay, well, it's actually a small sculpture I made from a piece of coral I found in Roatan, Honduras, glued to a wooden base. I have attached a photo of it. It doesn't really have much in common with an extra small Christmas tree, or a holly plant... Of course no one is 100%. Do you want to try again?"

"Yeah, I'll try again. That one was hard, Ben. We don't usually actually name our targets, just describe them. But I am for giving an actual prediction if it makes it more interesting. Let me know when you're ready."

Figure 10.2, the target object for the psychic's test.

"Well, as long as the descriptions are specific enough, (and there aren't too many of them, so that yes, a few are right, but the other 25 are wrong) I guess that's okay. I have selected a different target. Do you want a different set of numbers, or the same number?"

"Different numbers..." I chose different numbers and a second object, a small home fire extinguisher (see figure 10.3). "Okay, the target object is now out. The new number is 12065503. I'll get a photo shortly."

A few days later I heard from Lee again: "Ben, I'm going to ditch my original session for this one, in which the object was shaped like a brick. I looked at it this morning and it looks more like a tube to me. Six to eight inches long and roughly two inches in diameter, situated on its side."

That was awfully general, so I responded, "Okay. Any colors or other details? You want to make two guesses at what it is?"

"I think it's reddish brown and made of glass. One end looks as though it has a spout or a cap on it. If I were to guess, I'd say a glass bottle."

Figure 10.3, the second test object for the remote viewer.

I replied, "Hi Lee. Well, I really can't give you this one... you're right, it is generally a tube shape, and does have a spout or cap (though almost every tube-shaped thing I can think of has a spout or cap on it), but it's not reddish brown, not made of glass (in fact there's no glass on it), is well over eight inches long, is well over two inches in diameter, and is standing upright instead of laying down. The

Figure 10.4, the object for the third and final test of Lee B.'s psychic remote viewing ability.

overall tube shape is a hit, but a lot of things are tube shaped: pens, water glasses, toothpaste tubes, cans of soda, flashlights, batteries, etc. How about we try one more?"

"Sure, we can try as many as you like, I need the practice :)>"

I found one more object (Figure 10.4), and e-mailed him as soon as it was ready. "Okay, let's give it one more shot! Here's the number: 63071086. It's ready now!"

A few days later Lee sent me another URL with his information: "round disc; satin silver; compact disc; wristwatch; bottle cap; looking through a glass door; likely a satin stainless steel wristwatch."

I looked over the list and wrote back; he threw out a lot of descriptors and possibilities, and I couldn't just pick a random one and accept it as his answer, I needed him to give me his best guess—or two.

"Hi Lee. Okay, hmm. So, if you had two guesses, what would they be?"

Later that day I got Lee's response: "Ben, I'm not sure. I don't have time right now to do it properly. Let's skip ahead to the point I was going to get at: We are all psychic. That means you, Ben. I spent very little time on your targets, if you can't see the correlations, then you are trying not to see. I'm trying to open your eyes, my friend. I don't really care if you think I have psi, I'm trying to help you see. I felt like by asking me to actually name the objects, you were building a case against it."

I wrote back a short note, explaining that I wasn't trying to disprove his abilities, but to simply finish the test under the conditions we'd both agreed to. Instead of admitting that he was completely wrong, he suggested that I was being biased or obstinate if I didn't agree that a watch, a CD, a bottle cap, or a glass door were close in description to a wooden clothespin. It was clear he was feeling defensive, and I didn't want to hurt his feelings by pressing the issue. The point of the experiment was not to attack or challenge him, but instead to see what he could do.

He replied, "The end result is not about me having psi. I already know I do and I know you do too. I'd like to inspire you to use your psi, Ben. It would be a piece of cake for a guy with your intelligence. It bugs me when someone such as yourself doesn't know what he can do. It's right at your fingertips. I confess, I am out of practice right now, work is busy and the holidays are here. But remember, I said it is more of a skill than a power. Best holiday wishes to you as well Ben, I'd like to keep in touch." With that, the remote viewer and I parted ways to attend to our own holiday headaches, and our little experiment ended.

Commentary and Follow-Up

Lee's remote viewing information was typical of failed psychic claimants, consisting of many different guesses, later retrofitted to see how the information could be interpreted to fit the revealed target. Lee, who began our correspondence by claiming he could remote view with accuracy "every time," lost interest in the testing when it became clear he wasn't succeeding. Instead of giving me his best remote viewing information about the third and final test, he changed the subject from testing his abilities to telling me that I should develop my own.

I am convinced that Lee, like most psychics I have met, is a sincere, honest person who genuinely believes he has the powers he claims. The fact that he failed three times in a row didn't seem to shake his belief in his powers; instead he found excuses: he was tired, out of practice, and distracted by the holidays. And all that may be true, but if we repeated the experiment at another time with the same results, he almost certainly would have found another set of similar excuses.

Lee practiced his remote viewing powers at a Web site called Dojo Psi, "a private club for Mental Martial Artists for discipline, exploration, education, and pursuit of remote viewing world applications." As he stated, he was not used to actually *identifying* targets in his tests, but merely *describing* them. This provides an interesting clue into why he had such misplaced confidence in his abilities.

The problem is of course that *identifications* are by definition *specific*, whereas *descriptions* are by definition *general*. A given description—even one that appears very specific—might fit a wide variety of objects, greatly increasing the "success rate" while not truly demonstrating remote viewing ability. For example, if Lee described a target as something small with square corners and writing and/or colors on it, that could apply equally well to a deck of cards, a pack of cigarettes, a stack of CD cases, a book, a business card, a magazine, a dollar bill, a receipt, a drink coaster, a mouse pad, a pocket calculator, or dozens of other things. If any of those had been chosen as the target, Lee would likely be very impressed with the accuracy of his remotely viewed information. When you combine this generalization effect with the limited pool of likely candidates for a target (i.e., not a sofa or a dead dog, as described earlier), the occasional correct guesses are not so remarkable. Lee—and Dojo Psi—are simply unfamiliar with good scientific controls that are required to test phenomena such as remote viewing. Excellent discussions of how to do such tests correctly can be found in the work of Richard Wiseman (1995, 1997) and Ray Hyman (1989, 2003), among others.

This experiment was not some trap devised by me to disprove his powers; we had agreed to the testing protocols under conditions he himself set up. We treated each other fairly and with respect. Though I purposely avoided choosing target objects that might be very common (such as a miniature Christmas tree or a glass bottle), everything was conducted on a firm but friendly and cooperative note. Perhaps Lee was right. Maybe I do have psychic powers, and I could remote view if I wanted to. I'm willing to give it a try, as long as the standard for success is raised high enough that a success is meaningful.

CHAPTER 11
The Mysterious Pokémon Panic

Tokyo, Japan

Pokémon (a shortening of "Pocket Monsters," from the original Japanese name Poketto Monsuta) began as a video game for the handheld Nintendo Game Boy system, and, by the late 1990s, took the world by storm. More than a game, more than a movie, even more than a merchandising juggernaut, it was and remains a phenomenon. It has spawned countless video games, comic books, Web sites, video tapes, magazines, clubs, music CDs, books, trading cards, films, and, of course, an animated television series. It became such a cultural phenomenon that Time magazine featured Pokémon on its November 22, 1999, cover.

For kids it was an engaging pastime; for Nintendo, it was a multi-billion dollar money maker, possibly the largest marketing effort in the history of toys. (The theme song's refrain contained a catchy ode to merchandising, "Gotta catch 'em all!") Satoshi Tajiri, the creator of Pokémon, spent six years developing the game and world of Pokémon.

The series centered on young boys and girls who wander the world of Pokémon looking for small creatures (called Pokémon) to capture, befriend, and train for battle against other trainers (and their Pokémon). The ultimate goal is for kids to collect one of every species and become Pokémon Masters. There are hundreds of different Pokémon, and each creature has special powers and individual personalities. The most popular Pokémon, Pikachu, looks something like a yellow rat with a lightning-bolt tail and has the ability to shock its opponents with electricity.

Although largely forgotten and rarely mentioned in recent news accounts of "Pokemania," Pokémon wasn't always the benign cartoon whose worst threat was draining bank accounts. In December 1997, up to 12,000 Japanese children reported illnesses ranging from nausea to seizures after watching an episode of Pokémon. The attacks baffled doctors and scientists; nothing of its kind had been seen before (or since).

The Episode and the Attacks

On Tuesday night, December 16, 1997, Pokémon episode number 38, Dennou Senshi Porigon (Computer Warrior Polygon) aired at 6:30. The program, broadcast over 37 television stations, was already very popular in Japan, and held the highest ratings for its time slot.

In the episode, Pikachu and its human friends Satoshi, Kasumi, and Takeshi, have an adventure that leads inside a computer. About 20 minutes into the program, the gang encounters a fighter named Polygon. A battle ensues, during which Pikachu uses his electricity powers to stop a "virus bomb." The animators depict Pikachu's electric attack with a quick series of red and blue flashing lights. At about 6:51, the flashing lights filled the screens. By 7:30, according to the Fire-Defense agency, 618 children had been taken to hospitals complaining of various symptoms.

News of the attacks shot through Japan, and it was the subject of media reports later that evening. During the coverage, several stations replayed the flashing sequence, whereupon even more children fell ill and sought medical attention. The number affected by this "second wave" is unknown.

In all, millions watched the initial program. In one section of Japan, Aichi Prefecture, an estimated 70 percent of the 24,000 elementary school students and 35 percent of the 13,000 junior high school students watched the program, for a total of over 21,000 in Aichi alone (Japan Times 1997). In Tokyo, the local board of education investigated all public kindergartens, primary and middle schools in the area and found that 50,714 students, or 55 percent of the whole, watched the episode (Yomiuri Shimbun 1997c).

Doctors said that children "went into a trance-like state, similar to hypnosis, complaining of shortness of breath, nausea, and bad vision..." (Snyder 1997). According to the *Yomiuri Shimbun* newspaper, "Victim's families reported that children passed out during the broadcast, went into convulsions, and vomited" (*Yomiuri Shimbun* 1997b). Yet another gives a slightly different set of ailments: "Most children reportedly said they felt sick and had vision problems..." (Nextgeneration.com 1997).

Cartoon On Japanese TV Makes Young Viewers Ill

Japanese cartoon pulled after kids suffer seizures

Japan seeks reason why cartoon led to seizures

The victims themselves described their attacks thusly: Ten-year-old Takuya Sato said "Toward the end of the program there was an explosion, and I had to close my eyes because of an enormous yellow light like a camera flash" (MSNBC 1997); a 15-year-old girl from Nagoya reported, "As I was watching blue and red lights flashing on the screen, I felt my body becoming tense. I do not remember what happened afterward" (*Asahi Shimbun* 1997a).

Information regarding exactly how many children became sick (and when) and how many were taken to hospitals is piecemeal and at times contradictory, but, as with many aspects of this case, specific figures are known for certain areas. One hospital in western Tokyo started to receive children shortly after 7 p.m. A *Yomiuri Shimbun* newspaper story states that, "A total of six children aged between 9 and 15 were taken to the hospital Tuesday night....After treatment there, all six returned home before midnight."(*Yomiuri Shimbun* 1997d).

The Aftermath

The story of thousands of children having been made ill by their favorite cartoon raced through Japan. The following day TV Tokyo issued an apology, suspended the program, and said it would investigate the cause of the seizures. Officers from Atago Police Station, acting on orders from the National Police Agency, questioned the program's producers about the cartoon's contents and production procedures. The Health and Welfare Ministry held an emergency meeting, discussing the case with experts and gathering information from hospitals. Video retailers across the country pulled the series from their rental shelves.

Outraged mothers accused TV Tokyo of ignoring their children's health in the race for ratings, while other parents called for the implementation of an electronic screening device similar to the American V-chip that would block out intense animation. Even Prime Minister Ryutaro Hashimoto weighed in with a comment of dubious relevance: "Rays and lasers have been considered for use as weapons. Their effects have not been fully determined." Although a spokesman from Nintendo rushed to explain that the only link between its game and the cartoon was the characters, the company's shares dropped nearly five percent on the Tokyo stock market.

TV Tokyo put warning labels on all future and past Pokémon episodes. Despite the scare, both kids and adults soon missed Pokémon. It was back on the air by April, along with the new release of spring shows, and promptly climbed up to third in the ratings.

The Search for Answers

Several reasons were put forth to explain why the episode might have caused the problems it did. That bright flashing lights can trigger seizures in some epileptics is fairly well established. There seems little doubt that at least some children did in fact experience seizures and other afflictions from watching Pokémon. Researchers believe the technique of flashing lights caused the problem, perhaps made worse by the alternating red/blue color pattern. And Dr. Akinori Hoshika, a neurologist at Tokyo Medical College, confirmed that optical stimulation can produce some of the symptoms found in the Pokémon victims (Sullivan 1997).

In 1994, the Independent Television Commission (ITC) in Britain limited commercial television ads and programs to a rate of three flashes per second. The move followed a 1993 incident in which a Pot Noodle advert featuring fast-moving graphics and bright flashes sparked three seizures. The ITC also recommended that images should not dominate the screen, and repetitive psychedelic patterns should be avoided.

After several teens suffered seizures while playing Nintendo video games, the company began including warning labels on much of its software. The notice told users that the games' graphics and animation could cause a *shigeki*, a strong stimulation resulting in unconsciousness or seizures. A "Consumer Information and Precautions Booklet" that comes with the Game Boy product states in part, "WARNING: A very small portion of the population have a condition which may cause them to experience epileptic seizures or have momentary loss of consciousness when viewing certain kinds of flashing lights or patterns that are commonly present in our daily environment....If you or your child experience any of the following symptoms: dizziness, altered vision, eye or muscle twitching, involuntary movements, loss of awareness, disorientation, or convulsions, DISCONTINUE USE IM-MEDIATELY and consult your physician." (See figure 11.1.)

In the Pokémon case, though, there appeared to be few leads to go on. Although the bright flashes seemed to be the likely culprit, the flashes had been used hundreds of times before without incident. The technique, called paka-paka, uses different-colored lights flashing alternately to create tension. It is common in anime, the distinctive Japanese animation technique used in Pokémon (and many other cartoons, such as *Voltron*, *Sailor Moon*, and *Speed Racer*).

There was apparently very little difference between episode 38 and the other Pokémon episodes. The best

EPILEPSY WARNING

⚠ WARNING

READ THIS NOTICE BEFORE YOU OR YOUR CHILD USE ANY VIDEO GAME

A very small portion of the population have a condition which may cause them to experience epileptic seizures or have momentary loss of consciousness when viewing certain kinds of flashing lights or patterns that are commonly present in our daily environment. These persons may experience seizures while watching some kinds of television pictures or playing certain video games. Players who have not had any previous seizures may nonetheless have an undetected epileptic condition.

If you or anyone in your family has experienced symptoms linked to an epileptic condition (e.g. a seizure or loss of awareness), immediately consult your physician before using any video games.

We recommend that parents observe their children while they play video games. If you or your child experience any of the following symptoms: dizziness, altered vision, eye or muscle twitching, involuntary movements, loss of awareness, disorientation, or convulsions, DISCONTINUE USE IMMEDIATELY and consult your physician.

FOLLOW THESE PRECAUTIONS WHENEVER USING VIDEO GAMES:
• When using your NES®, Super NES® or Nintendo® 64 do not sit or stand too close to the television screen. Play as far back from the screen as possible.
• Play video games on the smallest available television screen.
• Do not play if you are tired or need sleep.
• Always play in a well lit room.
• Be sure to take a 10 to 15 minute break every hour while playing

REPETITIVE STRAIN WARNING

⚠ WARNING

Some people may experience fatigue or discomfort after playing for a long time. Regardless of how you feel, you should ALWAYS take a 10 to 15 minute break every hour while playing. If your hands or arms become tired or uncomfortable while playing, stop and rest. If you continue to experience soreness or discomfort during or after play, listen to the signals your body is giving you. Stop playing and consult a doctor. Failure to do so could result in long term injury.

If your hands, wrist or arms have been injured or strained in other activities, use of your system could aggravate the condition. Before playing, consult a doctor.

Figure 11.1, warnings added to video game systems after the Pokémon panic over photosensitive epilepsy

guess was that the sheer number of flashes or length of the segment (reported as five to eight seconds, depending on the source) made the difference. Producer Takemoto Mori had used virtually identical *paka-paka* in most of the previous episodes, with slight variations in color and background combinations. "During editing, that particular portion didn't call my attention or bother me," he said. All Pokémon episodes were prescreened before airing, and no problems were reported.

Toshio Yamauchi, an epilepsy expert at Saitama University of Medicine outside Tokyo, suggested that the symptoms could be a one-time attack triggered by optical stimulus, which is different from epilepsy: "There have been many similar cartoon programs in the past, and I don't understand why the program this time caused so many attacks." This seemed a genuine mystery.

Baffled Scientists

Despite all the furor and theories, a clear genesis of the Pokémon panic remained elusive. After four months Nintendo announced that it could find no clear cause for the outbreak, and Pokémon returned to the airwaves. Further research was left to doctors later that year. To date there have been only a handful of accounts and analyses of the Pokémon episode in scientific journals, three of them published in the *Annals of Neurology* (one by Takashi Hayashi et al., another by Yushiro Yamashita et al., and a much more in-depth piece by Shozo Tobimatsu et al.).

Hayashi et al. (1998) surveyed patients in the Yamaguchi prefecture (population 1,550,000) and found 12 affected children with no history of epilepsy. During the program, two had fainted and ten had tonic-clonic convulsions (in which the victims lose consciousness, usually with a stiffening of the body and forceful expiration of air, along with muscle contractions and other symptoms). Eleven of the twelve had "epileptic EEG abnormalities or photosensitivity." The researchers concluded that the children had latent photosensitive conditions that became seizures when induced by the flashing lights. They further estimated the incidence of seizures triggered by Pokémon was greater than 1.5 per 10,000, ten times the incidence found by British researchers (Quirk et al. 1995).

Yamashita et al. (1998) investigated all the children in 80 elementary schools in an area with a population of 470,807. Out of the 32,083 students, only one child had a convulsion, but 1,002 reported minor symptoms. As half of all boys and girls saw the program, Yamashita et al. suggest that 6.25 percent of the children were affected. This is similar to the percentage of children in the general population who show photosensitivity (8.9 percent).

Tobimatsu et al. (1999) studied four children who had been affected by Pokémon. The authors write that "The probable cause [of the attacks] was PSE [photosensitive epilepsy] because a tremendous number of children developed similar symptoms at exactly the same time in a similar situation.... However it is not clear as to why so many children without any previous seizures [75 percent] were also affected or exactly which components of the cartoon [caused the attack]."

None of the children had a previous history of convulsions before the Pokémon episode, and all were found to be more sensitive to rapid color changes than monochromatic ones. All were considered to have PSE. The researchers suggest that "the rapid color changes in the cartoon thus provoked the seizures." The researchers believe that the children's sensitivity to color—in particular rapid changes between red and blue—played an important role in triggering the seizures (Tobimatsu 1999). Four children, however, represent a very small sample and the results found may not be applicable to the general population. It is clearly a descriptive study, not an experimental one.

The childrens' viewing habits and the physical setup of Japanese homes exacerbated the effect. In a country with over 126 million people in an area the size of Montana and a population density of 865 per square mile, Japanese homes are typically quite small. Big-screen televisions are the norm, and most living rooms could aptly be described as small theaters. Many children sit very close to the television as well; one 14-year-old boy sitting three feet [one meter] from his big-screen television was struck unconscious.

The Mass Hysteria Link

While most doctors seemed to believe that PSE was ultimately the answer, others expressed skepticism at the reported breadth of the outbreak.

Dr. Yashudi Maeda, of a Fukuoka children's hospital, suspected that "the cases [regarding video game seizures] were most likely epileptic fits due to hypersensitivity to light, but I am not sure about the cases in which children just felt sick."

ABC News reporter Mark Bloch (1997) also found some scientists skeptical:

> In fact, epilepsy experts interviewed by ABCNews.com were skeptical the seizures experienced by hundreds of viewers were triggered by an epilepsy-like syndrome. 'I've never heard anything like it,' said Dr. Jeffrey Cohen, director of the Epilepsy Program at the Clinical Neuro-Physiology Laboratory at New York's Beth Israel Medical Center. He said it's possible that a few of the children watching may have experienced photo-sensitive-induced seizures. 'But it's hard to conceive that 700 did.' Rika Kayama, psychologist and author of a book on video games and health, told Kyodo news that the illnesses might have been caused by photosensitive epilepsy or "group hysterics."

To understand why the Pokémon episode may qualify as a case of mass hysteria, a little background is necessary. Mass hysteria (or mass sociogenic illness [MSI], as it is also called) begins when individuals under stress unwittingly convert that stress into physical ills. Peers, family members, or friends may also begin exhibiting the symptoms through contagion, in which the suggestion of a threat can be enough to create symptoms. Outbreaks are most common in closed social units (such as schools, hospitals, or workplaces) and where afflicted individuals are under social pressure and stress.

The victims are firmly convinced their illness is "real," although extensive tests and investigations fail to identify a cause for the symptoms. Victims are usually very reluctant to accept the diagnosis, however, and remain convinced of the legitimacy of their illness (Stewart 1991). It should be understood that the illness complaints are real and verifiable; the victims are not imagining their problems. Episodes of mass hysteria can last anywhere from a couple of hours to a few weeks, with many averaging about a week. The cases usually arise quickly, peak, and then sub-side just as quickly. Media reports and publicity help fuel the hysteria as news of the affliction spreads, planting the idea or concern in the com-munity while reinforcing and validating the veracity of the illness for the initial victims.

Solving the Mystery

As I investigated the mystery and gathered information from news sources and medical journals, I also suspected that the panic was the re-sult of mass hysteria. It seemed to fit most of the facts, but there was one gaping hole in that theory: The children were presumably in separate houses when they were stricken, so there would be little opportunity for the contagion to spread. Sure, within each household a few children might have seizures, and other siblings might also be affected by seeing it. But thousands? If it was mass hysteria, it could not have spread to so many at one time. Photosensitive epilepsy could not adequately explain the phenomenon, but nor could mass hysteria. It was impossible.

The solution to the mystery appeared as I began constructing a time-line of the Pokémon Panic. I realized that the popular conception of what happened was not quite accurate.

The jump in reported cases (see figure 11.2) is strong evidence for the role the media played in the panic. According to news accounts of the time, the number of children said to be affected stays around 700 the evening of the Pokémon episode (Tuesday night) and the next day. The next morning "Television and newspaper headlines were dominated by the reports. 'Pokémon panic,' screamed national newspaper Mainichi" (MSNBC 1997). Japanese children who hadn't heard about their peers from the news or their parents learned of it that morning, when the seizures "were the talk of the schoolyards" (*Yomiuri Shimbun* 1997 b).

The timing, it turned out, was the key to solving the mystery. Once the children had a chance to hear panicky accounts of what had happened through the media, their friends, and their schools, the number of kids reported the next day to have been affected —two days before, Tuesday night— shot up a staggering 12,000 cases. The first accounts of thousands

Chronology of
the Pokémon Episode

Tuesday, December 16, 1997, 6:30 PM
Pokémon episode 38 airs; flashing lights segment begins about 6:50 PM; Fire-Defense Agency claims that between 6:50 and 7:30 PM, 618 children were taken to hospitals with convulsions, headaches, and vision problems.

Tuesday, December 16, 1997, later that night
Evening news reports that hundreds of children were taken to hospitals from Pokémon fits; some news programs re-broadcast the flashing lights scene. A second wave of children (number unknown) is affected after hearing or watching the news.

Wednesday, December 17, 1997
Pokémon attacks are "the talk of the schoolyards." Television and newspaper headlines Wednesday morning were dominated by the reports. The number of victims reported by the mass media ranges from over 600 to over 700.

Thursday, December 18, 1997
Yomiuri Shimbun newspaper reports that nearly 13,000 children had "at least minor symptoms," with 685 taken to hospitals.

Friday, December 19, 1997
Yomiuri Shimbun newspaper reports on completed investigation by the newspaper and local boards of education, finding the number of children reported to have experienced "fits, nausea, and other symptoms" to be 11,870.

Figure 11.2, timeline of the Pokémon Panic

of students being affected appear only after extensive media coverage and the opportunity for contagion in the schools. And schools are among the most common places for outbreaks of mass hysteria to begin (Stewart 1991).

• Many of the Pokémon-induced symptoms reported (e.g., headaches, dizziness, vomiting) are less typical of seizures than of mass hysteria. Conversely, symptoms that are associated with seizures (e.g., drooling, stiffness, tongue biting) were not found in Pokémon victims. Three other symptoms (convulsions, fainting, and nausea) that were common to Pokémon victims are associated with both seizures and mass hysteria (see figure 11.3).

It is important to distinguish seizures from epilepsy. A seizure is a *symptom* of epilepsy, which in turn is a general term for an underlying tendency of the brain to produce a variety of electrical energy that disrupts brain function. Seizures can be brought about through various ways (e.g., a lack of oxygen, brain injury, high fever), and one seizure does not in itself establish epilepsy. There are several

Symptom	Gran Mal Seizure	Mass Hysteria	Pokémon Episode
Convulsions	Yes	Yes	Yes
Fainting	Yes	Yes	Yes
Nausea	Yes	Yes	Yes
Drooling	Yes	Yes	No
Sudden crying	Yes	Yes	No
Urination	Yes	No	No
Bluish skin	Yes	No	No
Biting tongue	Yes	No	No
Headaches	No	Yes	Yes
Blurry vision	No	Yes	Yes

Figure 11.3, comparison of the medical symptoms exhibited by sufferers of gran mal seizures, mass hysteria, and the Pokémon seizures.

types of seizures; research by Tobimatsu et al. found that the Pokémon victims they studied all had generalized tonic-clonic seizures, so that is the type I have used for comparison.

Furthermore, the incidence of photosensitive epilepsy is estimated at 1 in 5,000 (Cohen 1999). Such an incidence (.002 percent of the population) comes nowhere near explaining the sheer number of children affected (in some cases nearly 7 percent of the viewers). This is not to say that some children did not endure seizures, but clearly the vast majority of children did not.

• Stress frequently plays an important role in cases of mass hysteria, and Japanese youth are under tremendous academic and social pressures to achieve. Japanese schools in particular are known as high stress-generating institutions, and students with low (or even mediocre) grades have been known to kill themselves. The week the episode aired, many Japanese youths were preparing for high school entrance exams and therefore already under added pressure (*Asahi Shimbun* 1997a).

• In Japanese culture, there is strong social pressure to conform and follow what others are doing. Bob Riel (1996), manager at a Boston-based cross-cultural training firm, puts it this way: "One of the most important traits of the Japanese mindset is its collective nature. In Japan, we comes before I— a concept that's taught early on. Unlike Western children, who are taught to be independent self-thinkers, Japanese children are educated in a way that stresses interdependence, and reliance on others. Many Japanese habits and customs stem from this desire to maintain the group." This type of collective social order makes a fertile ground for contagion.

Although widely regarded as a simple case of mass epileptic seizures, the 1997 Pokémon panic is much more complex than that. With very few exceptions, much of the media overlooked the possibility of, and contributing factors to, mass hysteria. Several researchers have noted that mass hysterias are probably more common than currently recognized (see, for example, Jones 2000).

Acknowledgments

I would like to thank Dr. Shozo Tobimatsu of the Neurological Institute at Kyushu University in Japan for his help in obtaining materials, as well as Dr. Steve Novella and Robert Bartholomew.

References

Altman, Lawrence K. 2000. Mysterious illnesses often turn out to be mass hysteria. *The New York Times* (January 18) pD-1.

AOL.com. 1999. Parent's guide to Pokemon. On AOL.com, December 3.

Asahi Shimbun [newspaper]. 1997a. Popular TV cartoon blamed for mass seizures (December 17).

Asahi Shimbun. 1997b. TV Tokyo to set cartoon guidelines, December 19.

Bartholomew, Robert. 1997. Collective delusions: A skeptic's guide. *Skeptical Inquirer* May/June 21(3), p.29.

Bartholomew, Robert. 1999. Epidemic hysteria in Virginia. *Southern Medical Journal* August, 92(8), p762.

Bloch, Mark. 1997. Seizure or hysteria? ABCNews.com, April 15.

CNN Headline News. 1997. Cartoon-based illness mystifies Japan, December 17.

Chua-Eoan, Howard and Tim Larimer. 1999. Beware of Pokemania. *Time*, November 22, 154(21) p.81.

Cohen Jeffrey. 1999. Personal correspondence, September 20.

Takashi Hayashi et al. 1998. Pocket Monsters, a popular television cartoon, attacks Japanese children. *Annals of Neurology* September, 44(3) p.427.

Japan Times. 1997. 'Pocket monsters' shocks TV viewers into convulsions, December 17.

Jones, Timothy F. et al. 2000. Mass sociogenic illness attributed to toxic exposure at a high school. *The New England Journal of Medicine*. January 13, 342(2), p.96.

MSNBC. 1997. Japanese 'toon wreaks havoc. MSNBC.com, December 17.

Next-generation.com. 1997. Monster scare prompts Nintendo stock freeze. December 17.

Pharmaceutical Information Associates, Ltd. 1994. Video games trigger seizures. *Medical Sciences Bulletin*, May.

Quirk, James A. et al. 1995. First seizures associated with playing electronic screen games: A community-based study in Great Britain. *Annals of Neurology*. June, 37(6), p. 734.

Riel, Bob. 1996. Understanding the Japanese mindset in *Relocation Journal and Real Estate News* (October); accessed at www.relojournal.com.

Snyder, Janet. 1997a. Cartoon sickens children. Reuters report on ABC News, December 17.

Snyder, Janet. 1997b. 'Monster' TV cartoon illness mystifies Japan. Reuters report, December 17.

Stewart, James R. 1991. The West Bank collective hysteria episode. *Skeptical Inquirer*. Winter, 15(2), p.153.

Sullivan, Kevin. 1997. Japan's cartoon violence TV networks criticized after children's seizures. *Washington Post Foreign Service*. December 19.

Tobimatsu, Shozo et al. 1999. Chromatic sensitive epilepsy: A variant of photosensitive epilepsy. *Annals of Neurology*. June, 45(6), p.790.

Watanabe, Chisaki. 1998. Japanese fans mourn rocker's death. Associated Press report, May 7.

Whitlock, James A.1999. Seizures and epilepsy: Frequently asked questions. Northeast Rehabilitation Hospital (New Hampshire, Salem).

Yamashita, Yushiro, et al. 1998. Pocket Monsters attacks Japanese children via media. *Annals of Neurology*. September, 44(3), p.428.

Yomiuri Shimbun. 1997a. TV Tokyo to investigate 'Pocket Monster' panic, December 18.

Yomiuri Shimbun. 1997b. Govt launches probe of 'Monster' cartoon, December 18.

Yomiuri Shimbun. 1997c. Psychiatrists seek animation probe, December 19.

Yomiuri Shimbun. 1997d. 360 children suffer fits while viewing TV cartoon, December 17.

Commentary and Follow-Up

The Pokémon Panic case was one of my early successes, and it is the only one (so far) published in a peer-reviewed medical publication, *The Southern Medical Journal*. I don't recall why exactly I chose that case to look into; I think I was just intrigued by the idea that no one had yet definitively found a solution to the mystery. This case, unlike most in this book, is a non-paranormal one. The same principles of investigation apply to any mystery, paranormal or otherwise.

This case is interesting for a number of reasons. First, the Pokémon investigation was essentially a forensic one. By the time I began investigating the case in 2000, three years had elapsed since the seizures. I didn't travel to Tokyo to investigate the case, but I did make many trips to the local university medical library, photocopying dozens of medical journal articles about photosensitive epilepsy.

Second, it showed that an informed layperson could contribute to (and actually solve) a mystery that had baffled doctors for years. True, I had experience in researching mass hysteria from my background in psychology, but I was hardly an authority on the topic. People much smarter than I had looked into the case, and I remember thinking to myself, "This has been examined by doctors around the world. What do you think you're going to find that they missed?" I didn't know, but I wanted to give it a shot, just to satisfy my own curiosity.

Parts of the mystery had already been figured out: there were indeed seizures in people with photosensitive epilepsy, but that did not account for the massive numbers of reports. The mass hysteria idea had been proposed, but largely dismissed because no one was able to explain how it could have spread. All the clues were there; solving the mystery simply required a fresh look, putting the pieces together in a different way.

CHAPTER 12
The White Witch of Rose Hall

Montego Bay, Jamaica

*"I always believed that that was a foolish superstition
.... I never believed that mad story."*

—*The White Witch of Rose Hall, by H.G. de Lisser, p. 117*

At first sight, Rose Hall looks like something out of a film. Nestled high on a hill near Montego Bay in Jamaica, it is a mansion (or "Great House"), once the center of a sprawling sugar plantation covering over a thousand acres. In the 1800s it was the finest Great House in all of Jamaica, a beautiful stone mansion surrounded by terraced lush lawns. H.G. de Lisser described it in his 1929 novel *The White Witch of Rose Hall*: "It stood out.... with all its blatant assertion of opulence and power" (de Lisser, p.7).

The main house is a rectangular stone and timber framed structure, soaring three stories over the verdant landscape. A double set of stone steps comes down the slope like a ridged granite tongue, leading to the open double doors of Rose Hall. Much of the stone was brought over from England on ships as ballast. The upper floor contains posh bedrooms, connected by a grand mahogany staircase to the lower ground floor and its kitchen, living room, and dining area. The house has been restored to its former opulence, with elegant drapes catching the ocean breeze coming over the turquoise Caribbean waters.

The plantation was eventually purchased by John W. Rollins, an American politician and businessman, and now is a thriving tourist attraction. As you drive up the curving road, there is little from outward appearance that the Great House looming ahead was the scene of some of the most horrific acts of the era—and indeed "one of the most haunted places in the Western Hemisphere," home to the feared White Witch of Rose Hall.

The White Witch of Rose Hall

The story of how a beautiful young girl became the most feared and hated woman in the Caribbean begins with a novel. *The White Witch of Rose Hall* was published in 1929 by Herbert G. de Lisser, a middle-class Jamaican of African and European descent. De Lisser wrote several books, though this is his best known; it is a story of sex, murder, jealousy and revenge, set on a blood-drenched tropical sugar plantation.

De Lisser's tale begins in 1831 as a young English bookkeeper named Robert Rutherford is sent to the Caribbean to learn the sugar trade. He

The Rose Hall Great House in Montego Bay, Jamaica, said to be one of the world's most haunted places, and home to the feared Annie Palmer.

arrives at Jamaica's Rose Hall Plantation, surrounded by slaves and greeted by a beautiful young woman named Annie Palmer. Palmer's husband John had recently and suddenly died, leaving Annie as the owner and mistress of Rose Hall. A mutual attraction flares, and Rutherford is hired to help administer the plantation. Soon Rutherford learns more about his employer and lover: Annie had moved with her parents to Haiti as a young girl and learned black magic ("the voodoo priests there, who are versed in all the old African sorcery... have seen in this wonderful young girl great occult possibilities..." (p. 128) Her parents then died, and Annie moved to Jamaica where she soon met and married John Palmer, who owned Rose Hall. John Palmer, like two of Annie's previous husbands, had died mysteriously.

Rutherford, though entranced by Annie's stunning beauty and strong will, also had eyes for his young housekeeper, Millicent, the daughter of Takoo, the most feared Obeah (voodoo priest) on the island. Millicent warned Rutherford of Annie's evil nature, relating stories of Annie's cruelty, murderous nature, and occult powers. Rutherford dismissed the claims as superstition and jealously, but his skepticism waned as he saw more of Annie's nature: ("Pride, and the life she has led, and the power she has had over her slaves, may have unhinged her brain... inordinate vanity and fierce passions may have unbalanced her, or insanity may be her heritage. Or traffic with evil things in Haiti may have affected her brain." (p. 240)

Annie discovers the affair, and soon Millicent becomes deathly ill, cursed by the White Witch of Rose Hall. Takoo and a handful of slaves take murderous revenge on Annie Palmer, killing her in her bedroom and finally ending her evil. As one character notes, "Annie Palmer has lived out of her time... with her will and ability, she might have made a great name for her-

The legend of the White Witch began with a lurid 1929 novel by H.G. de Lisser.

This portrait, said to be of Annie Palmer (dressed in her favorite color, blood red) hangs in Rose Hall.

self, and her iniquities might have counted as venial offences even if husband-killing were included among them." (p. 239)

The book is a popular and breezy read. As for its literary themes, University of South Carolina Professor Kwame S.N. Dawes notes, the book is largely a morality tale about the evils of Caribbean culture: "Annie's evil is, significantly,....discovered in her being totally inscribed and initiated into the ways of Caribbean society" (Dawes, 10).

The Story Behind the Story

The White Witch of Rose Hall is, according to the book's preface, "A very striking and curious story, founded on fact." Yet there is another account of Annie Palmer, a supposedly more historical and accurate one, upon which de Lisser based his novel.

To get this story, I visited Rose Hall in 2005, led by a young woman named Diana. Adorned in a white peasant blouse and colorful blue and purple skirt, she led me through Rose Hall, pausing every few minutes at various places (portraits, bedrooms, hallways, balconies, and so on) to relay the true story of Annie Palmer. Though the guide's tale was obviously well rehearsed, many Jamaicans know the legend—or some variation of it—by heart. For generations, young children have been told that if they don't behave, the murderous ghost of Annie Palmer will get them.

The infamous Rose Hall actually began as a sugar plantation named True Friendship, founded in 1746 by a man named Henry Fanning. Fanning soon married Rosa Kelly, the daughter of a local pastor. Fanning died six months later, and Rosa remarried twice more before her final marriage to a man named John Palmer in 1767. John and Rosa Palmer built Rose Hall between 1770 and 1780. Eventually Palmer's grandnephew, John Rose

Palmer, inherited the home. In 1820, Palmer met and married Annie May Patterson (also known variously as Annie May Patterson; Annee May Paterson; Annie Mae Patterson; and Annie Mary Paterson)—later to become known as the White Witch of Rose Hall (Henry 2006). She was murdered in 1831 or 1833, again depending on the source.

If there was a Great House on the isle of Jamaica that should house a ghost, it would be Rose Hall. The old wooden floors squeak for mercy with each step, and long curtains billow and snap in the warm coastal breezes.

The house constantly moves and creaks, the smallest sounds amplified by the cavernous hallways and high ceilings. The vintage, baroque furnishings (added at a later restoration) only add to the spooky sense. It is in this setting that another story of Annie Palmer is told:

Annie was "beautiful beyond compare; she had a rich throaty voice with black penetrating eyes... Her complexion was smooth, and she could shift from a gentle smiling creature to a haughty, cruel, sensual, cat-like woman, gracefully exuding both anger and sensuality... Annie had strength besides her cruelty. She had the power of a mind trained in sorcery. She believed in spirits and had the ability to project death fears in her slaves. She was the one plantation owner on the island who was not intimidated by obeah (voodoo) magic." (Henry 2006).

The main room of Rose Hall, whose former owners are said to haunt the place.

As a young girl living in Haiti she had become the favourite of a high voodoo priestess, who taught her in the dark arts. In fact, "It was this woman who taught Annie to believe in spirits, to regard the air as charged with the supernatural, over which she could gain control. She attended forbidden voodoo orgies, summoned by eerie drumbeats in the dead of night" (Anon 1967, p. 12).

She moved from Haiti to Jamaica, and soon met and married Rose Hall master John Palmer. According to one account, "John Palmer lived for three years after their marriage. Annie claimed he drank, that the second husband went mad and the third married her for money. The slaves said poison, stabbing, and strangulation did them in one by one" (Anon. 1967, 13).

According to Jeff Belanger, in his book *The World's Most Haunted Places*, "Annie killed John Palmer with poison, and then she closed off his bedroom and would not allow anyone to enter it" (Belanger 2004, 40). Another account adds that Annie brought in her paramour to make love to her next to her dying husband. She then hid her husband's

Figure 12.1, Diana, a tour guide at Rose Hall, pauses near Annie Palmer's tomb to tell the story of Annie's murder and return from the dead

corpse, "most effectively, it seems, since it has never been found" (Anon 1989, 132); indeed, psychic medium Eileen Garrett confirms, "No grave for him has ever been discovered" (Garrett 1969, 151). As for Annie's fourth husband, he also died under murky circumstances. His fate was apparently sanguineous, for "the room in which he died received no visitors, as the blood stains could not be removed from the floors" (Henry 2006).

Annie not only left a trail of dead husbands, she also delighted in acts of unspeakable cruelty and perversion. Annie's sadism was legendary, her wrath feared by all. She was said to enjoy watching the slaves being whipped and beaten from her balcony before retiring for the night. Once, when a servant displeased her, Annie had the poor fellow's head cut off and placed on a bamboo stake, left to rot in the tropical sun, the bloated flesh and horrible stench a warning to others.

According to writer Mike Henry, Annie "mesmerized the slaves with demonic acts of sensuality" (Henry 2006) —in fact, "her sexual desires knew no boundaries" and included sadism, transvestism (she was said to put on male clothes and ride across the estate, whipping the slaves into submission). Their pleadings and cries of pain only aroused her further, resulting in ever more brutal beatings.

Another writer, John Spencer, writes that Annie's perversions extended to her own stepson: "John Palmer's son, Annie Palmer's stepson, with whom she was having a sexual relationship, was also having a relationship of his own with one of the slave girls" which eventually led to jealousy and the slave girl's demise at Annie's hand (Spencer 1992, 134). In this case, one among many, Spencer's "factual" account clearly borrows the intrigue from de Lisser's novel.

Finally Annie's depravity grew too much, her fury too hot. She was killed in 1831 by a slave, and buried in a tomb near trees not far from Rose Hall (see figure 12.1). According to another account, "In 1833, Annie Palmer was murdered, apparently by her latest lover.... Household slaves found her strangled, mutilated body in her bedroom. They set fire to her bed, and later refused to dig her grave" (Anon 1989, 132).

The Real Annie Palmer

It is these events, these people, that serve as the basis for the haunting of Rose Hall. Obviously no one expects de Lisser's fictional Annie Palmer to haunt the Hall; instead it is the real woman whom de Lisser based the character on: the cruel, sensual, sadistic murderess who terrified Jamaica and spawned the legend. A few events in the "true story" have obviously been confused with events in the novel, but if even half of the story is accurate, de Lisser's novel actually dialed down the debauchery.

Many people have sought—and apparently found—evidence that Rose Hall was indeed the site of multiple murders and mayhem. Dennis William Hauck, in his International Directory of Haunted Places, states that "People touring the basement dungeon often hear tortured screams or are overcome by feelings of sadness." Furthermore, in 1905, a maid was "pushed to her death from an upstairs window" by the ghost (Hauck 2000, 189); or, if you prefer, "One of the last caretakers of the estate broke his neck when he

---

The Sunday Gleaner, November 21, 1965

The true tale of 'The White Witch of Rose Hall'

Death of a legend

by GEOFFREY S. YATES

First of two instalments

THE melodramatic legend of Mrs. Annie Palmer of Rose Hall and Palmyra in St. James, a woman of unknown origins and of sinister beauty, who was murdered by her slaves as a retribution for her wickedness, is widely known and implicitly believed in Jamaica.

It is frequently retold in magazine articles, and visitors to the island are regaled with lurid stories of debauchery and death which are alleged to have taken place at the once splendid plantation house. Sometimes the scene of Mrs. Palmer's murder is transferred to a nearby property.

There have however, always been bold spirits who have questioned the conglomeration of inconsistencies, inaccuracies and over-writing which bedevils the whole affair. It is behind

officially appointed receivers.

The receivers saw to the administration of slave labour, providing plantation supplies, food, clothing, medical attention, (such as it was in those days), doled out punishment if necessary, sold and shipped the sugar and rum. They were responsible for submitting accounts which were officially lodged with the Court, and which survive in the Jamaica Archives at Spanish Town.

In all these accounts, there is no mention of any money being spent on repairing or maintaining either Rose Hall or Palmyra Great House. The receivers, who were men of pro-

fell down the stone steps into the cellar....pushed by the ghost of Annie Palmer" (Spencer 1992, 134).

During the tour, I asked Diana if she'd ever seen a ghost or experienced anything supernatural at Rose Hall. He smiled slightly and said no. I gently prodded further, asking if she'd ever heard of any of the other tour guides having seen Annie. Her sheepish grin reappeared and she shook her head no. "Other people send photos, though," she said, and soon we arrived at the gift shop to see the images.

A large glass case displays dozens of testimonials, letters, and photographs from tourists. Many of them begin something like this: "My family and I visited Rose Hall last month. We had a wonderful visit, and didn't notice anything odd at the time, but when we returned home from holiday and developed our photos, we were shocked to see that we may have photographed Annie's ghost! Enclosed are two images showing a mysterious white area..."

The tourism potential of their resident ghost has not been lost on the owners of Rose Hall. The bar in the cellar offers "White Witch drinks," and an impressive array of shirts, books, bags, videos, and other White Witch merchandise. There's even a "White Witch" perfume for sale. (Curiously, Rose Hall has also co-opted country singer Johnny Cash as their own, with Cash CDs and memorabilia for sale. Cash has no connection to Rose Hall, but was friends of the owners, and owned a home nearby.)

Ghost Hunters and Psychics

Rose Hall has drawn dozens, if not hundreds, of ghost hunters (including Ghost Hunters International) and psychic mediums over the years who have attempted to divine the secrets of the haunted mansion and communicate with the ghost of Annie Palmer. Eileen Garrett (1893-1970), referred to as one of the most respected mediums of the twentieth century, visited Rose Hall in 1952 and, she claimed, contacted the spirit of Annie Palmer on Christmas day. "Even before entering the house, I was overwhelmed by clairvoyant impressions," she wrote in her book Many Voices. Garrett described her psychic impression of Annie: "She is not at all as attractive as reported... she looks to me in her late forties when killed [with] black hair and very flashing, stimulating blue eyes.... She must have known her life was in danger, since she was trying to escape. When I stood near the tree, I got this feeling of her terror... . It was near this tree that she was beaten, violated, and finally killed. ... She suffered through the night." Through Garrett, Annie Palmer's ghost vowed that "Nothing will grow or flourish or come to fruit. No children will be born here. I died unhallowed, but the force of my life is not spent, only my blood" (Garrett 1969, 154).

Garrett was soon overpowered by the ghost of Annie Palmer; she fell to the ground, moaning terribly and seemed to go into a trance. Later she spoke in a throaty woman's voice different than her own, apparently channeling Annie herself: "Let no one think this is the end of me. My shrieks will live and those that would seek to inherit will find a curse upon them" (Anon 1989, 133). From that point on, Rose Hall was tranquil, Annie apparently finally laid to rest.

According to my guide Diana (and Beverly Gordon, manager of the Rose Hall Great House), another group of psychics visited Rose Hall in 1971. They gathered around her stone tomb not far from Rose Hall, contacting Annie's spirit and trying to lay it to rest. "They tried to raise Annie, and she was giving them a hard time... she came out of the tomb, they were trying to get her back in and they could not. On her tomb they placed three crosses on three sides. They wanted to trap her spirit back inside the tomb." (42) According to Dennis William Hauck (2000) in his International

Dictionary of Haunted Places, "In 1978, over eight thousand people arrived at the estate to watch famous mediums and psychics from around the world contact Annie Palmer's spirit" (2000, 189). There are several Web sites about hauntings that include sections on Annie Palmer and Rose Hall, where amateur paranormal investigators post their experiences and "ghost photos." More on this presently.

In the White Witch mythos we have de Lisser's novel of Rose Hall, as well as the "real story" behind it. Yet we are not done, for the true story of the real Annie Palmer has yet to be told.

The *Real* Real Annie Palmer

> *"It is all guess and hearsay,' murmured Burbridge*
> *[of Annie Palmer].*
> *'It is most of it conjecture,' admitted Rider.*
> *'I said as much at the beginning.'"*

The real story of Annie Palmer can be found in an obscure 1965 research report by Geoffrey Yates, an Assistant Archivist at the Jamaica Archives. The following is summarized from his account, "Rose Hall: Death of a Legend," published in the *Sunday Gleaner* in 1965.

Annie Mary Paterson was born in 1802 in England. She traveled to the Caribbean as a child, though instead of being instructed in the dark voodoo arts in Haiti, she had a rather unremarkable youth. She did indeed marry John Rose Palmer at the age of 18 on March 28, 1820; the couple moved into Rose Hall, but Palmer's fortunes had ebbed and their life was one of debt and want, not opulence. John Palmer died seven years after their marriage, in 1827 at the age of forty-two. Palmer died several thousand pounds in debt, and Annie inherited little or nothing. Though John Palmer died young by modern standards, in those days of poor medical care (several decades before Louis Pasteur would refine germ theory) dying of fever—especially in the tropics—was not uncommon. Research into accounts of the day reveal not even a hint of any foul play in Palmer's death; as Yates puts it, "there was no murder, no motive and no evidence." As for Annie, she soon moved out of Rose Hall to another part of the island and never married again, dying in 1846. She was buried in the church yard in Montego Bay on July 9. The truth is as simple and mundane as that.

Thus it's clear that virtually everything in the "true story behind the story" is wrong. John Palmer was not rich, nor murdered for his money. (Nor, for that matter, is his corpse missing; record of his burial can be found in the St. James Parish Register.) Annie Palmer never learned voodoo, nor engaged in any murder, cruelty, or debauchery; she had only one husband, and she was not murdered in 1831 (nor 1833) but died of natural causes some fifteen years later. Nor was she even buried on the plantation; her "tomb" on the Rose Hall grounds—from which psychics claimed Annie's ghost emerged—is in fact empty and not a grave at all. According to Jamaica's main newspaper, The Daily Gleaner, "it is hard to believe that she was buried at Rose Hall" (Gleaner, 1966).

So how, then, did the convoluted story of the White Witch of Rose Hall arise? Sharp readers may have already guessed part of the solution to the mystery: It was not Annie Palmer but Rosa Palmer—Annie's husband's great-uncle's wife, born nearly a century earlier—who had four husbands, none of them murdered. In fact, Rosa Palmer was "to all accounts a lovable and gracious lady" (Thompson and Nelson, 2007, 26). The process is classic legend-making. People blended a few facts of Rosa Palmer's life with a few facts of Annie Palmer's life, creating a wholly fictional person whose only connection to Annie Palmer is a shared name.

Yates laments the "conglomeration of inconsistencies, inaccuracies, and over-writing which bedevils the whole affair.... I state categorically that neither Mrs. Rosa Palmer nor Mrs. Annie Mary Palmer was ever murdered by slaves at Rose Hall, that there is no evidence that either of them was involved in debauchery or unnatural cruelty, and that the commonly held tales of luxury... are without any foundation whatsoever." Furthermore, Yates states, "Nowhere in the official archives of Jamaica is there anything I have yet discovered which links either Rosa or Annie Palmer with any form of crime, debauchery, or unnatural death" (Yates 1965). Indeed, *The Daily Gleaner* noted "that practically every statement about [the story of Rose Hall's] leading characters is contrary to the evidence contained in the records of the time" (*Gleaner* 1966).

Another Caribbean Studies researcher, Dr. John Gilmore, agrees that the Annie Palmer story is pure fiction: "There's no doubt the White Witch story has been built up as a mainstay of the tourist industry in the past thirty years. The story has now been so widely propagated that it is taken at face value by many Jamaicans" (quoted in Anon 2006). A 1934 book by Joseph J. Williams on ghosts, psychics, and occult in Jamaica makes no mention at all of Rose Hall nor Annie Palmer—a strange oversight indeed, given that the legend of the White Witch is known throughout the island. It seems likely that Williams was aware that de Lisser's novel (and indeed the legend itself) were without factual basis.

And what of the tales of sadism and cruelty? Yates suggests that likely came from a Revered Hope Waddell, a minister who interviewed slaves at Rose Hall in 1830. Waddell, an abolitionist, was gathering information about slavery and heard stories about mistreatment. However, by his own account, his knowledge of the local dialect was dodgy and he likely misunderstood at least some of what he heard. He had a political axe to grind, and likely slanted his reporting to emphasize the cruelty of plantation owners. Weddell's report was repeated in a 1868 article in the Jamaican newspaper *The Falmouth Post* by its editor, John Castello. That's when the sordid story truly gained credibility: "Because it was in print, it became believed as true and then people started to look for blood stains and ghosts and saw them" (Yates 1968). Sixty-one years later, the story served as the basis for *The White Witch of Rose Hall.*

The mangled and misattributed tales might have been sorted out decades ago had earlier writers on the subject bothered to do any real scholarship. After 1929, the legend was perpetuated by writers far more interested in sensationalism than careful investigation. This case demonstrates shockingly poor research and wanton indifference to the facts—if not outright mystery mongering. Clearly those who profit from the myth, either those at Rose Hall or those who write about it, refuse to look too closely into the mystery. As always, it's much easier to simply repeat and regurgitate legends and myths without making any effort to sort fact from fancy.

In one typical example of breathtakingly lax research, writer John Spencer gives a short recounting in his book *The Encyclopedia of Ghosts and Spirits*: "Late in life, at the age of 72, John Palmer met and married a 28-year-old girl from Tahiti called Anne, who became the second mistress of Rose Hall" (p. 134). Well, not quite: John Palmer died at age 42, so his marriage thirty years later seems unlikely. He was actually 35 when he married Annie (not Anne)—who was 18, not 28 at the time—and who was actually from England by way of Haiti, not Tahiti! It takes real craftsmanship to pack so many significant errors into one sentence. With such shoddy research, it's no wonder that the true story of Annie Palmer has been badly garbled.

It seems that most visitors to Rose Hall, including tourists, ghost hunters, psychics, and writers take the touristy legends and myths at face value. Writers (it's hard to call them "researchers") such as Belanger, Spencer, Hauck, the *Ghost Hunters*, and others seem to have made little or no effort to tell fact from fiction. While bits of fact and accuracy occasionally (and probably inadvertently) creep in, their accounts are almost wholly fiction presented as historical reality.

Return to Rose Hall

"Your spectral [visions] are nothing real;
merely something you think up...
They are visions to frighten negroes and children."

The ghost of Annie Palmer cannot possibly haunt Rose Hall, for she is a fiction. The Annie Palmer described in all the popular accounts is a made-up legend mistakenly believed to be real, and not based on the life, character, or history of any actual person. This Annie Palmer could no more have a departed spirit than could Sherlock Holmes, Superman, or James Bond.

How, then, can we explain the evidence of hauntings at Rose Hall? We must re-examine the "evidence" that so many authors seem to find for the White Witch of Rose Hall. How do we explain that many psychics claimed to communicate with the ghost of a woman who never existed? Garrett, one of the world's top psychic mediums of the era, was certain that she contacted the spirit of Annie Palmer, and even "confirmed" purely fictional details of Annie's suffering and murder! What of the dozens of ghostly photographs displayed at Rose Hall, taken by tourists and amateur ghost hunters? How can ghost expert Jeff Belanger conclude that Rose Hall is "one of the world's most haunted places"?

In the case of the psychics, there are two possible explanations: either 1) they intentionally fabricated the contact, creating a hoax for publicity; or 2) they succumbed to the power of suggestion, and simply imagined their communication with Annie Palmer from the Great Beyond. I believe that the latter is far more likely: The so-called sensitives were simply hearing voices in their heads and mistaking them for otherworldly contact. Knowing the legend, it would be easy to imagine the contact and unwittingly improvise the story, giving plausible details. Suggestion combined with imagination is powerful indeed, and if you are of such a mind, it's easy to feel a slight unease or chill when you enter an area reputed to be haunted. Those feelings are subjective, and no more based in reality than the jangled nerves one may get while watching a suspense or horror film.

Even the least skeptical observer can find humor in a group of psychics gathered around "Annie's tomb," contacting her spirit with all the attendant gravity, pomp, and melodrama, only to later find the tomb was a tourist decoy with no connection to the real Annie Palmer. No wonder the psychics who gathered at Annie's tomb said her ghost was "giving them a hard time"—they weren't even at her grave!

This is a perfect example of why psychics have no role in scientific paranormal investigation.

Investigating the Ghost Photos

The terrifying tale is in tatters and the psychic mediums who claimed to communicate with the ghost of a person who never existed are discredited. But what of the other evidence, the haunting phenomena still reported to this day? Despite breathless claims of "tortured screams" emanating from the dungeon and rare sightings of Annie, it seems that those phenomena are apparently long gone (if they ever existed at all outside of writers' fancy). According to out guide, the Annie Palmer ghost experience has been reduced to "ghost" photographs taken by tourists and ghost enthusiasts. The amateur photographers may take dozens or hundreds of photos during a tour of Rose Hall, and often upon close inspection they will find a few that seem odd for some reason and conclude that they have captured a ghost.

One investigator who goes by the handle of Scuttles (at www.scaryplace.com) wrote of a Rose Hall ghostly image that was "taken with a digital camera I keep with me. It is a simple one that does not have the ability to do a 'double exposure'" (Scuttles, ND).

All cameras—even the simplest ones—can easily create double exposures. Given this person's obvious unfamiliarity with the basics of photography, it's not surprising that many of the images (such as orbs, haze, or streaks) would be interpreted as mysterious.

Most commonly, images are seen in a mysterious white form on Annie's bed (though it wasn't actually her bed, virtually all the original items having been destroyed in a fire). People also reported odd white forms in photos of mirrors and picture frames.

I examined the ghost photographs of Annie Palmer on display at Rose Hall. I instantly recognized most of the supposedly supernatural images as obvious camera artifacts. They were typical ghost images caused by light bleed, double exposures, long exposures, unnoticed flash reflections, pareidolia, and so on. Within half an hour I had duplicated most of them; below are three of the ghost photos offered at Rose Hall, along with brief explanations and my duplicate images.

Annie's Bed

Photographs of the bed in Annie Palmer's bedroom sometimes shows an eerie white light near the headboard. Nearly a dozen photos on display show this odd phenomenon. Some people see faces or other forms in the light, though the image has a simple explanation. The varnish on the wooden headboard is simply reflecting camera flash. Compare the original "ghost image" on the left with my photograph on the right. (See figure 12.2)

Ghostly Picture Frame

In an adjacent room, photographers have captured what appears to be a glowing ball of light above a bed. Some speculated that they had captured an image of the restless spirit of one of Annie's husbands above the bed in which he met his murderous demise. In fact, as you can see from my photograph, the light is simply another flash reflection off the glass on the picture on the wall behind the bed. (See figure 12.3)

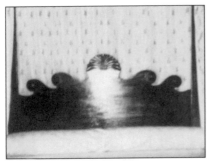

Figure 12.2, left, one original photo of a "ghostly presence" above a bed; on the right is the author's replication of the same effect.

Figure 12.3, left, one photograph of a ghostly white image on a picture frame; on the right is the author's replication of the same effect.

Figure 12.4, left, a "ghostly" photograph of a spooky glowing white streak or loop; on the right is the author's replication of the same effect.

Staircase ghost

The Rose Hall staircase has also been the site of a few ghostly images, most of them like the one shown here: a glowing white ribbon of light. This is a common image in ghost photography, and one of the easiest to explain. It is simply the flash reflection of a camera strap accidentally placed in front of the lens. (See figure 12.4)

Conclusion
"Men, alas, are not guided by logic!"
It is an irony that spirits at Rose Hall, "the most haunted house in the Western Hemisphere" (Time-Life 1989) and indeed one of "the world's most haunted places" (Belanger 2004)—as confirmed by a famous psychic medium—is in reality merely myth passed off by careless writers as fact. Some acknowledge that there is much legend and myth in the ghost story (it's hard to deny, given the heavy influence of de Lisser's book), but the mistake they make is assuming that somewhere amid the lurid stories and obvious folklore themes there must be some truth. While such stories sometimes contain a grain of truth, that is not always the case. Sometimes—I daresay often in "true account" ghost literature—pure fantasy is passed along as truth. All that glitters is not gold.

"Is it a sort of ghost, a fiend, some wretched African belief? Why do you people believe such horrible things?"
Though the ghost of Annie Palmer—like Annie Palmer herself—is a fiction, the story of the White Witch of Rose Hall has left victims and done damage to the credibility of some writers, psychics, and ghost hunters. But perhaps more tragically, the legacy of an innocent woman has been forever blighted by careless research and false accusations. As Terry Hawkins, a researcher whose uncle was an engineer on the Rose Hall restoration notes, Annie "was the blameless lady who has been constantly slandered by generations of ignorant people and whose very name is still being exploited to sell admission tickets to Rose Hall Great House. I hope that both James Castello and H.G. DeLisser, who originated and embellished this legend in

1868 and 1929 respectively, are spinning in their graves." (Hawkins 2008). Imagine if, a century from now, due to some strange mix of myth and circumstance, people describe you as a cruel, perverted, sadistic serial killer. Psychics claim to contact your spirit, and relay your sensational confessions to the public.

Still, some hold out hope that one day the truth will out. "Though Annie Palmer has been identified as the 'White Witch', it is possible that her name, like Rosa Palmer's, will be cleared, since no one so far has managed to unravel fact from fiction" (Thompson and Nelson, 2007, 27).

Finally, however, fact has been largely (if not wholly) separated from fiction in the case. Piece by piece, myth by myth, fact by fact, the mysterious and mad mosaic of the White Witch of Rose Hall finally comes together and is solved. The White Witch never was, and will never be.

References

Anon. 1967. *The Legend of Rose Hall*. Rollins Jamaica Ltd., Jamaica, pp. 3-13.

Anon. (n.d.) 'Visions in Paradise' (*The Metro*, London); available online at http://www.metro.co.uk/weird/article.html?in_article_id=17777&in_page_id=2.

Belanger, Jeff. 2004. *The World's Most Haunted Places*. Franklin Lakes, New Jersey: Career Press, pp 39-43.

Cornadle, Diana. 2006. Author interview, Rose Hall, Jamaica, November 21.

The Daily Gleaner. 1966. Rose Hall. May 27, p. 16.

Dawes, Kwame S.N. 1994. 'An Act of 'Unruly' Savagery: Re-Writing Black Rebellion in the Language of the Colonizer. H.G. de Lisser's The White Witch of Rosehall' in *Caribbean Quarterly* (March) 40(1).

DeLisser, Herbert G. 1929. *The White Witch of Rose Hall*. Ernest Benn Ltd., London.

Hauck, Dennis William. 2000. *The International Dictionary of Haunted Places*. New York: Penguin Books, p.189.

Henry, Mike. 2006. *Rose Hall's White Witch: The Legend of Annie Palmer*. LMH Publishing Ltd., Kingston, Jamaica, pp v-viii.

Garrett, Eileen. 1969. *Many Voices, The Autobiography of a Medium*. New York, New York: Dell.

Gordon, Barbara. 2004. Quoted in Belanger 2004.

Hawkins, Terry. 2008. *The True Story of Rose Hall* (book review posted at Amazon.com, May 8).

Liston, Richard. 2003. 'Trail of the Unexpected: Witchcraft, Voodoo, Sex and Murder at Rose Hall in Jamaica' in *The Independent- London*, 12 July.

Mackie, Erin. 2006. 'Jamaican Ladies and Tropical Charms.' In *Ariel* (April-July) 37(2), p.189.

Radford, Benjamin. 2007. The (Non)Mysterious Orbs. In *Skeptical Inquirer*, September/October.

'Scuttles' (pseud): Rose Hall Investigation. Available online at http://www.scaryplace .com/JamaicaTrip.html.

Spencer, John, and Anne Spencer. 1992. *The Encyclopedia of Ghosts and Spirits*. London, England: Headline Books, pp. 133-134.

Thompson, Orville, and Andrene Nelson. 2007. *The Preservation of Great Houses in Jamaica: Who Benefits?* (Case study from Global Travel and Tourism Partnership, New York); available online at http://www.gttp.org/docs/casestudies/2007/jamaica.pdf.

Time-Life. 1989. Hauntings in *Mysteries of the Unknown* series. Time-Life Books, Alexandria Virginia, pp. 132-133.

Williams, Joseph J. 1934. *Psychic Phenomena of Jamaica*. New York, New York: Dial Press.

Yates, Geoffrey. 1965. Rose Hall: Death of a Legend. *The Sunday Gleaner* (Jamaica), November 21, p. 7.

Acknowledgements

The unprecedented task of sorting myth from fact in the legend of the White Witch of Rose Hall was helped by various researchers and librarians, especially Timothy Binga of the Center for Inquiry library in Amherst, New York and Jenna Griffith. Thanks also to Jennifer Lawrason for her assistance.

Commentary and Follow-Up

The Rose Hall story is well-known, and appears in countless books on ghosts and hauntings (and Season 2 of *Ghost Hunters International*). I investigated the haunted house as a side trip to Jamaica, and, as with all field investigations, it's best to get as much material as you can then and there. Often mystery spots that are tourist attractions will have books, pamphlets, maps, brochures, etc. I usually purchase everything I can that might be relevant. You may think that you can get a book at a later time for a better price, but in many cases the materials (especially regional ones) simply are not available once you get home.

Sometimes in the course of an investigation I find that the mystery has already been solved (or partly solved) by a previous researcher whose work has been overlooked or ignored. Such is the case here, and it demonstrates the importance of doing thorough research. Had I not come across Geoffrey Yates's research from over forty years earlier, a big part of the Annie Palmer mystery would have been missing. To completely duplicate the work that Yates did on the true story of the Palmers might have cost a small fortune and taken weeks or months, if I could have done it at all. One of the pleasures (and duties) of doing investigations is giving credit to earlier researchers.

Will the definitive debunking of the White Witch of Rose Hall have any effect? Tourists will continue to go to Rose Hall seeking ghosts; tour operators at the Great House certainly have no reason to tell the true story of Annie Palmer. The *Ghost Hunters* team could have saved themselves some embarrassment if they had done any research on my investigation three years earlier (watching the investigators talk to the ghost of a fictional character is priceless). But what of future "true" ghost books and their writers—will *they* tell their readers about the careful, scientific investigation demonstrating that the Annie Palmer they describe was never a real woman but instead a mostly fictional hybrid of fact and fancy?

I know for a fact that Jeff Belanger (of Ghostvillage.com, "the Web's most popular paranormal destination") is aware of my Rose Hall investigation, because I sent it to him in 2008 as a professional courtesy. Yet in his 2009 book *Encyclopedia of Haunted Places: Ghostly Locales from Around the World,* the Rose Hall Great House appears on page 254—without a word about the mystery being solved. It is presented as a complete mystery, a spooky ghost story that no one had really investigated.

Will future writers on Rose Hall simply copy from Belanger's books and others, assuming that if the case had been solved (or at least credibly investigated), surely some writer would have mentioned it? As this case shows, one should never assume that previous writers or investigators on any paranormal subject did any research at all. Anything can be made to seem mysterious if you withhold some of the known facts. Examples like this demonstrate how the public is often misled about paranormal subjects.

This case is also interesting because, as with the Santa Fe Courthouse Ghost, the evidence is definitive that the ghost does not exist. Since people who never existed can't have ghosts or spirits, the story of Annie Palmer falls apart. I wish I could attribute my solving this mystery to investigative genius, but the truth is that anyone who took the time, did good research, and approached the topic analytically could have done the same. In fact, had any of the dozens of previous writers on the topic over the past forty years bothered to do more than a cut-and-paste job, they, not I or Geoffrey Yates, would be credited for solving the mystery of the White Witch of Rose Hall.

CHAPTER 13
Slaying the Vampire
Solving the Chupacabra Mystery

Puerto Rico, USA

B igfoot, the mysterious creature said to roam the North American wilderness, is named after what it leaves behind: big footprints. Bigfoot's Hispanic cousin, the chupacabra, is also known less for what it is than for what it leaves behind: dead animals mysteriously drained of blood. Goats are said to be its favorite prey (chupacabra means goat sucker in Spanish).

The creature first gained international notoriety in 1995 after an eyewitness in Puerto Rico, Madelyne Tolentino, provided a detailed description of what would become the world-famous chupacabra. The animal seemingly sprang into existence from out of nowhere, and many believe it is the product of aliens or secret U.S. government experiments in the jungles of Puerto Rico. The menancing goatsucker had a heyday of about five years, when it was widely reported in Mexico, Chile, Nicaragua, Spain, Argentina, and Florida, among other places in the southern United States and Latin America. In 2002, one writer noted, "Not since the advent of crop circles has a strange phenomenon been so quickly assimilated into popular culture. Chupacabra is now equal

The chupacabra sighted by M. Tolentino in Puerto Rico, from a drawing by J. Martin, 1995. It is close, but not entirely faithful, to Tolentino's description.

to the Loch Ness Monster or Bigfoot as a cultural icon" (Chupacabras 2002). Though the chupacabra is well known, it has been the subject of remarkably little serious, empirical research. While a few authors write with some scholarship on the chupacabra, the vast majority of information on the subject is rife with error, mistaken assumptions, and misinformation. In the world of chupacabra, proven facts and wild speculation mix freely and indistinguishably. Researcher Karl Shuker (2009) lamented the "immense confusion and contradiction" surrounding the chupacabra, making it "almost impossible to distinguish fact from fiction, and reality from hearsay and local lore." I took Shuker's statement as a challenge, to see if I could be the first person to definitively solve the mystery.

The Investigation Begins

One of the first steps in this investigation was finding out what, exactly, people believed the chupacabra to be. Since no one is certain what the beast is, the issue became what people were reporting as chupacabra-related phenomena.

Having spent many years investigating mystery animals, I had a pretty good idea of what the "standard" chupacabra looked like. Tolentino said the chupacabra she saw had dark eyes that went up the temples and spread around the sides; it was about four feet high, walked like a human on two legs, and had thin arms and legs, with three fingers and toes at the end of each limb. It had no ears or nose, but instead two small airholes, and long spikes down the creature's back. A sketch by Jorge Martin based on her description (but with a few inaccuracies, such as muscular instead of thin legs) was widely circulated.

I discovered that, while this was the most common description, there were many variations. Depending on which book you read (or whose eyewitness account you believe) the chupacabra has either a "powerful tail" or it has no tail at all; it either spends most of its time flying in the night skies—or doesn't, since it lacks wings. It might have three fingers on each hand, or four; it might have a row of distinctive spikes running down its back—or it might not. Its ears are either "big" or they are "small or absent." At least one person suggested that the chupacabra had language skills and could understand spoken Spanish (including profanities; Corrales 1995, 107). A farmer named Rafael Moreno was concerned that a chupacabra had taken sexual liberties with his cows. (Loren Coleman, in his 2003 book *Bigfoot!*, included reports of Bigfoot raping cows as well.)

Most of these descriptions were from Puerto Rico around 1995, but when the beast was later reported in other countries, it took on a very different form. A few were found dead (for example in Nicaragua and Texas), and the carcasses turned out to be small, four-legged beasts looking very much like a hairless dog or coyote. I also noted another curious element: many, perhaps most, of the chupacabra reports were not sightings of the mysterious monster at all, but merely of animals whose deaths were *assumed* to be caused by the beast.

Tracking the Chupacabra

The next step was identifying and analyzing the central claims about the chupacabra, including 1) Where did the chupacabra come from, and why did it suddenly appear in 1995 Puerto Rico?; 2) Why were the original Puerto Rican chupacabra sightings so different from the dead "chupacabras" found in Texas and elsewhere?; 3) What killed the victims of the suspected chupacabra attacks?; and 4) What did the DNA tests on the found "chupacabra" reveal, and is there any way to know if they truly are samples of the Hispanic vampire beast?

Over the course of several years, most of these questions were answered through research. For example, the question of what mysteriously mutilated (and/or exsanguinated) livestock was answered decades ago in the context of cattle mutilations (see, for example, Stewart 1977). Furthermore, a close examination of chupacabra victims by Puerto Rican veterinarian David Morales revealed that, contrary to popular claims, the animals had *not* been drained of blood (Morales 2005). The investigative principle Hyman's Categorical Imperative states that before we investigate why or how a phenomenon occurred, we must first be sure that it *did* occur. In this case, there is no evidence that "mysterious" blood loss actually occurred, so I turned my investigation efforts to understanding why people would *think* that it had occurred. To address that question I consulted forensic and veterinary textbooks, and interviewed a forensic pathologist at the Office of the Medical Examiner in Al-

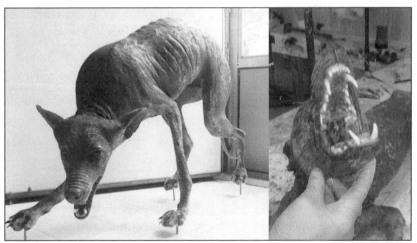

Photos of one of the Texas chupacabras, this one found in Blanco, Texas. This one was later displayed at a creationist museum. Photos courtesy of Jerry Ayer.

buquerque, New Mexico. As it turns out, confirming blood loss is impossible without conducting a professional necropsy (Geberth 1996 and Cunliffe 2009).

This information also helped to answer the next question: If there was no mysterious blood loss or unexplained element to the deaths, then what *did* kill the animals? To answer this question, I researched the subject of wildlife predation. I tracked down obscure, out-of-print government publications containing descriptions and photographs of predation by dogs and coyotes (see, for example, Wade and Bowns 1984). I also interviewed experts including the state director for Texas Wildlife Services, who confirmed that the marks found on animals killed by dogs and coyotes can look exactly like those found on suspected chupacabra victims. The principle of Occam's Razor suggests that if the marks discovered on a dead goat's throat could have been made either by coyotes (animals that are known to exist and proven to kill livestock), or chupacabras (creatures never proven to exist), then coyotes are the logical explanation.

Also through researching original sources it became clear why the Puerto Rican chupacabra was so different from later incarnations of the same beast: Eyewitnesses were seeing a wide variety of different things and referring to them all as *chupacabra*. The four-foot-tall bipedal creature with spikes down its back originally seen in Puerto Rico could not be the same coyote-like animal found dead on Texas ranches.

The solution to another mystery—the biological identities of the dead, found "chupacabras"—was answered through research and investigation. I consulted information on Web sites and podcasts, obtained copies of the DNA results in several cases, and interviewed both chupacabra owners and the scientists who conducted the genetic testing on their carcasses. I also investigated the issue of whether or not it was physically possible for the dead beasts to have vampirized their victims in the signature chupacabra style; the answer was no.

Since the bloodsucking chupacabra has a strong cultural aspect (for example it is almost exclusively seen in Spanish-speaking countries and regions), I also researched Latin American, Hispanic, and Puerto Rican vampire folklore. This helped me understand the cultural background and social environment from which the chupacabra emerged.

Investigating New Reports

Investigating the chupacabra took several years, and by paying close attention to news stories about the vampire beast I was able to track down each new sighting immediately after it occurred. In the case of the most famous beast, the "Cuero chupacabra," I was asked to be part of the History Channel television program *MonsterQuest* and flew to San Antonio, Texas, to examine the frozen monster. I spent about a week interviewing the chupacabra's owner, Phylis Canion, and examining her creature.

I live in the Southwestern United States, where several chupacabra reports appeared almost literally in my back yard. For example, in 2002 a man found what he believed to be a dead chupacabra on a sunny mesa west of Albuquerque, New Mexico. When I saw the news report, I immediately identified the "chupacabra" from an identical sample in my personal collection of cryptozoological artifacts, and then contacted the news media to help explain the creature. In 2007, only a few miles from where the 2002 chupacabra was found, a strange dog-like animal that resembled the chupacabra found in Cuero was seen and photographed near the Rio Grande river.

In 2008 I conducted an extensive field expedition in search of the chupacabra. I studied the history of sightings, in order to find the most probable place in the world where chupacabra animals, if they exist, might still be living. I ruled out Puerto Rico, as no sightings had appeared there in many years (Downes 2008); and reached a similar conclusion about Texas, since the recent sightings had been identified as dogs and coyotes. I concluded that the best place to find an extant population of chupacabras would be in the jungles of Nicaragua, near the San Juan River, on the border with Costa Rica. Two colleagues and I searched the rainforest for several days and hired an expert tracker to seek evidence of the beast (Radford 2010).

The Missing Piece of the Puzzle

By the summer of 2009 my research had answered nearly all of the central questions about the chupacabra. But one key mystery remained: why did the goatsucker appear more or less out of the blue (some say out of the Puerto Rican jungle) in 1995? There are no other animals in the world that are claimed to have spontaneously appeared (and certainly not in so specific a place and time). Even Bigfoot and the Loch Ness monster may have existed in anecdotal reports and legends long ago (though evidence for this is dubious; see Radford and Nickell 2007). Real, living creatures simply do not appear out of thin air, and even if the chupacabra is a product of folklore, it still must have come from *somewhere*.

Solutions to some parts of the chupacabra mystery were proven or hypothesized elsewhere, but the monster's origin had been an impenetrable mystery since 1995. I had already done far more investigation and research than anyone else on the subject, but I felt that if I couldn't explain its origin, any solution to the mystery I proposed would be incomplete. To figure out where the monster came from I'd have to return to its original sighting.

A young woman named Madelyne Tolentino of Puerto Rico gave

the most important chupacabra description on record, not only because of its remarkable detail but also because it is the "original" eyewitness description upon which almost all images of the creature are based.

Tolentino claims that she saw the creature near the street from her mother's house during the second week of August, 1995. Her account appears in Scott Corrales's book *Chupacabras and Other Mysteries* (Corrales 1997). Upon reading this story (and making lots of notes in the margins) it soon became clear why most writers only briefly summarize Tolentino's description: this "eyewitness account" is riddled with implausible observations, contradictions, and inconsistencies.

To give just one example, after Tolentino claims she saw the monster with alien eyes and spikes down its back, she didn't panic, but instead joked to her mother about the chupacabra's apparent lack of an anus. That she could possibly have noticed such a detail from a distance defies credulity, but in any event she later screamed, and her mother then ran into the street to catch the monster. She failed, but Tolentino says a local boy chased it into a nearby wooded area where he grabbed the menacing chupacabra and pried its mouth open before releasing it into the wild.

There was not a shred of evidence to support Tolentino's incredible story, and it seems her mother and the young boy who gave the monster a dental exam were apparently not even interviewed. Yet her "eyewitness report" was treated as valid and truthful by the media, and her description became the "standard" chupacabra image known worldwide.

This revelation spelled real trouble for the chupacabra; the entire goatsucker phenomenon began with Tolentino and her sighting; if this most important eyewitness account is not credible, her description—and much of the information that followed it—is irrefutably tainted. If large parts of her story were almost certainly not true, what other parts weren't true? Was any of it real? Was Madelyne Tolentino lying, telling tall tales, or did she actually see something unknown? If it was a hoax or hallucination, where did she come up with such a detailed description? I felt tantalizingly close to the answer, but I was unable to locate her for an interview, and anyway the mystery of why the creature was suddenly sighted in August 1995 remained unanswered.

Tolentino's story was clearly suspect, but unless I could prove beyond any doubt that her report was false, the case would never really be closed. Whether or not the chupacabra is entirely a product of culture can be debated, but the monster's strong pop culture element is undeniable. I searched for something—anything—that might have appeared in Puerto Rico around the time of the first chupacabra sighting that plausibly explains its origin. I researched the history of Puerto Rico, especially in the months leading up to Tolentino's "sighting." I uncovered many things, from a looming hurricane to a dengue fever outbreak, and finally I discovered a clue.

Left, the chupacabra that eyewitness M. Tolentino described seeing in August 1995. Right, the monster from the film *Species* which was seen in Puerto Rico by Tolentino and others at the height of the chupacabra panic. Illustration by the author.

Just before Tolentino's sighting, a new element was added to the island's social and cultural mix—something that had not existed there before and could have spawned chupacabra sightings. The creature Tolentino described bears no resemblance to any known animal. It does, however, look almost exactly like a *fictional* creature seen by hundreds of thousands of people in 1995: Sil.

What Species Is the Chupacabra?

Sil is the name of the alien creature played by Natasha Henstridge in the science-fiction horror film *Species*. *Species* was released in Puerto Rico on July 7, 1995—less than a month before Tolentino reported her chupacabra sighting. The creatures looked very similar; could the original chupacabra eyewitness have simply described a monster she saw in a movie? It's certainly possible; other monster witnesses have described "real-life" monsters that they actually saw in films (see, for example, Loxton 2009).

This lead seemed promising, but I needed more information. I reviewed the movie's press kit and production notes, and interviewed the film's production coordinator for insight into the development of the Sil alien design. I also bought a book on the making of the film (Giger 1995), which contained excellent reference material, including dozens of photographs of artist H.R. Giger's designs for the Sil creature. The art could have been used as a blueprint for creating a chupacabra. Sketches of the chupacabra's long, thin fingers and claws appear on page 24; the goatsucker's distinctive spine spikes can be seen on the *Species* creature on pages 25 through 29 and throughout the book; and so on.

I carefully reviewed Tolentino's description and compared it to the *Species* alien, identifying over a dozen morphological similarities, including the large, oblong head; large, wraparound eye shape; black or red eyes; a small or nonexistent nose; the absence of ears, the bipedal stance; long, thin arms; long thin legs; thin, clawed fingers; a small, lipless mouth, large spikes down the spine; lack of a tail, and so on. The resemblance of Sil to the Puerto Rican chupacabra is unmistakable.

The more I researched the alien monster in *Species*, the more similarities to the chupacabra emerged—they even have identical origin stories. The two main explanations for the chupacabra are that it is either an extraterrestrial alien life form, or the result of top secret U.S. government genetics experiments gone wrong. These happen to be *exactly* the two origin explanations of the *Species* creature: Sil is *both* an extraterrestrial alien *and* the result of top secret U.S. government genetics experiments gone wrong. Oh, and the first scene of the film is actually set in Puerto Rico. The parallels could not be clearer, and this seemed to be a strange case of life imitating art.

I had more or less proved a direct connection between the film *Species* and the Puerto Rican chupacabra, but just because the film was seen in Puerto Rico right before the chupacabra was first reported does not prove that Tolentino's eyewitness description of her chupacabra sighting was influenced by the film. Unless I could prove for certain that Tolentino saw the movie—and was thus exposed to its chupacabra-like alien—prior to her report, the link was strong but not conclusive.

As luck (and good research) would have it, I was able to prove that Madelyne Tolentino saw *Species* before her chupacabra sighting. She stated it very clearly during a 1996 interview with two researchers, reprinted in *Chupacabras and Other Mysteries*. Tolentino said that she saw "a movie called *Species*... The movie begins here in Puerto Rico, at the Arecibo observatory." In fact, Tolentino herself described Sil and the chupacabra she saw as looking nearly identical: "[The monster] was a creature that looked like the chupacabra, with spines on its back and all....The resemblance to the chupacabra was really impressive." Tolentino said, "I watched the movie and wondered, 'My God! How can they make a movie like that, when these things are happening in Puerto Rico?'" She was then asked, "In other words, does it [the film] make you think there might have been an experiment in which a being escaped and is now at large? [at the time of the interview, in 1996 Puerto Rico]" Tolentino's answer is "Yes."

Thus it seem that Tolentino believed that the creatures and events she saw in *Species were actually happening in reality in Puerto Rico at the time*. Remember, *Species* was seen by the Puerto Rican public at the exact same time that the chupacabra hysteria occurred. This confusion between fact and fiction, reality and fantasy, says much about her credibility.

Sometimes truth is stranger than fiction, and sometimes fiction influences reality. The popular image of the chupacabra—the one appearing on thousands of books, magazines, and Web sites as a credible eyewitness description—is in fact based on a science fiction film.

Did Tolentino make the story up? Did she dream the whole experience, and convince herself and others that it was real? Did she actually see something unrecognizable, and unconsciously fill in the details with memories of the monster from the *Species* film? Or did she actually see a chupacabra that, by some astronomically unlikely coincidence, just happened to look exactly like a monster in a film she'd recently seen? Short of a confession of hoaxing, there's no way to know for certain what happened, but logic and our ever-sharp Occam's Razor logic tool tells us that the chupacabra legend was started by a young woman who confused reality with a monster movie.

The fact that it took fifteen years to uncover this information is curious as well. All the clues were there, but nobody had taken the time and effort to put the pieces together, and often that's all that's needed to solve a mystery. Perhaps the chupacabra researchers, recognizing that their gold standard eyewitness account had serious credibility problems, chose not to look too closely at her story. Or perhaps no one bothered to do any real research or investigation. Whatever the reason, the last piece of the solution to the chupacabra mystery fell into place.

The idea that something mysterious had been killing Puerto Rico's animals had existed for some time, but before Tolentino's report no one had put a form to the phantom menace. *That* was where the original chupacabra came from. If Tolentino had seen a different alien or monster film at the same time, the world would have a different image of the chupacabra. With the final piece of the puzzle in place, the chupacabra mystery crumbled and the solution was complete. The next task was to collect my information and write up my findings; the result was a 60,000-word book on the topic published in 2011 by the University of New Mexico Press.

Note: This chapter is a section of investigative highlights condensed from my detailed and exhaustive book on the chupacabra. I have of necessity summarized much, and if readers have any questions about statements made in this chapter, they should consult the complete book for full details and references.

References and Further Reading

"Chupacabras Rides Agains Again." [sic] 2002. *Fortean Times* magazine, 156.

Corrales, Scott. 1997. *Chupacabras and Other Mysteries*. Greenleaf Publications.

Cunliffe, Dr. Clare. 2009. Interview by the author, October 27.

Downes, Jonathan. 2008. "Re-evaluating the Chupacabra" talk at the 2008 UnConvention. Available at www.youtube.com/watch?v=7BK8myjdltc.

Geberth, Vernon. 1996. *Practical Homicide Investigation: Tactics, Procedures, and Forensic Techniques*, 3rd edition. New York, New York: CRC Press. Pp. 216-222.

Giger, H.R. 1995. *Species Design*. Morpheus International. Beverly Hills, California.

Loxton, Daniel. 2009. "The shocking secret of Thetis Lake". *Junior Skeptic*, Number 35.

Morales, David. 2005. Quoted in Is It Real? Chupacabra. *National Geographic Television.* Airdate October 12.

Radford, Benjamin, and Joe Nickell. 2007. *Lake Monster Mysteries: Investigating the World's Most Elusive Creatures.* University Press of Kentucky, Lexington, Kentucky.

Radford, Benjamin. 2010. "Tracking the goat sucker". *Fortean Times* magazine (No. 257, January), 48-53.

Shuker, Karl P.N. 2009. *The Unexplained.* New York, NY: Metro Books.

Stewart, James. 1977. "Cattle mutilations: An episode of collective delusion". *The Zetetic,* Spring/Summer 1(2):55-66.

Wade, Dale A., and James E. Bowns. 1984. *Procedures for Evaluating Predation on Livestock and Wildlife.* Document B-1429. Published by The Texas A&M University System though the United States Fish and Wildlife Service, Department of the Interior.

Commentary and Follow-Up

While some paranormal investigations can take a few hours or weeks, my research on the chupacabra was conducted over the course of approximately five years. As I noted, when I began my investigation some parts of the solution had already been proposed. I didn't need to start from scratch, and doing good background research allowed me to find and make use of important earlier work. My real job was solving the last few pieces and putting it all together.

The chupacabra mystery was probably the highest-profile investigation of my career. To be honest, I had my doubts about my ability to solve the case because, as Karl Shuker noted, there were mountains of myth and misinformation to sort through. With dozens of contradictory reports and sightings, and information on television shows, in books and magazines and on Web pages, it was a daunting task. But the amount of useful, credible information was much smaller, and focusing on that was helpful.

This case was multifaceted, involving everything from folklore to forensics, from Andean vampire stories to what physically happens after an animal dies. But one thing in my favor was the specific, limited scope of the subject. Because the entire mystery was only about fifteen years old, there was a finite amount of information on the subject. There were only so many reports to read, only so many found "chupacabra" carcasses to examine, only so many sources to interview, and only about a half-dozen main claims. There's no way anyone could claim to "solve" the entire mystery of ghosts, for example. There are simply too many aspects to treat the subject comprehensively.

When I went to Texas for MonsterQuest, I had a meeting with the show's producer on the night of my arrival. He visited me in my hotel room to discuss the shooting schedule and call times. I was happy to discuss all of that, but I was more interested in explaining to him how the pieces of the chupacabra puzzle fit together. I laid it all out for him and said that his could be the first documentary TV show to give the full, accurate story on the subject, instead of just another typical treatment. He listened for a bit, but it soon became clear that entertainment would once again trump truth. Whether I could explain every single mystery about the chupacabra or not, the show had a script to follow—and I didn't write the script.

Of course, just because a mystery is solved doesn't mean that everyone knows about it, or that many people won't think the mystery continues. We see this over and over again; the Bermuda Triangle is a good example of a "mystery" solved decades ago, yet will likely forever remain known in the public's consciousness as unexplained. Just as visitors to Jamaica's Rose Hall Great House will continue to find ghostly evidence of a woman who never existed (Chapter 12), people will continue to report seeing and finding animals they mistakenly believe are chupacabras. Thus the chupacabra will live on.

Conclusion

"Supposing is good, but finding out is better"
~Mark Twain

I am a passionate believer in finding out. Finding out about the world and finding out about myself. I have an intense curiosity about the world, a profound thirst for understanding. To me, the world is a wondrous, endlessly fascinating place full of amazing and mysterious things. I want to understand as many of them as my short time on earth will allow. When confronted with things that we don't understand, we could just wonder about them and go on our way. We could just shrug our shoulders and tend to other issues, things that provide easy answers or don't challenge us intellectually. Or we can try and understand, to wrap our minds around puzzles and mysteries, to poke and prod and test and study until finally, in this one minuscule area of the world, this mote of controllable and examinable area, nature yields a secret and we are enlightened. We see why or how that works, we understand the process. We may not understand it completely, or in every aspect, but we can get a foothold on the truth because we are willing to ask and investigate.

Marcus Aurelius, Stoic philosopher and one of the greatest Roman scholars and emperors, wrote in his book *Meditations*, "Never let anything pass without having first examined it and tried to understand it; be an exact examiner of mankind and his actions." He also discussed his desire for truth, reflecting a central tenet of skepticism and scientific inquiry: "If any man is able to convince me and show me I do not think or act right, I will gladly change; for I seek the truth that by which no man was ever injured. But he is injured who abides by his error and ignorance."

Ultimately, of course, whether paranormal investigators choose to use the scientific methods and strategies I describe here is up to them. Ghost hunters, crop circle aficionados, Bigfoot hunters, and others can continue to use the same methods and strategies that have for decades consistently failed to yield a shred of hard evidence. They are welcome to ignore this information, but they can't complain that no one has offered a valid, science-based paradigm for investigating the paranormal.

Ignorance is the default condition of mankind. Solutions and explanations are precious, while problems and mysteries are common. I respect and encourage anyone who makes a sincere, informed effort to solve problems and mysteries around them, and I hope this work helps. I believe that if ghosts, Bigfoot, aliens, and psychic powers exist, they are important and deserve to be taken seriously. If investigation is to be done, it should be done right.

Index

Credits

The following chapters are revised, updated, and expanded versions of materials published elsewhere:

Chapter 5, The Demonic Ghost House of Buffalo, includes material adapted from "How to 'Haunt' a House," published in *Skeptical Inquirer* magazine, 32(1), September/October 2006.

Chapter 6, The Psychic and the Serial Killer: The "Best Case" for Psychics, includes material adapted from "The Psychic and the Serial Killer," published in *Skeptical Inquirer* magazine, 34(2), March/April 2010.

Chapter 8, Ogopogo, the Bloodthirsty Lake Monster, includes material adapted from "Ogopogo the Chameleon," published in *Skeptical Inquirer* magazine, 30(1), January/February 2006; and part of Chapter 7 in *Lake Monster Mysteries: Investigating the World's Most Elusive Creatures* (University Press of Kentucky, 2006).

Chapter 9, The Mysterious Santa Fe Courthouse Ghost, includes material adapted from "Santa Fe 'Courthouse Ghost' Mystery Solved," published in *Skeptical Inquirer* magazine, 31(5), September/October 2007; and "Capturing the Santa Fe 'Courthouse Ghost'," published in Fortean Times magazine, 229, November 2007.

Chapter 10, The Amazing Lee B., Remote Viewer, includes material adapted from "The Remote Viewer," published in *The Skeptic* (Australia), March 2009.

Chapter 11, The Mysterious Pokémon Panic, includes material adapted from "Pokémon Panic," published in *Fortean Times* magazine, 149, August 2001; "The Pokémon Panic of 1997," published in *Skeptical Inquirer* magazine, 25(3), May/June 2001; and "Pokémon Contagion: Photosensitive Epilepsy or Mass Psychogenic Illness?" published in the *Southern Medical Journal*, 94(1), February 2001.

Chapter 12: The White Witch of Rose Hall, includes material adapted from "The White Witch of Rose Hall,' published in *Fortean Times* magazine, 239, August 2008.